Philosophy and Theatre

The relationship between philosophy and theatre is a central theme in the writings of Plato and Aristotle and of dramatists from Aristophanes to Stoppard. Whereas Plato argued that playwrights and actors should be banished from the ideal city for their suspect imitations of reality, Aristotle argued that theatre, particularly tragedy, was vital for stimulating our emotions and helping us to understand ourselves.

Despite this rich history, the study of philosophy and theatre has been largely overlooked in contemporary philosophy. This is the first book to introduce philosophy and theatre. It covers key topics and debates, presenting the contributions of major figures in the history of philosophy, including:

- what is theatre? How does theatre compare with other arts?
- theatre as imitation, including Plato on *mimesis*
- truth and illusion in the theatre, including Nietzsche on tragedy
- theatre as history
- theatre and morality, including Rousseau's criticisms of theatre
- audience and emotion, including Aristotle on catharsis
- theatre and politics, including Brecht's epic theatre.

Including annotated further reading and summaries at the end of each chapter, *Philosophy and Theatre* is an ideal starting point for those studying philosophy, theatre studies and related subjects in the arts and humanities.

Tom Stern is a Lecturer in Philosophy and the Academic Director of European Social and Political Studies at University College London, UK.

Philosophy and Theatre

An Introduction

Tom Stern

Routledge
Taylor & Francis Group

LONDON AND NEW YORK

First published 2014
by Routledge
2 Park Square, Milton Park, Abingdon, Oxon OX14 4RN

Simultaneously published in the USA and Canada
by Routledge
711 Third Avenue, New York, NY 10017

Routledge is an imprint of the Taylor & Francis Group, an informa business

British Library Cataloguing in Publication Data
A catalogue record for this book is available from the British Library

Library of Congress Cataloging in Publication Data
A catalog record for this book has been requested

ISBN13: 978-0-415-60450-5 (hbk)
ISBN13: 978-0-415-60451-2 (pbk)
ISBN13: 978-1-315-88751-7 (ebk)

Typeset in Garamond and Gillsans
by Taylor and Francis Books

MIX
Paper from
responsible sources
FSC
www.fsc.org   FSC® C013056

Printed and bound in Great Britain by
TJ International Ltd, Padstow, Cornwall

Contents

Acknowledgements

My thanks, first of all, to those who gave me comments on the manuscript, the proposal or related material: Gabriel Doctor, Sebastian Gardner, Raymond Geuss, Lucy O'Brien, Sarah Richmond, Jonny Thakkar and the anonymous Routledge reviewers. On every page, I see improvements they made and, regrettably on my part, justified criticisms to which I have not done justice. This book has benefited enormously from conversations I've had with Harry Adamson, Michael Frayn, Rory Madden, Hugh Mellor, Véronique Munoz-Dardé, Lydia Wilson and the students in my class on philosophy and theatre – my thanks for their time. I am grateful to Tony Bruce and Adam Johnson at Routledge for their help and support. Various friends and family members have been kind enough to ask how the book was going ('was it on something, theatre and something?'), of whom some have been indulgent enough to listen to the answer. Without the hard work and support of my UCL colleagues – academic and administrative, Philosophy and European Studies – I doubt this book could have seen the light of day. Thanks, finally, for all this and more, to Andrea Haslanger.

Preface

Philosophy and theatre emerged from the same place at the same time: Ancient Greece in the 6th century BC. They are both Greek words: 'philosophy' is the 'love of wisdom', 'theatre' is the 'place for viewing'. The first philosopher, Thales, died in approximately 546 BC. Little more than a decade later, Thespis, the first playwright, won his first prize, having reputedly invented acting (as we now understand it) along the way. Like many developing twins, philosophy and theatre had a complicated relationship. The case of Socrates is instructive. The earliest source we have for Socrates is his appearance as a character in Aristophanes' comedy, *The Clouds* – indeed, that is the only source that dates from during his lifetime.[1] It is not a flattering picture: Socrates is to be found measuring the size of a flea's foot or stealing his students' clothing; worse, he convinces his students to abandon traditional Athenian religion and he turns promising young Athenians into immoral tricksters. One source suggests that Socrates saw Aristophanes' play and may have found the whole thing amusing – in any case, he was hardly the first Athenian figure to be mocked by Aristophanes.[2] But, in a changing political climate, the punishment for Socrates' philosophising and its perceived influence went from public ridicule to execution: Socrates was put to death for corrupting the youth and for not believing in the gods of the city – the very things for which he had been mocked in Aristophanes' play.

While Socrates was still alive, so one source claims, he had worked together with Euripides to write tragedies; he had also convinced a young tragedian called Plato to give up writing plays and become a philosopher.[3] After Socrates died, Plato wrote a defence speech on Socrates' behalf – the *Apology*; it doesn't mention Aristophanes directly, but it does emphasise the false rumours and prejudices that made Socrates' conviction all but certain. This is taken by many to be a reference to Socrates' depiction in *The Clouds*. Plato, in turn, would go on to unite Socrates and Aristophanes as characters in his *Symposium* – Socrates out-thinks and out-drinks his comedian adversary; and in *The Republic*, as we shall see, Plato would attack contemporary Athenian theatre – but he would do so in the form of a dialogue, using the character of Socrates as his mouthpiece. Many scholars think that Plato's pupil, Aristotle, wrote his *Poetics* by way of a response to Plato's criticisms of theatre; certainly, Aristotle's *Poetics* was the single most influential theoretical treatise on theatre, interpreted and reinterpreted by modern European playwrights in many traditions and used to inform how they wrote their plays. It may be speculative – but it really isn't very speculative – to say that philosophy as we now know it would be unrecognisable without theatre and that theatre as we now know it would be unrecognisable without philosophy.

The case of Socrates also reminds us that the relationship between philosophy and theatre has ranged from highly antagonistic to highly collaborative – often at the same time, even in the same person. Plato, who attacked the theatre, wrote his attacks in dialogue form; centuries later, Rousseau would criticise the theatre – often adapting Plato's arguments – but he would also make his name as a playwright. So, although it is easy to find philosophers condemning the theatre and playwrights mocking the pretensions of philosophers, it is just as easy to find plays that are informed by philosophical approaches and philosophers who are committed, in some way, to the theatre.

This book presents a series of philosophical topics, problems or questions that arise in relation to theatre and that, taken together, are meant to offer a comprehensive overview and introduction. My hope, in each case, is that readers will be presented with the main issues, that they will come to know where the principal contributors stand and that they will know where to look should they want to pursue these topics in more detail. I do not assume background knowledge in the academic study of philosophy or of theatre; hence, some material in this book may be familiar to students of philosophy although completely unknown to students of theatre, whereas the reverse is likely to be true for others. But for those with a background in theatre, the book should offer a grounding in the relevant philosophical discussions and the means to explore them further. And for those with a background in academic philosophy, the philosophical study of theatre – these days given relatively little airtime compared with fine art, music, novels or films – will require looking at otherwise unfamiliar topics and texts that bring to light new concerns or that cast new light on old ones.

My approach to the topics in this book has been governed by two major considerations. On the one hand, I have always tried to keep an eye on the sorts of questions that everyday spectators and those who work in theatre might ask – which, indeed, I have heard around me before and after theatrical performances – and that philosophical approaches might assist in answering or, at the very least, clarifying. At a production that makes drastic alterations to a well-known play text: 'Should directors be allowed to get away with it?' At a highly abstract, symbolist production: 'How "realistic" was the performance and how much does that matter?' At a play about climate change denial: 'Shouldn't playwrights stop messing with politics and stick to writing *good* plays?'[4] On the other hand, I have considered the philosophers, past and present, who have written on theatre. Philosophers who write about theatre are not hard to find: Plato, Aristotle, Hume, Hegel and Nietzsche are just some of the most recognisable names. Several philosophers were also notable playwrights in their own right, including Seneca, Machiavelli, Voltaire, Diderot, Rousseau, Lessing, Schiller and Sartre – at least four of them belong to the first group, too. There are countless others who have contributed to philosophical discussion about theatre in one way or another. Sometimes, of course, philosophers address the sorts of questions I just mentioned, directly or at least indirectly. Often, however, they offer new conceptual tools, new terminology, new distinctions and indeed new questions of their own. The aim of each discussion is to find a balance between these two considerations – to tread the path between clarifying or answering everyday questions and engaging seriously with the philosophical contributions at hand. Sometimes, the path was already well trodden; often, I have had to clear it for myself. In either case, it goes without saying that many deserving thinkers and thoughts have not found their way into a book of this size and scope; the suggestions for further reading are intended to minimise some of the damage. Specific recommendations are to be found along the way in the notes to each chapter. The selection of 'further reading' at the end of each chapter offers those I take to be particularly useful or, failing that, unavoidable in some sense.

Aside from the first chapter, 'What is Theatre?', the book is divided into two sections. The two sections correspond to two directions of fit: 'from the world to the stage' and 'from the stage to the world'. Loosely speaking, then, the topics in the first section are about the (mis) representation of reality on the stage; those in the second section are about the effect that the stage has upon its audiences. This is a cursory distinction, which doesn't do much more than give me an organising principle for the chapters – as we shall see, answers on each side will clearly impact upon answers from the other – but I hope it's clear why questions about truth, imitation or historical accuracy belong on one side, whereas questions about ethics or the political efficacy of theatre belong on the other. Although the book is intended to be read from start to finish (and the chapters frequently refer to one another), readers should certainly feel free to turn straight to chapters of particular interest.

There are innumerable ways of approaching theatre from an academic point of view and there are plenty of ways of approaching it that aren't obviously academic at all – watching and performing plays are surely among the best. As for the academic approaches, readers will understand that this is not a work of theatre history; nor do I offer criticism of individual plays or performances. The choice to construct the book around particular topics – like 'politics' or 'truth' – has meant that I do not offer a chronological account of the development of the philosophy of theatre. Nor, in general, do I dwell on the very different customs and practices associated with particular kinds of theatre at particular times (although I have tried to bring out relevant details at certain points). Although theatre practices have changed enormously over time, the problems, arguments and conceptual clarifications offered in these chapters are wide-ranging enough, I hope, to stand up on their own. Whereas many writers on theatre view it under the general scope of 'performance' – taken to include theatre, but also sports, religious rituals, political rallies and even the kinds of 'performances' that we all might be said to put on in everyday interactions with each other – I focus relatively narrowly on theatre, the art form. Much that is discussed in these pages could bear upon other kinds of performance and upon other forms of art, but I have found that there's plenty to say about theatre alone.[5] Nor, finally, do I explore various recent trends that take philosophy itself to have something essentially theatrical, dramatic or performative about it; such an omission should not be taken as a dismissal of these views, which in any case are highly varied: to give them their due would take us in a completely different direction.

It is my conviction that the philosophical approaches set out in this book can help us to clarify our thoughts about theatre and provoke us into thinking in new ways. But there's no reason to think that philosophers are uniquely positioned to shed light on theatre, and this book makes no such claim. Instead, I hope that the reader will find these philosophical enquiries to be one instructive mode of thinking about theatre – to be combined, fruitfully, with many others. That, in any case, has been my experience.

Further Reading: General

For those who are inclined to begin at the beginning, reading Aristophanes' *The Clouds* alongside Plato's *Apology* and *Symposium* is a highly rewarding experience. As for modern introductory texts: Carlson (1993) is an extraordinarily comprehensive, chronological survey of theatre theory in all of its various guises from Aristotle to the twentieth century – far broader in scope than the present volume; Brown (1995), Williams (2006) and Brockett & Hildy (2010) are extremely helpful introductions to the history of theatre, together with further reading; Balme (2008) introduces theatre studies to unfamiliar readers, while Bial (2004) does the same for performance studies. Barish (1981) remains an important and accessible study of theatre-bashers, beginning with Plato and including Rousseau and Nietzsche. For a brief, light-touch account of the different approaches taken by contemporary philosophers and theatre or performance scholars, see Saltz (2001b). Among recent publications on philosophy and theatre, Woodruff (2008), although idiosyncratic, is the most far-reaching and accessible; but see also Puchner (2010), Hamilton (2007) and Rokem (2010); Zamir (2007) focuses on Shakespeare. For a critical review of some recent work on philosophy and theatre (including some of these books), see Stern (2013).

Notes

1 Plato and Xenophon knew Socrates, of course, but wrote about him after his death.
2 See Claudius Aelianus (1997) *Varia Historia* trans. D. O. Johnson, Lewiston: E Mellen Press, p. 40; for discussion of this and other references to Socrates' engagement with theatre, see Puchner (2010: 3–9).
3 At least, according to the (probably apocryphal) anecdote in Diogenes Laertius, *Lives of Eminent Philosophers*, trans. R D Hicks, Harvard: HUP, 1972, vol. I, Book III, p. 281.
4 For what it's worth, I have heard versions of each of these questions asked by people around me at recent productions, although in some cases I have written them up in a slightly sanitised form.
5 On theatre and its relation to other art forms, see Chapter 1.

1   What is Theatre?

Throughout this book, we consider philosophical problems that arise in relation to theatre. The broad aim of this chapter is to answer the question: what is theatre? Giving an answer – and looking at answers proposed by others – helps us to understand what a broad range of activities can be associated with 'theatre'. One way to answer our question would be to say: 'there's no single, useful definition; it's the label for a loose, rag-tag bundle of social and cultural practices that more or less began in Ancient Greece but that had probably been going on long before in various different guises and under various different descriptions'. This is perfectly true, even if exactly the same answer, word for word, could be given for 'What is democracy?', 'What is history'? and 'What is philosophy?', amongst other questions. The point, then, is to come up with something a little more concrete than that, but that pays attention to the enormous variety of things that have been and still are called 'theatre'. We don't need a watertight definition, but we do need something that will carry us through the rest of the book. We'll look at the question 'what is theatre?' in three different ways. First, we examine the 'typical elements' of a theatrical performance. Second, we look at some standard definitions of theatre. Third, we look at theatre compared with other art forms. Finally, we look at the relationship between play texts and theatrical performances.

Typical elements

One approach is to think about the typical elements of theatre. To call these elements 'typical' is not to say that theatre is impossible without them. Indeed, it quickly becomes clear that few, if any, of these elements are really necessary for a theatrical performance. The idea, then, is both to introduce what I take to be the typical elements of a theatrical performance and to highlight the kinds of theatre that try to do without them.

If we write a list of the most common and frequently discussed elements of a theatrical performance, it might include some of the following: a play text; characters and a plot; spoken words; a director; scenery and stage; lighting and sound; an audience; actors; finally, the building itself – the theatre. Yet theatrical performances are possible without many of these common elements. The most prominent of these is, of course, the play text, which is often held to be an important contributor to theatrical performances, but is obviously not a feature, say, of (completely) improvised theatre. Despite general agreement that plenty of theatrical performances don't use play texts at all, the relation between play texts and theatrical performances has been the subject of some philosophical debate, to which I return towards the end of the chapter. Plot and character do not feature in any conventional sense in many kinds of avant-garde theatre. Spoken words are absent, for example, from mime theatre. The director – understood as a distinct and independent artistic role – is more or less an invention of the twentieth century. Other elements, harder to dismiss, deserve a closer look: these are the theatre, the actor and the spectator.

   The first element is the place itself – the theatre. The word 'theatre' can refer in general terms to the artistic institution, as an equivalent of 'classical music', 'poetry' or 'dance'. That is how it is used in the title of this book, for example. But a 'theatre' is also a location, often enough a purpose-built construction like the Theatre of Dionysus or the Globe. As part of the theatre, we normally find the place for the spectators and the place for the actors to perform – the latter, of course being the stage with its set and scenery. It's clear, though, that theatrical performances frequently take place without theatres in this sense. In the mediaeval period, there simply were no purpose-built theatres as we understand them now; but theatrical performances took place in churches, in town squares or in processions along main streets. Modern companies use abandoned industrial complexes, parks, streets and tunnels to stage performances. As for the set and scenery, a play can take place without any of these; plenty do. In short, a theatre isn't required for theatre. In a more expanded sense, of course, one might say that in all of these cases a theatre is created by the company. The abandoned warehouse is not a purpose-built auditorium with purpose-built stage, but the performance still makes it a theatre in a sense. In all these cases, that is, the theatrical performance is *located* somewhere. The word 'theatre' comes from the Greek word *theatron* – a 'place for viewing'. In all of these cases, there is a space carved out for the viewers and a space carved out for the viewed. Understood broadly, it isn't always clear which space is which, and these spaces could shift during the course of the performance, as with the medieval procession play moving through the town. Here, we find something much closer to a requirement for a theatrical performance: a certain kind of viewing space. Yet even so, it's possible to find putative examples of theatre that don't have that. The 'radio play', if it counts as a kind of theatre, doesn't obviously have a 'place for viewing', or even a dedicated or significant 'place for listening' (i.e. auditorium). Of course, some theatre theorists might well discount it as a species of theatre on just those grounds.

A second feature is the actor – the person on stage performing a certain role. In what I'm taking to be the typical performance, the actor is one who impersonates, pretends to be or plays the role of someone or something she is not. Laurence Olivier plays Hamlet; Nina plays The World Spirit. But one certainly finds actors – which is to say, people playing a certain role in the performance – who aren't exactly impersonating or 'playing' anyone or anything else. The actors might simply appear as themselves, making claims to the audience that they take to be true;[1] or it might be unclear whether or not they are playing a part; members of the audience may be asked to take part in certain ways and, again, it may be unclear if these are 'plants' or not. If stand-up comedy counts as a kind of theatre – which for some theorists it clearly does[2] – then, depending on the performer, it may or may not involve impersonation or pretence.[3] Finally, some kinds of theatre don't seem to require human agents at all. Balme describes 'the scenographic theatre of G. N. Servandoni (1695-1766) which consisted primarily of spectacular scene changes and did without performers altogether.'[4] Puppet theatre uses human puppeteers, of course, but not human actors in a standard sense. Some recent experiments with 'robot theatre' have attempted to do away even with this human element, leaving (say) computers to chat to each other, thus forming a kind of live, evolving dialogue, which may be different at each performance.[5] As with abandoning the spatial element, abandoning human performance altogether does put pressure on what we count as theatre; but there is no reason why robot or computer theatre couldn't become increasingly significant as the technology develops.

A third element is the audience. Typically, the theatre – the place for viewing – has those who are viewed (actors) and those who view (spectators). An audience needn't be the quiet, reverential, rather passive audience of conventional, contemporary theatre. Nor must spectators be cordoned off from performers so that it's always clear which are which. One difficult question, especially in the light of twentieth-century experiments with theatre, is whether the spectator must be aware that she is watching a performance. Some 'street theatre' performers put on plays in public places: an argument might be staged about some topical issue, the idea being to raise awareness or encourage debate, without onlookers realising that the argument is (initially) staged. Onlookers are either unwitting spectators or, if they get caught up in the argument, they become unwitting performers. It's clear that even in this non-conventional setting, there is an audience. Some forms of theatre attempt to do without the audience altogether. 'Closet dramas' are plays that are written to be read, not to be performed; often they are excluded, as theatre, for precisely this reason. Brecht wrote *Lehrstücke* – 'teaching plays' – which, he claimed, were designed to help the actors to learn, not for the benefit of any audience.[6] Some of the 'happenings' organised by Allan Kaprow in the late 1960s certainly included, as part of the overall event, activities that did not have any spectators whatsoever.[7]

We have seen that each of these three elements – location, performer, spectator – may be dispensed with in certain non-typical forms of theatre. Nonetheless, we'll take it that all three are typically present. (When they are present [when the performer and spectator are together in the theatrical space] we also find a fourth element: something like 'liveness', which I discuss when comparing theatre with other art forms at the end of this chapter.) This discussion helps us when we turn to some of the better-known definitions of theatre, which we are now in a position to assess.

Definitions

The earliest definitions of theatre focus on the concept of *mimesis* (roughly: imitation); for Plato, theatre is characterised by imitation without narration. I can describe what Agamemnon and Clytemnestra said and did; I can describe what they did and also include some of their speeches, during which I might impersonate them and others; or I can cut out the description altogether and pretend to be Agamemnon, while my friend pretends to be Clytemnestra and we talk to each other, becoming the story ourselves for the benefit of a third party. Theatre, for Plato, is the latter. Because it plays such an important role in philosophical discussions of theatre, we look at *mimesis* in detail in the following chapter. But as we have already seen, there are recognisable forms of theatre in which imitation or impersonation do not play a significant role. So although *mimesis* merits close attention, we shouldn't think that theatre is impossible without it. For similar reasons, Eric Bentley's celebrated definition of theatre – 'A impersonates B while C looks on' – seems unnecessarily restricted in its appeal to impersonation.[8]

For a definition that does not appeal to imitation or impersonation, we can turn to Peter Brook's famous claim: 'I can take any empty space and call it a bare stage. A man walks across this empty space whilst someone else is watching him, and this is all that is needed for an act of theatre to be engaged.'[9] In this minimal set of sufficient conditions, we find the three central elements that we examined above: location, performer, spectator. One or two features of Brook's claim are importantly ambiguous and we might respond to this differently depending on how we are meant to understand him. The most important ambiguity, it seems to me, is what the 'performer' and the 'spectator' know about their situation: does the watcher know that the empty space has been called a 'bare stage'? Does the walking man know that he is walking across the 'bare stage' and that he is being watched? When I first taught a class on what theatre is, we followed Brook's instructions: we designated the centre of the seminar room a bare stage; one student walked across the room; others watched. It may not have been the best theatre – but theatre it was. Looking out of the window of my office, I see plenty of students walking past, and I see others watching them; and, even if I designate the concrete path a 'bare stage', it doesn't seem much like theatre to me. Many theorists of theatre speak of the mutual awareness of performers and spectators as an essential component, thus of theatre as a kind of collaboration between the two. Hence, Grotowski emphasised the 'actor–spectator relationship, a perceptual, direct living community' irreducibly at the heart of theatre.[10]

Does every event that consists of a marked-out location, with performers and spectators who know about each other, amount to a piece of theatre? Most of us, I take it, would say that it does not. For one thing, plenty of non-artistic events look like they would count: sports, public ceremonies, board-room presentations, political rallies, courtroom trials and public executions all arguably contain these basic elements. These sorts of events, together with theatrical performances, may be studied under the broad, umbrella term of 'Performance Studies' – performance being deliberately chosen as a broader and less culturally specific category than theatre. For some, then, it's a feature of theatre – but not necessarily a feature of performance in general – that what's going on is a kind of playing (which doesn't necessarily involve impersonation, as we have seen). Hence, Balme writes that, 'reduced to the simplest common denominator, theatre, or more generally a theatrical event, consists of a simultaneous and mutually conditioning act of playing and watching by performers and spectators gathered together in a common space'.[11] There's a clear sense in which the public execution is not 'playing', in the way that the execution scene in *Danton's Death* certainly is.[12] Others, though, have been drawn to the conclusion that 'theatre' should be used to cover all such artistic and non-artistic events. Thus, when Paul Woodruff defines theatre as 'the art by which human beings make or find human action worth watching, in a measured time and place,' he deliberately intends to revise and redefine it, to include weddings and football matches within the category of theatre.[13] Within this broad category of 'theatre', Woodruff identifies what he calls 'art theatre' (the art form commonly known as 'theatre') as a sub-category – one that is important in some ways and unimportant in others. The appeal of such an approach to theatre is evident, in that theatre becomes something much broader and arguably more significant. It also has some historical support: certainly, in medieval texts, the Latin term *ludi* is found to refer both to plays and sports, which might suggest the lack of a distinction that we now seem to find significant.[14]

Nonetheless, this book looks at theatre as a form of art that sits along-side others, like film, painting or poetry. It is true that non-artistic, public events such as football matches and political rallies may be described as 'theatrical' and that they involve performance; but that doesn't mean that they are instances of theatre. In fact, the term 'theatrical' is often used pejoratively in such cases, to mean insubstantial, just for show, pre-planned in a way that such a thing ought not to be, and so on. And in sport, for example, there's clearly a difference between the effectiveness of the spectacle and the demands of the game: it is frequent enough to hear a commentator at a football match remark, of the winning team, that, although the game wasn't that good to watch, 'they had a job to do and they did it'. It's not clear that the same could be said of a company performing *Hamlet*. When we speak of a theatrical performance, I take it we typically mean something much narrower: an artistic event that takes place in a particular location, with mutually aware performers and spectators engaged in some kind of play. But notice that this is not intended to be a watertight definition – just something to work with for the purposes of this discussion.

A final word on definitions. Philosophers, now and in the past, have taken very different views about what a definition is and what it's useful for. Defining something can be two different kinds of activity: a back-wards-looking one, describing what it is; a forwards-looking one, saying what it ought to be ('define X as ... '). Definitions often combine these elements, including enough common sense to account for the descriptive element, but enough normative grip to get at what the definer wants. Approaching something as historically complex as theatre – a multi-faceted and relatively continuous, but ever-changing tradition stretching back at least to the Greeks – one is unlikely to come up with a satisfactory descriptive definition that captures just exactly what it is that makes something 'theatre'. Looking at the varied activities that might count as theatre even in this brief discussion, we can already see why that would be. So those who offer a definition of theatre often aren't really trying to include everything that could be counted as theatre; often, they have a particular aesthetic or philosophical goal in mind – a certain view of what theatre ought to be, rather than a descriptive account of what it is. Thus, for example, Brook's set of sufficient conditions, in the context of his book, is the launch platform for an aesthetic manifesto; Eric Bentley is offering an imagined prehistory of theatre, in order to emphasise certain elements of performance; Woodruff has a broader project, to connect theatre with the ethics of everyday life.[15] Creating a definition with a particular aesthetic or philosophical goal in mind is not a crime. But nor should these definitions be conceived of as neutral descriptions of a cultural practice. Debates about definitions of theatre are, often enough, really debates about what matters and what ought to matter.

Theatre and other art forms

The focus on typical theatrical elements serves well to explain why certain art forms do not count as theatre. Paintings, sculptures and architectural constructions do not feature performers and spectators. The same typically holds for novels and poems, when read silently.[16] Although many playwrights are counted as major literary figures, they have less creative control than their equivalents in other literary arts. Novels and poems do not typically make use of staging, lighting, scenery and so on. They are not collaborative in the same way. Nor do they require collaboration on the part of a group of spectators. This reliance on others to complete the artwork contributes to a further distinctive feature of theatre (in the broad sense). Compared with films, novels and poems, theatrical performances change and develop over time, both within a production (as ideas are explored) and across different productions. The modern reader of an old novel may not have exactly the same experience of that novel as a contemporary reader would have had (amongst other things, because of cultural changes, lost references, historical ironies); but at least she knows that she is making contact with more or less the same object that an original reader would have consumed. The same is true for the modern-day viewer of an old film. The spectator at a modern Shakespeare performance – even one that attempts to recreate renaissance practices – can hardly say the equivalent: think of the different accents, performance rituals, crowd behaviours and so on. This is not to deny that editions of novels or cinematic projection techniques differ over time – but this is nothing like the changing experience of the theatregoer. The changing nature of theatrical performance over time means that particularly well-known plays like *Hamlet* have a kind of life of their own: there are always new ways to adapt or develop the play and it's never going to be possible to exhaust it; this contrasts it with the equivalent film or novel. Indeed, the theatregoer knows that the performance she sees is, in an important sense, a one-off. This is evident in the case of those improvised or immersive performances that develop based on direct interaction with an audience; but generally, no matter how much a performance has been rehearsed and planned, it could go much better than the previous night, or much worse.

By way of making a contrast with film in particular, much has been made of the 'liveness' of theatre, which we have already mentioned. A theatrical performance can go wrong in a way that a film can't: actors can get put off, forget lines, corpse; equally, actors may put on a better or more inspired performance one night than they do the next. Improvisations or fortuitous slips can frequently be adopted in later performances. The performance of the film actor is mediated by the camera and by the editor in a way that the performance of the stage actor cannot be; hence, Walter Benjamin writes that, in the case of film (not theatre), 'the audience's identification with the actor is really an identification with the camera'.[17] 'Liveness' also entails that the theatre audience can have more of an effect on the artwork than can, say, viewers of paintings or films. Actors respond to audiences differently on different nights. Even conventional, passive audiences have a role to play in creating the artwork. Many spectators identify the excitement of theatre with its liveness – the sense that their cooperation is required, that the experience is shared. Similarly, others describe a feeling of awkwardness or an acute awareness of the pretence of theatre, which they do not associate with film. In my experience, bad theatre produces an embarrassment on the part of the spectator that does not find its equivalent in bad film: you mustn't look too bored or too distracted, because they can *see* you.[18] It's a peculiar feature of theatre, then, that you can offend the artwork.[19]

Theatre in the narrow sense and theatre in the broad sense

We have seen why some art forms should not count as theatre. Notice, though, that if a piece of 'theatre' is an artistic event that takes place in a particular location, with mutually aware performers and spectators engaged in some kind of play, then theatre, as defined, includes opera, dance and performance art. There is a sense in which this is absolutely right; I'll call this category of artistic performance 'theatre in the broad sense'. Much of what we said about theatre, compared with films and novels, also applies, say, to dance: one can offend dancers; dance performances change from one evening to another; dance is live. But clearly, 'theatre' also has a narrower sense – one that has the function of *distinguishing* a theatrical performance (the performance of a play) from an opera, a dance performance or a piece of performance art. Pinning down just what it is that distinguishes theatre in the narrow sense is particularly difficult and may well be best described in cultural and historical terms, rather than in the abstract. Plenty of instances of theatre in the broad sense could fit under a number of different categories, including performance art, theatre (in the narrow sense) or dance.

However, there are some general trends. Opera suggests an emphasis on music; dance, of course, on dance. As for theatre in the narrow sense, a 'play' typically suggests more of an emphasis on the spoken word than do the other kinds of performance under consideration (but, then again, the spoken word is often a feature of other kinds of artistic performance – and plenty of plays do not have words). One way to back up this intuition is to think about who tends to be identified as the 'artist'. In the case of opera, for example, it is the composer whose name tends to be attached to the artwork; in the case of dance, depending on the context, it may be the company, composer or choreographer.[20] When we broaden this to television and film – which obviously are not kinds of theatre, but which make use of many of the same artistic techniques – we find a similar disparity: the name associated with film tends to be that of the director or actor, with television perhaps the channel, production company or main actor. So although I might go to a Tarantino film or watch a BBC costume drama or see an early Wagner opera, I would be more likely to describe myself as seeing an Ibsen play or the new play by Butterworth or Churchill.[21] Similarly, theatre directors are often described as giving 'interpretations' of play texts, whereas it is rare to find film directors described as doing so in relation to film scripts.[22] Indeed, scriptwriters for film and television are frequently unknown to millions who see their films, unless they happen to be directors or playwrights as well.

To be clear: there are plenty of exceptions in all of these cases; what's more, the fact that these cultural trends exist doesn't show that they are particularly deep or important; they might merely be convenient labels for artworks that are clearly collaborative and for which no single 'artist' could be found – and we've already seen that playwrights aren't necessary for theatre; the texts they write can be used in all sorts of ways and, as we shall see, the relationship between a text and a performance is by no means clear. In as much as the association between the playwright and the performance does represent a tendency, it suggests a greater respect for the artistry of the writer of the words than for equivalents in related art forms like film, television and opera.

The philosophical discussions in this book explicitly relate to theatre in the narrow sense, about which there is plenty to say. When I use the term 'theatre', that is what I have in mind unless otherwise stated. Often, though not always, the issues raised could apply to theatre in the broad sense, too. Furthermore, given the range of performances covered by the notion of 'theatre' (even in the narrow sense), some of the issues under discussion simply will not arise for certain kinds of theatrical performance.[23]

We should end the discussion of theatre in relation to other art forms by noting that part of the interest in theatre comes not from its distinctiveness as such, but from the way that it incorporates and interacts with the other arts. It would not be unusual for a theatrical production to make use of painting, sculpture, design, music, dance, fashion, film or poetry, while architects have played their part in creating beautiful or unusual theatre buildings.[24] Plays are adapted as films and vice versa, used as the basis for operas, as inspiration for dance performances. We don't need to think of theatre as separate and completely independent from all of these things.

Theatre and drama

At this point, it may be helpful to say something about 'theatre' and 'drama' – two words that are frequently used interchangeably. 'Drama', like 'theatre', comes from the Greek (an 'action' or 'doing'). Like theatre, the range of things that may be referred to by drama is enormous. This means that aggressively policing some purportedly unique distinction between the two of them would probably be a waste of time. Nonetheless, some differences should be addressed; we'll look at three related but different ways of drawing the distinction.

A good way into thinking about the first difference comes from considering the corresponding adjectives, 'theatrical' and 'dramatic', both of which can be applied to real-world incidents but with different meanings. Suppose there is a fire in my neighbour's house and the emergency services are called in to rescue her: if I call the rescue operation 'dramatic', I might mean it was tense or daring; but if I call it 'theatrical', I probably mean that the rescuers were showing off or unnecessarily making a spectacle of it. Following this, one might think that 'drama' suggests something to do with a plot or the internal development of an action: a dramatic incident is one in which events unfold over time in a particular way. 'Theatre', on the other hand, puts the emphasis on the combination of location, performer and spectator discussed above – for theatre, then, one doesn't need a coherent narrative or the unfolding of events in a particular way. One example of the latter might be Peter Brook's suggestion (quoted above) that the man walking across the 'bare stage' would be an act of theatre; it's not clear that this would necessarily count as 'dramatic' in the sense that we are discussing.

If 'drama' suggests something about the narrative or unfolding of events, then it might also emphasise the creator or 'dramatist' of the narrative more than it emphasises the performers; whereas if theatre emphasises the spectacle, then it might place more emphasis on the performers. This explains why theatre historians often refer to the 'drama' of a certain period to mean those plays that were written (or, generally, created) during that time; the 'theatre' of the period would refer to what was performed – including, of course, plays from a much earlier period. So, if a theatre historian speaks of 'post-war British drama', she may be speaking of playwrights like John Osborne, John Arden and Harold Pinter, whereas 'post-war British theatre' might suggest a focus on theatres and companies like the Old Vic or the Stratford Festival Company.[25]

The Old Vic's 1960 production of *Romeo and Juliet* would, on this understanding, be renaissance drama and post-war theatre. We can see why this way of drawing the distinction is related to the previous one: in both cases, drama emphasises formal elements such as plot and character, whereas theatre emphasises performance. But what makes a performance 'dramatic' in the first sense goes well beyond the 'dramatist' in the second: whereas the performers in The Old Vic's *Romeo and Juliet* are not a necessary condition for the 'drama' in the second sense, they certainly are for the 'drama' in the first.

A third and related difference is that 'drama' has traditionally been used to indicate a certain literary genre (along with 'epic' or 'lyric'). There is a sense, then, that describing a play text or a performance as 'drama' appeals to (primarily Western) literary norms and expectations – perhaps, following the second distinction, with a concomitant emphasis on the *written* word – which do not necessarily apply to theatre. Hence it isn't unusual, in academic discussions, to read of 'non-dramatic' or 'postdramatic' theatre; and for this reason, many contemporary theatre theorists and practitioners are keen to distance themselves from what they take to be the traditional restrictions of 'drama', compared with the relative openness of the term 'theatre'. But note that the term 'drama' can, in some cases, be broader than the term 'theatre'. For our purposes, one important example is that 'drama' also indicates a genre for television and radio programming, typically denoting something both fictional and serious; 'theatre', on the other hand, can include performances which may be neither fictional nor serious, but excludes television programming. So we can see that theatre and drama frequently overlap, but they do not have to: a typical performance of *Hamlet* may be both theatre and drama; television 'dramas' are not theatrical performances; and some theatrical performances do not count as 'dramas', on this understanding. On the terms set out by any of these three overlapping distinctions, this book is about philosophy and theatre; but much of the discussion also relates to drama.

Play text and theatrical performance

Plenty of theatrical performances, such as plays that are completely improvised, don't have corresponding play texts at all. Conversely, some works of dramatic literature are not written to be performed (so-called 'closet dramas', like those of Seneca), even if they may be adapted for the stage. So nobody would claim that every theatrical performance must necessarily stand in some relation to a play text or vice versa. As we saw in the discussion of the terms 'theatre' and 'drama', many writers on theatre (and performance) seek to distance themselves from the association between theatre and the 'play text' – partly because that association lends itself to a narrow, traditional focus on a Western literary canon, to the exclusion of other, marginalised forms of theatre that do not make use of such a text. There is thought to be, then, a political agenda (broadly speaking) to what counts as theatre, or what 'deserves' to be studied and taken seriously. Even when there is a well-known play text, there's no *aesthetic* law saying it must be used in a conventional manner – by which I mean: each character assigned to an actor, each actor uttering the words assigned to his or her character, stage directions diligently followed, and so on.[26] There are many non-conventional ways of using play texts to create performances, and even within the conventional model, there is a huge variety, depending on artistic goals as well as on budget and location.[27] So there's no reason to think that there is one text/performance relationship or that there ought to be such a thing. Nonetheless, for right or for wrong, most of the plays discussed in the course of this book do have corresponding play texts and that is the model I take as typical – partly because that is the model assumed by most of the philosophers whom I discuss and partly because that is still, to my mind, the dominant model on contemporary stages. What's more, the question of how to characterise the relationship between play texts and performances has been subject to some debate and it deserves a place in our discussion. These debates sometimes attempt to use philosophical approaches to say what sort of a thing a play or a theatrical performance is (ontology or, broadly, metaphysics) and then move from there to discuss the role of the text. Such discussions, it seems to me, are broadly motivated by two concerns: the first is a philosophical puzzle about what constitutes 'the work of art' in the case of theatre; the second is an aesthetic debate about the significance of the play text in relation to the performance. We'll look at each in turn.

On the face of it, we all know what *Hamlet* is: a play, written by William Shakespeare at the start of the seventeenth century. But what exactly is the play? It can't just be the written text, because there are three different extant versions, with significant differences; and there is no simple or uncontroversial way of choosing which one should be the standard version or uniting all three into one definitive edition. In any case, quite apart from these texts, *Hamlet* is often something people think they can go to see at a performance: I can 'see *Hamlet*' in way that I can't 'see *War and Peace*'. But when I see a performance of *Hamlet*, it is rare to see any one of the three surviving texts performed without any editing or alterations to the words; and there's plenty on the stage that has not been specified or implied by the text (examples might be scenery, staging, casting, costumes). Nonetheless, I want to maintain that the performance I see is a performance of *Hamlet*: I have seen *Hamlet*, not merely an adaptation of *Hamlet* or a performance of something else, which happens to be inspired by *Hamlet*. So could *Hamlet* just be the performance I am going to see? Not really: this performance differs considerably from another performance I have seen; but they are both *Hamlet*; so this performance isn't all there is to *Hamlet* any more than the written text is all there is to *Hamlet*. As 'art objects', then, plays are harder to pinpoint than other kinds of art: it's pretty clear, in contrast, what the Bayeux Tapestry is and where to find it; but *Hamlet* seems to hover somewhere between a set of unchanging texts (albeit open to changes in the editing process) and an open-ended series of performances and productions stretching back to Shakespeare's time and on into the future. Reflections on our different attitudes to text and performance have led some to suggest that *Hamlet* the text and *Hamlet* the performance should be thought of as different works of art. David Saltz, for example, writes that '"to read Hamlet" and "to see Hamlet" denote such different experiences that we might well ask whether the word Hamlet has the same reference in the two expressions'. He continues: 'If I have seen a play twice, and read it three times, is there some single "thing" that I have encountered five times?'[28] Plenty of people, myself included, think the answer to this question is obviously 'yes': namely, *Hamlet*. But, it must be said, if *Hamlet* is a thing, then it's an odd one: one can encounter *Hamlet* in the texts or in the performances, but in neither case has one completely exhausted its possibilities. These are the sorts of considerations that might lead to further investigation on the part of philosophers and theorists about the relationship between the play text and the performance. But, of course, there's no reason to think that *Hamlet* needs to be identical with the text or with the performance (which it isn't), or that it needs to be an object like the Bayeux Tapestry (which it obviously isn't); it could just be a kind of imagined, abstract construction out of texts and performances – or a useful label that nonetheless doesn't pick out any one unique thing in the world. The question of exactly what *Hamlet* is may never be answered in the way that a similar question about the *Bayeux Tapestry* could be. And why would anybody expect such an answer or seek to find it?

There is, as I suggested, a second, aesthetic motivation for discussion of the text–performance relationship. This is an aesthetic conflict about where the artistic value of theatre lies. Put in extreme form, one side views play texts – primarily works of dramatic literature – as the central aesthetic focus. They are to be revered as literary constructions: words on a page, like poems and novels; unfortunately, sitting on top of works of dramatic literature, and threatening to obliterate them, there has developed a sort of glamorous, unsightly mould comprising actors, directors, critics and theatregoers, not to mention lighting technicians, sound engineers, costume designers and so on. The other side treats theatrical performances as the locus of artistic merit: theatre is basically akin to music and dance, for reasons we have discussed; techniques of literary analysis are mostly irrelevant; any attempt to tell performers what to do, based on the words of some playwright (dead or alive), is an unwelcome trespass into the realm of artistic freedom.

Perhaps nobody holds these views to these extremes. But moderate versions of some of them can certainly be found. Historically, Aristotle, as we shall see, shows himself to be far more interested in the written elements of the tragedy – the plot and the characters – than the elements relating to the performance alone, which he considers peripheral. Lessing, although writing on behalf of a theatre, gives Aristotle's claim a qualified endorsement.[29] Some scholars, notably the Victorian essayist Charles Lamb, have argued that Shakespeare's plays in particular are better read than performed. Nietzsche's account of ancient tragedy in many ways takes the opposite view to Aristotle: to look primarily at the play texts associated with Attic tragedy is to miss its significance.

Where the relationship between a performance and a play text is relatively conventional, it's clear that the truth lies somewhere in the middle. Viewing play texts as the aesthetic focus ignores or downplays the artistry of performance; crucially, it also, more often than not, downplays the artistry of the playwright: playwrights have often been active participants in theatrical performances – as actors, producers, directors – and wrote with them in mind.[30] You miss something if you read their work and ignore the theatre; and, in fact, good literary criticism of play texts rarely ignores the theatre. The difference between reading a scene and watching it performed well can be striking. To give just two brief examples: the significance of Nora's dance in *A Doll's House* is easy to miss on paper and very difficult to miss if you see it happening in front of you. Another oft-cited example is that of silence: to the solitary reader, the word 'silence' on the page means very little and may be skipped over; but silence in a packed auditorium means a great deal. (Teachers will know the difference between peaceful, solitary silence and the awkward silence of a classroom.) One can always imagine such things, but actively imagining something and actually witnessing it are different. On the other hand, ignoring the literary elements of a text – when that text is being used in a traditional way as the basis for a performance – can lead to disappointing performances, and the line between artistic freedom and the vanity project of a director trying to make a splash is not always easy to draw.[31] Performances are subject to various market pressures: theatres need to draw in crowds, they are subject to fads and fashions, they use famous but not necessarily talented actors to gain publicity. Productions of very well-known plays must often be seen to do something new for the sake of novelty alone. Lessing, although an admirer of the stage, suggests that well-known actors tend to favour mediocre plays, which give them more of a chance to shine as individuals than they would in a well-crafted work.[32] None of these pressures obviously applies to play texts as works of dramatic literature – so one can see why reading a play text might be thought to offer a purer experience.

This conflict, implicitly or otherwise, plays its part in discussions by philosophers and others about the relationship between play texts and performances. Such discussions are often presented as though they might settle the aesthetic dispute alluded to above, or at least contribute in some way. They tend to compare the text–performance relation with some other kind of relation in order, supposedly, to clarify it. The text–performance relation has thus been compared with the relation between a mould and sculpture, a musical score and performance, a recipe and meal, an ingredient and a completed meal, an original text and its translation into another language, an artwork and its interpretation.[33] The relationship between a play text and a performance is, of course, identical with none of these relationships; but they may be helpful in drawing out what appeals to one side of the conflict or the other. The idea that the play text is like a mould clearly places too little weight on the artistry of performance; more than that, it misunderstands what a play text is: no matter how carefully two independent companies tried to perform *Hamlet* according to the text of the play (of which in any case there are a number of versions), they would be forced to make choices – about, say, casting or costume – that aren't specified in the text and that would inevitably alter the resulting performances. Conversely, one might think that viewing the text merely as a recipe for the performance undermines something central or significant about the artistry of many play texts: often, reading a tragedy does have many of the same effects as watching a performance – for Aristotle, reading a tragedy has all of the significant emotional effects; but nobody gets full or gets nourished from reading recipe books – indeed, they tend to make us hungrier.[34]

Such discussions and comparisons are doubtless helpful in thinking about the ways that play texts and performances interact; we cannot give each position the attention that it deserves. The debate is understandable, as I have suggested, in the light of the deeper aesthetic concern about the artistry of theatre. Sometimes, indeed, a clear attempt is made to link philosophical arguments to the aesthetic debate: both Saltz and Hamilton suggest, for example, that their analyses are intended to combat what they call the 'hegemony of the text'[35] – the prominent role that the text plays in the minds of theorists, critics and spectators when thinking about theatrical performance. One of Saltz's claims, then, is that 'only in performance do we actually encounter an instance of the play proper'[36] – the text alone can never offer full access to what Saltz calls 'the play'.

I would like to sound one note of caution. The aesthetic debate is, it seems to me, just that – a debate about aesthetics. Nobody denies that directors and theatre companies *can* make all sorts of creative decisions about how to use the text of *Hamlet*, including using it in traditional performances and creatively adapting it in unconventional ways, such that the performance is radically distinctive. Perhaps, on extreme occasions, a critic may object that 'That isn't *Hamlet*!' More often than not, though, the objection will be: 'That's a bad *Hamlet*!' or just 'That's a bad play!' In the former case, the critic evidently acknowledges that she has seen a production of *Hamlet*, and in the latter case, the relation to the *Hamlet* play texts doesn't seem significant. Where objections are made, it is often to the particular way in which it has been done, rather than as part of a universal view of what the text–performance relationship must be or what the 'play' necessarily is. Where there is a suggestion that performances ought to be faithful to play texts like a translation is faithful to the original or interpret the text in some way, this is probably best understood not as a descriptive claim about what the text–performance relationship necessarily is, but rather as an aesthetic claim about what the relationship ought to be, whether generally or in this particular instance. In other words: it is an open question whether philosophical discussions of the text–performance relationship can add to the aesthetic debate outlined above, or whether they merely mirror it in more complicated prose. And if questions about the deep nature of the text–performance relationship do not help us on with the aesthetic debate, then one may wonder what, if anything, is really at stake here.[37]

Conclusion

We have explored the question 'what is theatre?' by looking at typical theatrical elements, by analysing proposed definitions and by comparing theatre with other kinds of art. We also looked at the peculiar ways that a play text can interact with a theatrical performance. It can be no surprise that no single, clear, unambiguous, universal definition of theatre has emerged. A final way to answer the question is just to explore theatre's variety exactly as we have done, to remind ourselves of its flexibility and its resistance to strict or final limitations.

Further Reading

Balme (2008: 1–62) and Lennard & Luckhurst (2002) both offer a helpful starting point for those who have not thought about the variety of activities that go by the name 'theatre'; readers should also consult 'Further Reading: General', above. Those interested in pursuing philosophical discussions of the nature of theatre should look at Saltz (1995) and (2001a); Hamilton (2007); Woodruff (2008: Ch. 1).

Notes

1 For a sample case, see Hamilton (2007: 47), who describes a scenario developed from Handke's *Offending the Audience*. Certain forms of Asian theatre are often cited as featuring actors who do not impersonate.

2 Balme (2008: 4).

3 For a helpful discussion of performing with and without acting, see Kirby (1995).

4 Balme (2008: 55).

5 Annie Dorsen's *Hello Hi There* (2010) does this, taking as its starting point a conversation between Chomsky and Foucault.

6 See e.g. Brecht (1964: 79–80). One might wish to say, in such cases, that the actors are the audience.

7 See Sandford (1995).

8 Bentley (1964: 150).

9 Brook (2008: 11).

10 Grotowski (1969: 15).

11 Balme (2008: 2); see also Lennard and Luckhurst (2002: 2)

12 This is obviously not to deny that there are elements of 'show' or 'performance' in the public execution – which evidently there frequently are.

13 Woodruff (2008: 18).

14 Wiles (1995: 66). Though obviously *ludi* would not cover all that Woodruff intends with 'theatre'.

15 I discuss Woodruff's project in more detail in Stern (2013).

16 When performed to an audience, of course, they may count as theatre of a sort; note that tragedy and comedy were originally categorised as types of poetry.

17 Benjamin (2007: 228).

18 On theatre and embarrassment, see Ridout (2006: 70–95).

19 The notion of 'liveness' is more complicated than it may seem: after all, many theatrical performances are highly scripted, pre-planned, rehearsed and so on, which, in one sense, makes them less 'live' than 'live TV'; so-called 'live' concerts are often pre-recorded. For critical discussion of the concept of 'liveness' see Auslander (1999).

20 Performance art is a more general term covering all sorts of performances, of course, but the 'artist' associated with the performance is often a combination of writer, performer, producer and director.

21 See Balme (2008: 148).

22 Saltz (2001a: 302). The context of Saltz's remark is a challenge to the idea that giving interpretations of play texts is a central function of theatrical performances.

23 To give some obvious cases: Chapter 2 discusses *mimesis*, although some theatre is not mimetic; Chapter 5 looks at the ethics of acting, although not all performers are 'actors' in this sense.

24 Another historical interaction between theatre and painting was the deliberate recreation of famous paintings by freezing the actors in the appropriate poses. I have only seen this once: at a Globe Theatre production of *The Mysteries*, in which Jesus and his disciples posed to recreate Da Vinci's *The Last Supper*.

25 This is standard practice, for example, in Brockett and Hildy (2010), in which one finds separate accounts of the drama and theatre in most given historical periods. Note that even so, the choice as to under which heading to place some person or play can still seem more or less arbitrary and the two are frequently merged.

26 There are, of course, certain actual laws applying to performances of plays that are still under copyright, but that is another matter. It is not uncommon for theatrical performances to count as 'derivative works', the 'original' being the play text. Permission for directorial decisions such as cuts, alterations to staging directions, switching the genders of the characters and so on must often be sought in writing before performance.

27 See Hamilton (2007: 41–50) for an extremely helpful set of examples, using the text of *Hedda Gabler*.

28 Saltz (1995: 267). Saltz goes on to put forward a theory of what *Hamlet* the play is; play texts have only a small role, according to him, in identifying which play is being performed on a given occasion.

29 Lessing (1962: Section 80)
30 Loosely (i.e. anachronistically) speaking, this is certainly true of Sophocles, Shakespeare, Molière, Brecht, Beckett, Pinter.
31 For a polemic against directorial freedom (and directors trying to make a splash), for example, Ziolkowski (2009).
32 Lessing (1962: Section 25, p. 67).
33 See, for example, Saltz (1995); Saltz (2001a); Hamilton (2007); Woodruff (2008) Ch. 1; see also Lennard and Luckhurst (2002: 9–21).
34 Nobody, I take it, would extend Aristotle's claim to every play text.
35 Saltz (1995: 273)
36 Saltz (1995: 267). I simply note that this has odd consequences. Even ignoring the peculiarly artificial ring of 'encountering the play proper', it would be odd, upon asking someone if she had 'encountered' *Hamlet*, to be told: 'No, I haven't; I have only read it.'
37 In the broadly analogous field of 'musical ontology' – philosophical discussion of what musical performances 'really' are – Ridley (2003) argues that philosophical arguments offer nothing at all to the realm of aesthetic appreciation and understanding. My instinct is that much the same may turn out to be true for philosophical discussions of what theatre 'really is' or what the text–performance relationship 'really is'. Your aesthetic view of whether an experimental performance of *Hamlet* is refreshingly creative or a distasteful abomination has nothing to do with a deep view about theatrical ontology. Of course, I do not take myself to have established this – I merely report an intuition. In the absence of an equivalent piece on theatre, Ridley's piece is highly recommended.

Part I

FROM THE WORLD TO THE STAGE

2 Mimesis: Imitation and Imagination

The writings of two philosophers – teacher and pupil – have shaped our politics, our religion, our art and our science. And although we should not flatter ourselves into thinking that either of them considered it the most important of topics, Plato and Aristotle both wrote about theatre. In many respects, their concerns set the tone for large parts of this book, whether we address them explicitly or not. I've already argued that it's not going to be possible to come up with a perfect definition of theatre. But when these two Greek philosophers tried to define it, they were quick to identify one word as central: *mimesis*. Apart from that, Plato and Aristotle agree upon little else. As we'll see, they don't even agree on what *mimesis* is, when it comes to theatre. But both agree that, where there's theatre, there's *mimesis*. Even before we acquaint ourselves with the various meanings of *mimesis*, we can get a sense of it by thinking about a typical theatrical performance. When you watch a play, actors dress up and speak like kings, sets make the stage look like Thebes or Verona. The whole play is an enacting, an acting out, an imitation (however inaccurate) of what the story might have looked like if (or when) it happened; and you, an audience member, are engaged in a kind of pretence that the story is unfolding before your very eyes. Each of these various activities could be described as *mimesis*. This chapter uses Plato and Aristotle to begin our analysis of philosophy and theatre. Through their opposing views about *mimesis*, we open up a much wider debate about what theatre is and what it can do.

Meanings of *mimesis* – imitation

Unfortunately, English doesn't have a word that's the equivalent of *mimesis*. The closest we have is 'imitation', a word I'll use for part of our discussion; but it's not quite right. The important thing to note about *mimesis* is that it can be used to describe a family of different notions, which can be broadly grouped in the following way. First, visual imitation: the columns on that building look like palm trees. Second, behavioural imitation: when husbands commit adultery, their wives often imitate them or follow their example. Third, impersonation or mimicry: Dionysus gets dressed up like Heracles in order to fool people into thinking he's Heracles; a human can mimic perfectly the sound of a nightingale. Fourth, imagination or play-acting: children imagine that they are their favourite heroes and re-enact a famous story.[2] Finally, a slippery notion of 'metaphysical mimesis', which involves some kind of correspondence relation between the world as it seems to be and the world as it really is.

There are some features that all of these cases have in common. We can discern, in each example, an original and a kind of copy: the palm trees (original) and the pillar (copy); the husband and the wife; Heracles and Dionysus; hero and child; the real world and the world as it appears to be. We should add two points about this copy. First, it should be obvious from the examples that 'copy' here means something other than 'exact replica down to the last detail': the adulterous wife is probably not doing *exactly* what the adulterous husband did; Dionysus doesn't look *exactly like* Heracles – just enough to pass for him. So the copy needn't be an exact copy – just a copy in some relevant way. But, to move to the second point, we shouldn't go to the other end of the spectrum and claim that the copy needn't correspond in any way to the original. Despite the different kinds of example, we can say that the copies do more than merely *represent* the originals. On a treasure-map, the symbol, 'X', marks the spot where the treasure is buried. The correspondence between the 'X' and the treasure is merely symbolic, conventional. It could have been an 'O' or a 'T'. But the examples of *mimesis* that we've seen are something more than that: the copy corresponds to its original in more than a merely conventional or symbolic way. The copy is, in some sense, *like* the original.

Common features can also be identified among a subset of the meanings of *mimesis*. Visual imitation, behavioural imitation and impersonation lie more or less comfortably within our standard use of 'imitation'. This is less true for the last two, for play-acting and metaphysical mimesis. If we saw a group of children playing at being characters from films or players on a football team, we wouldn't naturally say that they were 'imitating' those characters; we'd say that they were pretending to be them, or imagining that they were them. As for the final category, metaphysical mimesis, we'd have to use up more space than is available understanding the metaphysics in each separate instance to understand what is implied and whether it's covered by 'imitation' or some other term.

Setting the metaphysical aside, and concentrating on the first four conceptions of *mimesis*, it may be helpful to think of the first three kinds (visual, behavioural, impersonation) as occurring at the third-person level, and the fourth, imagination, as occurring at a first-person level. It is to a *third party*, that is, that the columns should look like palm trees and the voice sound like a nightingale. In the case of the adulterous spouses, it's not that the imitation is *designed* for a third party (as in the previous two); but, at the very least, it's available to be recognised by a third party. Although, as we've seen, there are many differences among them, I shall refer to this group collectively as kinds of 'imitation-*mimesis*'. With imagination, however, the story is different. The children pretend to be their heroes. They aren't trying to look like their heroes, or to pass themselves off as their heroes. The crucial point, therefore, is the imaginative act of pretending that takes place within each child. Note that to say the pretending is 'first-person' doesn't mean it is necessarily first-person *singular*. There's no reason why a lone child can't successfully engage in play-acting; but many types of play-acting involve more than one person, imagining together. I shall refer to this as 'imagination-*mimesis*'. Now that we have some hold on the various meanings of *mimesis*, we can move on to consider what Plato says about its relation to theatre.

Plato on mimesis

Plato's claims about theatre are not always clearly distinguished first of all from his comments about other kinds of art, such as painting, and from his claims about other kinds of poetry. But tragedy, in particular, comes in for a lot of attention in Plato's *The Republic*; and this attention is famously and almost exclusively negative. Plato did not intend to give a careful definition of theatre, but he takes some time to explain the kind of *mimesis* that he thinks is at work, and it is helpful to spell out his claims.

The context of Plato's most famous remarks on theatre is *The Republic*, a dialogue between Socrates and a number of Athenian youths, including Glaucon and Adeimantus (Plato's brothers). As always, Plato does not speak directly in his dialogues, but rather explores the ideas through the figure of Socrates, who can neither be identified with Plato nor be completely isolated from Plato's own views. The conversation turns to the concept of justice, and Socrates, with the help of his interlocutors, begins to describe an ideal, just city. The rules for how this ideal city is set up have a variety of implications for education, family, political organisation and, of course, for poetry (tragedy and comedy being, for the Greeks, a kind of poetry). There is some debate about whether Plato intends to ban all mimetic poetry, or whether it is only certain kinds, but clearly, he subjects the most significant and successful Greek poets to scathing attacks and (imagined) censorship.[3] Theatre comes in for particular criticism. For now, the important thing is that Socrates' criticisms of theatre depend upon his understanding of what theatre requires compared with other kinds of poetry. What it requires is *mimesis*.

Some kinds of poetry, Socrates explains, involve narration; others involve narration and *mimesis*; others involve *mimesis* only. By narration, Socrates roughly means an indirect description of the story, in the third person: 'the priest asked the Greeks to return his daughter for a ransom'. By *mimesis*, in this instance, he clearly means somebody pretending to be the priest, seeming grief-stricken, and desperately uttering words along the lines of: 'I'm begging you Greeks to give my darling Briseis back. I'll give you anything you want.' It's clear from *The Republic* that readers of Homeric epics would often deliver speeches from Homer imitatively, so one could imagine a combination of narrative ('the priest went to the Greeks and said...') and *mimesis* ([*wailing, desperate*] 'I'm begging you...').[4] However, the *mimesis* of the Homer-reader (known as a 'rhapsode') was part of an overall act of story-telling or narration. Tragedy and, by extension, theatre in general is always a matter of *mimesis* without narration – at least according to Plato.[5]

Having explored some various senses of '*mimesis*', we might wonder what Plato has in mind here. In fact, Plato correctly discerns that theatre typically makes use of both *mimesis* as imitation and *mimesis* as imagination. As for imitation: scenery made to look like the front of a house and its garden; actors impersonating various people, dressing up, mimicking accents. As for imagination: the actors are pretending that they are Agamemnon, Clytemnestra and so on. These two senses of *mimesis*, although distinct, could well be related.[6] We'll have more to say about their relationship once we've looked more closely at each in turn – first, at Plato's account (and criticism) of imitation-*mimesis*; second, at the kinds of imagination that take place in theatre.

Mimesis as imitation

Our starting point here is the question of *what* is being imitated. Plato develops, in *The Republic*, what has come to be known as his theory of forms, according to which there are single, unchanging, ideal so-called 'forms', which are instantiated by objects in the world. In one example, he explains that there is one (eternal, unchanging) form of a couch, to which all (transient, impermanent) couches in the world correspond (and are imitating). When the carpenter makes a couch, he is in some sense modelling his creation on this single couch-form. The claims about theatre, then, follow on from an analogy with painting. When the painter paints a couch, he is making an image of the carpenter's couch, which is in turn a copy of the form of the couch:

SOCRATES: We have these three sorts of couch. There's the one which exists in the natural order of things [i.e. the form]. This one, I imagine we'd say, was the work of a god. Or would we say something else?

GLAUCON: No, I don't think we would.

SOCRATES: Then there's the one made by the carpenter. [...] And then the one made by the painter, isn't there?

GLAUCON: Let's take it there is.

SOCRATES: Painter, carpenter, god, then. Three agents responsible for three kinds of couch.[7]

The 'imitator' (i.e. the painter or his theatrical equivalent), Socrates goes on to say, makes that which is 'two removes from nature' – in other words, from the form. So, when imitation happens in poetry, it, like painting, is the imitation of an imitation – two removes from the real thing. And theatrical poetry, unlike other kinds of poetry, is exclusively imitative. Plato sets this up in order to lay his charges against imitative poetry and imitative art in general.

[handwritten margin note: imitater is already twice removed from the object]

First, a metaphysical charge, based on the forms. Imitation-*mimesis* is never as good as the real thing (the thing it's imitating): no couch is as perfect as the form of a couch and no couch-painting as perfect as a couch. Second, an ignorance charge. The poets and painters don't really need to know about the things they imitate – they just have to know about the superficial appearances of those things: to write a play about a carpenter you don't need to know how to build a table. This, in itself, would not be so bad, if it weren't for the third, 'spectator's gullibility' charge. People tend to take the false or deficient poetic imitations for the real thing or, perhaps, they put too much faith in or are not sufficiently sceptical about the imitations.[8] It's important to note the complexity and variation in the notion of *mimesis* invoked by Plato, which underlies his charges: plays use imagination-*mimesis* on the part of the actor and the audience (the actor imagines being the priest and says: 'I, the priest, would like my daughter back'. and he sounds like he means it; the audience imagines that he is the priest) to create a kind of imitation-*mimesis* (what the play looks like to the audience) of a world (ours) that is, itself, a *mimesis* of another world (of forms).[9] A further sense of *mimesis* invoked in the third charge is that naïve audience members may go on to use characters from plays as role-models, falsely taking them to be the real thing (or sufficiently like the real thing).

Looking over these criticisms, it's clear that some are directed at imitation-*mimesis* as it tends to occur (and as audiences tend to respond to it) in Plato's context; but some seem directed at imitation-*mimesis* as such, with little scope for better or worse kinds. As for the former: much of Plato's discussion of poetry in general and theatre in particular focuses on ways in which the famous poets get things wrong – for example, they misrepresent the gods in showing them to be deceitful and unjust. Furthermore, it's widely acknowledged that in Plato's time, poets were often appealed to for practical advice and education as well as for models of virtue, in a way that is unthinkable today.[10] In an attempt to bridge this gap, modern interpreters of Plato have likened his concerns about tragic poetry to modern concerns about the influence of television or popular music.[11] We might worry that exposure to soap operas and romantic comedies gives a young person a hopelessly unrealistic and ultimately harmful notion of human relationships; we might worry that her attitudes to others might be adversely affected by the songs she listens to, which glorify violence and sexism; we might worry that a child who wants to become a doctor as a result of watching medical dramas on TV has no idea what a real doctor's life would be like. Undoubtedly, these are Platonic concerns. This family of concerns is not exactly aimed at theatre (or dramatic *mimesis*) as such, but rather at the effect of particularly popular and widespread forms of theatre or popular entertainment and the attitudes of audiences towards them. It would be possible in principle, if aesthetically scandalous, to insist on a certain kind of accuracy in imitations, such that (say) dramas about doctors really did reflect the life of a typical doctor. Then the child who grew up wanting to be a doctor based on dramatic portrayals would have less to worry about. More generally, these objections are more about which kinds of imitation-*mimesis* are good and which are bad; they do not attack the *mimesis* itself.

However, some of Plato's concerns seem to be aimed at *all* imitations, no matter the accuracy: imitations take us further from the forms, so, *however* accurate they are, they can never be as good as the things that they imitate; this, for Plato, is their fatal flaw. This flaw is clearly a function of imitation-*mimesis*, as the comparison with painting demonstrates: the painter might try to make his portrait look like the subject; but neither the painter nor the portrait is pretending to be the subject in any obvious way. As far as Plato is concerned, then, theatrical *mimesis* is aiming to copy or imitate precisely the appearance of the original. This accounts for his criticisms of theatrical *mimesis*: however good the imitation, it's still just the imitation of an appearance.[12] Notice that one doesn't need to agree with this second, metaphysical objection (about the forms) in order to make the first objection (about theatrical *mimesis* and role-models); as it happens, though, Plato offers both.

Interpreting The Republic

Before I explore some criticisms of Plato's claims, a note on the interpretation of his arguments in *The Republic*. Few texts have been examined in as much detail, or with such varied results, as this one. I have presented the relevant part of his argument against theatre-as-imitation as it seems to me to be presented in the text and in a way that is not idiosyncratic. However, there are some reasons to be suspicious of this mode of presentation, which it seems appropriate to flag up at this point.

First, I note that I'm taking a very strict, rather literal and perhaps therefore ungenerous interpretation of his comments on theatre. There are many signs in *The Republic* that Plato's understanding of and appreciation for *mimesis* is not nearly as one-sided as I have suggested. For one thing, I'm assuming that Plato is using Socrates as his mouthpiece, which is always a dangerous assumption to make. I'm also not addressing the very reasonable point that Plato, in choosing to write a dialogue, makes use of much that is 'theatrical' in his own work.[13] Recall the story (of questionable accuracy) that Plato himself was a playwright before he met Socrates; even if this was just a rumour, it is ancient enough to indicate a regard for Plato's artistic abilities. Furthermore, since many of the conversations he writes involving Socrates took place in Plato's absence, it's hard to take seriously his (or Socrates') claim that there are just true stories or false stories. Plato's dialogues often tell stories – both stories about the characters in the dialogues and, more interestingly, myths about the afterlife or about how the world was made; indeed, *The Republic* itself ends with a myth. Are these stories true or false? The answer, of course, is somewhere in between.[14] Indeed, within the imagined, just city described in *The Republic,* Socrates and his interlocutors certainly allow for the *rulers* to make claims or tell stories to the rest, which only the rulers know to be false, but which serve some kind of higher purpose or general benefit.[15] This is the so-called 'noble lie' or 'noble falsehood'. Although it is depicted as part of Socrates' imagined just city, it has been tempting for commentators to take the dialogues themselves or the myths within them to be a kind of 'noble lie' told by Socrates to his interlocutors or by Plato to his readers. At least, they leave open the intriguing possibility of a mimesis that Plato is happy to sanction.[16]

The question of the truth or falsehood of particular dialogues should also give us pause for thought. In the case of *The Republic*, for example, it has been shown that the combination of real people and real events brought together in the dialogue would have been historically impossible – as Plato and his contemporary readers would probably have known.[17] Elsewhere, Plato's *Symposium* reports a drunken evening, in celebration of the playwright Agathon's victory in a dramatic competition. During the evening, Socrates argues with Agathon, a tragedian, and Aristophanes, a comedian (amongst others, of course). The reader of the dialogue is told the story by Appolodorus, who wasn't there, but has heard it from Aristodemus, who was. Much of what Socrates says is a report of a conversation he has had with Diotima, sometime before the event takes place. As Freddie Rokem points out, Plato's attempt to distance us from the true event puts us twice removed from the 'real thing', just as mimetic art for Plato is twice removed from the reality it attempts to portray.[18] Whatever Plato meant by repeatedly distancing himself from the events of his dialogues, it's clear that he doesn't share Socrates' claim that either a story is true or it is false. Barish puts it nicely: 'The Platonic dialogues, in general, one suspects, would have trouble with the proposed Platonic censor.'[19]

Finally, I have separated Plato's claims about the copying of appearances (imitation-*mimesis*), which primarily occur in Book 10 of *The Republic*, from his criticisms of what I'm calling imagination-*mimesis*, which primarily occur in Books 2 and 3. Again, although this is not an unusual division, we should note that Plato does not explicitly distinguish them as I have done, so many critics have taken on the challenge of trying to unify these notions of *mimesis* together with the criticisms Plato applies to them. Because there is little agreement on how this should be done, and because it invariably requires an intense examination of the whole of *The Republic*, together with other Platonic dialogues, I have chosen not to pursue this line here.[20]

Despite these important reservations, Plato's claims about *mimesis* as twice-removed from reality – broadly speaking as I have presented them – are clearly and forcefully put. Certainly, they have been taken very seriously by philosophers interested in theatre. For that reason, it seems appropriate to offer some criticisms of Plato's arguments when interpreted in this way.

Problems for Plato - Criticism of Plato's arguments

Metaphysical presuppositions

First of all, Plato's claims about *mimesis* in theatre do not come from nowhere. He has a metaphysical theory about how the world is: the three-tiered structure described above. And he has a theory about what we ought to be doing about it: turning towards what he considers the *real* world (of forms) and away from the one that we take to be real but isn't (i.e. the world of regular, carpenter-built couches). This is what he considers the task of philosophy – to direct our attention away from what most people take to be the real world.[21] As Socrates puts it: 'nothing in human affairs is worth taking that seriously'.[22] Philosophy and theatre, then, pull in completely opposite directions: one brings you closer to reality, whereas the other drags you away from it. Hence, one strategy to combat Plato is to deny that his metaphysical claims about the forms are correct. If there isn't this world of forms of which the everyday world is a kind of imitation (or *mimesis*), then theatrical imitations of the everyday world are not imitations of imitations. Of course, few philosophers (myself included) would now take Plato's metaphysical claims about the forms seriously; but we are more concerned with his claims about theatrical imitation, so I won't pursue his metaphysics here. In any case, as we have seen, many of the objections he makes to theatre may be removed, intact, from his metaphysical arguments.

Imitation as simple verisimilitude

A second challenge to Plato would consider more directly his concept of imitation-*mimesis* as applied to theatre. Indeed, the notion of imitation-*mimesis* at work in Plato's description of the playwrights is simplistic, but it's worth spelling out. As we've seen, the best imitations are those that seem most like the original – i.e. that resemble most closely its appearance (such that they may fool gullible people into thinking that they are the real thing).[23] The most successful imitation would therefore look and sound just like the depicted events would have looked or sounded like to someone who was there. Hence Plato's criticism that it's only the *appearance* that's being imitated and, therefore, that poets don't need to know about the real thing. Nehamas puts this nicely: 'it is almost as if the imitator lifts the surface of the imitated object and transfers it into another medium.'[24] Broadly speaking, such a notion falls under the concept of verisimilitude. Verisimilitude, in general, means 'truth-like' – bearing a likeness to truth or having the appearance of truth. Plato's account of theatrical imitation-*mimesis* is that it means being as verisimilar (as true-seeming) as possible (although, being a copy, it must ultimately fail). Of course, the notion of verisimilitude is a general one. But in Plato's case, he is appealing to what I'll call 'simple verisimilitude': the imitation on stage must, in terms of how it looks and sounds, seem to be as much like the real-life events it is depicting. This notion of theatrical mimesis as simple verisimilitude has been a powerful one in the history of theatre theory, but when we consider it in more detail, it can quickly become problematic.

First, even accepting that Plato is right about theatrical imitation – that theatre aims at imitating the appearance of the everyday world as closely as possible – we should remember that this in itself is not an uncontroversial task. In the history of theatre theory and criticism, verisimilitude (in this simple form) has been appealed to on both sides of a number of debates. For example, when setting a play, should one keep the action in the same place or allow different scenes to be set in different locations? (This is the debate about so-called 'unity of place'.[25]) One can make an argument from verisimilitude in either direction. On the one hand, it could go against verisimilitude to expect the stage to represent a room in an English palace at one moment and then an open field in

France in the next (as in *Henry V*). It's hardly an everyday, life-like experience to see a single place (the stage) change from a palace to a plain. On the other hand, if the stage represents the same room all the way through the play, then the plot can be stretched to breaking point by expecting all the significant events of the story to take place in the same room. Are we really to believe (as in Racine's *Phèdre*) that Phèdre and Hippolyte just happen to reveal their respective secrets to their respective companions and that Thésée calls down his terrible curse in exactly the same location?

Equivalent points have been made about the unity of time: in a sense it's more verisimilar to perform a play in 'real time' – such that one hour on stage represents one hour of action; but, then again, if one tries to write about a significant dramatic event that takes place only in the time allotted to the play, it can end up feeling artificially compressed and hence not verisimilar at all. By convention, French tragedians in the seventeenth century would write plays depicting no more than sunrise to sunset. This drew criticism from both sides: if it's necessary to make theatrical time correspond to real time, then why can we stretch two hours to become more like sixteen hours? Or, if we're allowed to stretch two hours to sixteen hours, then why can't we stretch it to a week or, as in Shakespeare's *A Winter's Tale*, sixteen years? As with the unity of place, forcing all the action to take place in one day can also lead to very compressed plots; hence, Lessing's complaint that playwrights who claim to respect the unity of time often do so by not letting their characters go to bed.

The debate about verisimilitude even crops up in unexpected and apparently clear-cut cases. The (now practically obsolete) debate about whether to use masks on stage featured arguments from verisimilitude on either side. On the one hand, obviously, people in everyday life don't wear masks – so masks aren't verisimilar. On the other hand, as Lessing argued, masks have the advantage of hiding the accidental expressions of the actors – tiredness, frustration, annoyance – expressions that the characters they portray would not in fact exhibit in real life.[26] (If this seems completely counterintuitive, then think of the potentially distracting effect of having real children or real animals on stage, as opposed to having dolls, which at least won't get bored or start acting up.) All of this goes to show that, even if Plato were right about the aim of theatre, there'd be a lot more to say about how it should go about achieving that aim. Of course, for Plato, the aim itself is a suspect one, and so how the aim is achieved is of comparatively little importance.

Second, though, Plato's account of theatrical imitation, taken as simple verisimilitude, is a poor description of what plays, including those in Plato's time, are attempting. Theatre in Athens was part of an elaborate religious festival originally associated with a festival of new wine (and the god of wine – Dionysus). In its mature form, this festival hosted plays in an open-air theatre that could seat about 14,000 people. Plays included song and dance and often depicted supernatural events. None of this is in any way conducive to imitating real, everyday life.[27] Aeschylus could hardly have thought that the best way to imitate the disastrous return of Agamemnon from Troy as accurately as possible (in Plato's sense) was to begin with a masked actor pretending to be a watchman, shouting to himself about the stars. Watchmen on duty do not typically speak in such a way that they can be overheard by 14,000 people. And if the idea is to imitate the action as accurately as possible, then why all the singing and poetry?[28]

Even once all of these things have been discarded (as many subsequently were in Western theatre), one still has a stage and an audience and a number of insurmountable obstacles to ever finding on stage a simple imitation of how the world is. Diderot asks us to imagine a foreigner who has never heard of theatre being brought to a performance and watching it through a grille (so as not to see the audience). The foreigner, Diderot claims, wouldn't think for a moment that the events were real. The reasons for this are many, but they include the strange way the actors speak (so as to be heard) and the impossible amount of action condensed into such a short space of time. Not to mention that the play is often 'set' somewhere other than its actual location. What would the foreigner make of all these people talking as if they were in Thebes or Trézène, when they're actually in Athens or Paris?[29] Even supposing that the foreigner would never be tricked into thinking that the play was real, one might imagine that plays could be more or less verisimilar; hence, some of the debates mentioned above might find a place. But theatre doesn't look like real life and it doesn't seem like a very good description of the work of most playwrights to say that this is what they are intending. If that's the case, then it may count against Plato's analysis of what theatrical imitations are (his metaphysical objection), and also against his criticisms of their effect on gullible audiences (his 'audience gullibility' charge). If we know that what we're seeing isn't (and isn't trying to be) a copy of everyday life, then perhaps we won't have such a gullible attitude towards it.

main argument [handwritten marginal note]

Imitating a deeper truth

Plato claims that imitation directs our attention away from the universal, unchanging world of forms. We've already seen two ways to combat this claim – first, to deny the world of forms; second, to deny that Plato's understanding of imitation is the correct one. But as a follow-up to the second point, the idea of theatre as an imitation that *in some sense* aims at displaying the world to its audience can survive (and has survived). It's just that the simplistic notion of a theatre that tries to be as true to the appearance of life as possible isn't terribly convincing. Hence, a third line of response to Plato: obviously, theatre can't and shouldn't try to imitate the appearance of the world as closely as possible; but it can still, via imitation, tell us about the world. As Hegel remarked, if all art wanted to do was to imitate nature, then it would be just like a worm chasing after an elephant.[30] And in such a case, Hegel adds, we could only admire the artist for his sleight of hand – never for any ultimate, successful achievement. But supposing we accept that theatre isn't aiming at simple verisimilitude. Perhaps, then, theatre can still imitate certain selected features of the world; perhaps, in fact, it can do this very effectively and convincingly. And perhaps, in doing so, it can lead to a greater understanding of (aspects of) the world, which would otherwise be harder to grasp – harder, say, than if confronted in the swirl of everyday existence.

The first response to Plato amounts to a denial that his metaphysics is correct. The second response denies that his analysis of what playwrights are doing (and how audiences respond) is correct. But this third response is compatible with his views on both of those subjects (although it doesn't presuppose them). We could accept that there's a 'more real' world, say, of forms; it's just that theatre needn't direct us away from that real world – it can bring us closer to it. And part of the reason that it brings us closer to the real world is that audiences take these imitations seriously (if not uncritically). This, then, amounts to more than just a defence of theatre against Plato. It suggests that Plato, on his own terms, would do well to take theatre seriously.[31] There is, not accidentally, a parallel here with Christian debates about art in general: art can direct the viewer's attention away from the message of the gospels; or perhaps, if used in a certain way, it can highlight and emphasise certain key messages, hence playing a crucial role. Still, just as with Plato, whose account of the world (as forms and their imitations) led to his views about theatrical imitation, so with the other philosophers we'll consider: what you think theatre can and should imitate depends on what you think the world is and ought to be like. What I want to consider now is a response of this third kind, written by Plato's pupil, Aristotle.

Aristotle *on* mimesis

Aristotle writes about theatre in his *Poetics*. Again, a word about the text. The *Poetics* doesn't read like a completed, published volume, but rather as a series of notes, possibly unfinished. The aims and context of Aristotle's writing are hard to know with any certainty, but the *Poetics* is obviously directly concerned with theatre (and tragedy in particular – it refers to a parallel text on comedy, which, if it was ever written, has not survived) in a way that *The Republic* is not. Aristotle does have brief comments to make about epic poetry, but dramatic poetry is his main focus. The *Poetics* has much to say that may be taken in response to Plato's *The Republic* – and indeed some critics take him to be responding directly to Plato's text – but all agree that Aristotle goes far beyond Plato and many of his concerns are independent of *The Republic*.[32] To state one obvious point: Aristotle is interested in what makes one play superior to another play. This is of no interest to Plato, because, as we've seen, all plays involve imitation and as such are to be condemned. So Aristotle can offer us not only a response to Plato, but also some new thoughts about theatrical imitation.

Aristotle's celebrated definition of tragedy has imitation at its heart:

> Tragedy is an imitation of an action that is admirable, complete and possesses magnitude; in language made pleasurable, each of its species separated in different parts; performed by actors, not through narration; effecting through pity and fear the catharsis of such emotions.[33]

The centrality of imitation (*mimesis*) to this definition might initially seem akin to Plato's claims about theatre. But Aristotle's claim for poetry (and he has tragedy foremost in his mind) is that it 'tends to express universals', which means that it presents 'the kind of thing that would happen'.[34] In claiming that theatre can present universals, Aristotle may be seen to answer Plato's objections.[35] For Plato, theatre takes its audience one step further away from the world of forms than they already are in the world of everyday objects. Both Plato and Aristotle posit larger or more general truths beyond our everyday world. If we loosely equate Plato's world of forms with Aristotle's universals (both offering a kind of fact or truth that cuts across everyday experience and goes beyond the specifics of time and place), then we can take Aristotle's claims about theatre and universals to be a response (of the third kind, above) to Plato: theatre doesn't take us further away from universals; it brings us closer to them.[36] But in turning to universals as the focus for tragedy, Aristotle rejects Plato's idea that what matters in theatrical imitation is simple verisimilitude. He does this in two important ways: first, theatrical imitation can leave things out; second, imitation is permitted to be, in various ways, untrue.

First, Aristotle is clear that the playwright needs to be selective in what he presents on the stage. You can't tell the whole story, so you shouldn't try. If you do try to present, say, *everything* that happens to a particular character, then you will certainly fail and, in the process, end up with something that's unnecessarily complicated (and probably very long).[37]

Aristotle is clearly interested in describing a skill that Plato doesn't acknowledge: playwrights have to select which parts of a story to imitate on the stage, because they can't try to imitate everything. Hence, for example, we may not need to know all that much about Hamlet's relationship with his father or exactly where it is that Hippolyte and Phèdre are talking. In both these cases, one could argue that leaving out this information makes the plays better. The audience might suffocate under the weight of too much information. We all have, as Aristotle notes, a limited memory for details.[38] So a part of the playwright's skill lies precisely in *omitting* details. This may be connected with the goal of presenting what is universal: unnecessary detail would simply be clutter, obscuring the significance of 'the kind of thing that would happen' – which, after all, is what's most significant about the drama.

Second, theatre for Aristotle can imitate falsely in a way that Plato obviously doesn't allow. This has two different features. First, the subject of the play – what is to be imitated – can be something that is not and never was the case:

> The poet is engaged in imitation, just like a painter or anyone else who produces visual images, and the object of his imitation must in every case be one of three things: either the kind of thing that was or is the case; or the kind of thing that is said or thought to be the case; or the kind of thing that ought to be the case.[39]

Of these three options, Plato only seems to rule out all but the first. He is critical of poets for getting their facts wrong (e.g. about the gods); although he is then critical even of factually accurate imitations, on the grounds that they are still imitations.[40] However, for Aristotle, plays can imitate not only what is (as in Plato) but also what is not. Like Plato, he draws a comparison between the poet's and the painter's imitating – but they are no longer merely imitating how the world appears to be. Instead, they *may* imitate things people *say* are the case and they may imitate things that *ought to* be the case. Now, of course, much of what people say is false; and, sadly, much of what ought to be the case is not. Again, we may understand this with reference to the poet's aim of expressing the universal: Aristotle clearly holds that a story that never took place may well be a better expression of the universal than a true story.[41]

The second way that theatre can imitate falsely is not spelled out clearly in the *Poetics*. But what Aristotle does say is that imitations are relative to a purpose. So, to borrow his example, if the purpose of an imitation is zoological, then one has to depict the correct (anatomical) features of an animal in order to train students of zoology; but if the purpose is theatrical or artistic (perhaps to have a greater emotional effect on the audience or viewer) there may be overriding reasons to get some details wrong. A painter, for example, might deliberately alter the proportions or perspective of her subject in order to produce a certain effect (examples of this are easy enough to find in the work of modern painters). This is rather different from the first case, in which the playwright tells a story that isn't true. For Aristotle might allow the playwright to write about a mythical or fictional event, without allowing him to alter such basic things as anatomical details of animals. If such alterations can be part of successful artistic imitation, then Aristotle has obviously moved far beyond Plato, for whom the artist was merely trying to copy as closely as possible the appearance of things. Clearly, Aristotle doesn't make the same demand on imitation that Plato had made.

I am suggesting that Aristotle's claims about imitation are connected with his claim about poetry and universals in two ways: first, the claim that poetry expresses universals provides an answer (of sorts) to Plato's criticisms of imitation; second, the differing way that imitation is licensed in Aristotle, as opposed to Plato, is a result of his commitment to the expression of universals in drama. Nonetheless, Aristotle's claim that dramatic poetry expresses universals may be separated from his analysis of theatrical imitation. Criticisms of his claim about universals are explored in Chapter 2, in the context of a discussion about truth on the stage. But one can criticise (as I shall) his account of theatrical universals, whilst maintaining that his view of imitation is superior to Plato's. As Aristotle correctly saw, playwrights do not merely seek slavishly to reproduce the appearance of everyday events: in producing imitations of actions, they omit parts of the story, they invent a great deal, and, on occasion, they imitate falsely because it improves the artistic value of their work.

Mimesis and imagination

As we've seen, the imitation element of *mimesis* is given extensive treatment in Plato's and Aristotle's accounts of theatre. We saw how, for Plato, the imitation of the everyday on stage takes us further from the true world of forms; and how, for Aristotle, the notion of imitation is much broader and encompasses artistically necessary inaccuracies as well as omitting irrelevant subject matter. But, as we saw at the start of our analysis of Plato, there's another sense of *mimesis* that is clearly involved in a typical performance: namely, a kind of imagining, play-acting or pretending. This kind of *mimesis* is also discussed in Plato and Aristotle, in relation to theatre. It contains, I would suggest, a cluster of rather different notions, which it is helpful to distinguish. Having done so, we can go on to say something about the relationship between the two different types of *mimesis*.

So far, all we've said is that, <u>in addition to imitation-*mimesis*, theatre involves some kind of imagining or play-acting</u>. These terms could then be used to describe two different things: what the audience is doing and what the actors are doing. Plato, for example, seems to be concerned with what actors do; for example, he is worried that the guardians of his ideal city, in pretending to be evil or immoral people, would take on the characteristics of those people.[42] Regardless of whether Plato's concerns are justified, we can see why he holds that actors in some sense pretend to be or imagine that they are some particular character. But there's no doubt that the audience is also engaging in a kind of *mimesis*. When we sit at the theatre, the curtain goes up and a person walks out onto the stage, we see that person not (or not merely) as some old British actor whom we once saw on a TV show about people who spend too much money on their pets, but as *Oedipus*, by now a blind old man who has suffered at the hands of fate. We do not see him as Oedipus because he looks like Oedipus (imitation-*mimesis*). Nor do we see him as Oedipus because the actor is himself pretending to be Oedipus. Indeed, no matter how much the actor pretends to be Oedipus, no matter how much he behaves as Oedipus would behave, we still won't engage with him in the right way unless we, too, are (in some sense) imagining that he is Oedipus.[43]

The kind of *mimesis* that takes place on the part of the actor is different from that which takes place on the part of the audience. First of all, actors are encouraged in some sense to respond (physically) to what is going on. Oedipus is old and blind, so the actress playing Antigone must guide him and help him sit down. The audience pretend that they are seeing a blind man aided by his daughter; but they aren't supposed to help him out, or physically respond in any obvious way. On the other hand, in a typical performance, the actors are under relatively strict instructions to respond with certain words, gestures and actions; these limits do not apply to the audience members, who, within the confines of their seats, are free to respond as they wish. It's perfectly normal for audience members to check their watches, for example – a freedom that does not extend to actors. A second point about the difference between audience and actor *mimesis* is obvious: actors need practice and training, whereas the audience doesn't.[44] At least part of the training of that actor, one might suppose, consists in learning how to pretend, imagine and so on, in relation to different parts (or types of parts). Finally, although human actors (I would suggest) are engaged in pretending when they're on stage, there are successful performances in which the characters are played by machines or puppets. In such cases, the audience is still required to play their part in the *mimesis*, but clearly the 'actors' are not in any reasonable sense 'pretending' or 'imagining'. For this reason, I shall look more closely at audience-*mimesis* than at actor-*mimesis*; we have a chance to discuss actors in more detail in Chapter 5.

Imagination and make-believe

So far, we have discussed imagination, play-acting, make-believe and pretence, without really distinguishing between them. I don't intend to draw careful distinctions between all of these terms, but some distinctions are relevant to our discussion of theatre. First, I'll say something about imagination, then about make-believe.

Imagination

Philosophers writing about imagination have had a wide variety of targets in mind. First, one can talk about the imagination of the artist – in other words, her creativity or ingenuity. We might praise the imagination of, say, Goethe or Strindberg; and in doing so, we suggest that there's something innovative about them – that they have created new genres, or that they are notable for writing in an unusual variety of styles. This focus on the creative imagination of the artist finds particular attention in Kant's *Critique of the Power of Judgement* [46–50]. However, our current focus is the audience at a theatrical performance, and clearly this is not the notion of imagination that we want. When I watch a play, I engage imaginatively with what the author and actors produce; but I myself am not thereby being especially imaginative or creative.

A second notion of imagination is not concerned with artworks in particular, but rather with our everyday engagement with the world. When we watch a plane disappearing into a cloud, we do not immediately assume that the plane has *really* disappeared; we are able, instead, to 'fill in the gaps' in our perception. This 'filling in the gaps' is a kind of imagination: the plane-watcher uses the information she has, but adds some suppositions of her own and draws a sensible conclusion. Hence Hume, for example, holds that the imagination is what, in everyday situations, 'convinces us of the existence of external objects when absent from the senses'.[45] The key point about this kind of imagination is that it is not only typical, but it might even be necessary for everyday functioning. We *need* to think that objects that disappear from sight are still there – not being able to do so would make (e.g.) riding a bike down a street a difficult exercise. Note that this kind of imaginative engagement with what is not directly present to the senses can extend beyond the plane behind the cloud – that was merely the simplest case. One could argue that this imagination is in play when we think about past events or about people who are far away.

This kind of imagination is not about making things up that aren't true, or pretending; it's a necessary feature of correctly understanding the world: if you imagine the plane moving in the cloud, you might well guess accurately when and where it's going to emerge from the cloud. This makes it different from the first, artistic kind of imagination. The artist might well be fanciful or creative with her imaginings; but that is not required of the person who correctly uses imagination to fill in the gaps in sensory perception. The gap-filling imagination is certainly required of the theatre audience; but it's not peculiar to theatre, or to art in general – as we've seen, it's something we make use of all the time.

What we're looking for is what audiences typically do during a theatrical performance (but don't typically do once the performance is over). And here, it seems, we're talking about imagining that fills in gaps, to be sure, but does so in a less sober manner than the Humean version we just discussed. In the prologue of *Henry V*, the Chorus asks the audience for help: they must supplement the action with their imagination:

> O pardon, since a crooked figure may
> Attest in little place a million,
> And let us, ciphers to this great account,
> On your imaginary forces work.
> Suppose within the girdle of these walls
> Are now confined two mighty monarchies,
> Whose high upreared and abutting fronts
> The perilous narrow ocean parts asunder.
> Piece out our imperfections with your thoughts.
> Into a thousand parts divide one man
> And make imaginary puissance.
> Think, when we talk of horses, that you see them
> Printing their proud hoofs i'th' receiving earth.
> For 'tis your thoughts that now must deck our kings,
> Carry them here and there, jumping o'er times,
> Turning th'accomplishment of many years
> Into an hour-glass[…].[46]

What the Chorus asks of the audience is a kind of gap-filling, to be sure, but it isn't the same as what's required of the plane-spotter. There's obviously a difference between imagining the plane in the cloud and imagining that one man is an army. The kind of day-to-day, spatial imagination would tell us that there's one man there (and that he doesn't completely evaporate when he exits stage right); it isn't what we're doing when we turn the single man into an army. I do not wish to assign to Shakespeare (let alone to 'the Chorus' of *Henry V*) a particular notion of imagination, but the Chorus could be asking the audience for help in a number of different ways. Consider the following three cases:

1. I imagine seeing horses in front of me. (Sensory) ~visualising~
2. I imagine that there are horses in front of me. (Propositional)
3. I act as if there are horses in front of me. (Make-believe)

Setting aside 3 for the moment, it will be helpful to spell out the difference between 1 and 2 – a difference commonly noted by philosophers.[47] In the case of 1, the imagination is a matter of visualising, or seeing 'in the mind's eye'. When I imagine the horses, I am imagining a visual perception of the horses.[48] In the case of 2, the imagination involves supposing that some statement is true (without necessarily believing that it is true). The point is that imagination of the second kind (propositional) is possible without imagination of the first kind. I can imagine, say, that somebody other than Shakespeare was in fact the author of *Henry V,* without using any kind of sensory imagination. Of course, I *could* also use sensory imagination in relation to this thought – I could imagine (or visualise) Shakespeare tiptoeing into someone's room, stealing a manuscript and so on. But I don't have to. Looking back to the words of the Chorus, we see that both sensory imagination and propositional imagination are suggested. The audience is invited to imagine *seeing* the horses, their hooves pressing into the ground. But it is also to imagine that certain facts are the case, for example that years have passed in the space of a couple of hours. When the audience imagines that years have passed between scenes, this is obviously not a matter of visualising the years passing, but of supposing or accepting the claim that years have passed.[49] If interpreted in this way, the Chorus' request seems general for theatre: the audience has to imagine seeing certain things, and it has to imagine that certain things are the case.

Make-believe

The third category, above, was a kind of make-believe response – acting as if something is the case. Following 3, I would behave as if there were a horse there, using appropriate gestures and so on. When Aristotle speaks of the pleasure that children take in *mimesis*, it is not clear which of the many meanings of the term he has in mind; after all, children like drawing, copying and play-acting.[50] But, regardless of what Aristotle meant, we can be reasonably sure that even young children show an impressive capacity to engage in make-believe, with relatively elaborate rules.[51] What distinguishes make-believe or play-acting from the kinds of sensory and propositional imagining is its focus on *action*. Make-believe, at least in an everyday sense, suggests an emphasis on responses to certain imagined states of affairs. If two children play a game in which they make believe that a tree-stump is a bear, then the important point seems to be that they act as if it's a bear. This is not the same as visualising the bear; nor is it the same as simply supposing (entertaining the proposition) that the stump is a bear. An important feature of make-believe is that, unlike sensory imagination, it can occur at a group level. I can play a make-believe game of catch with a friend, and our imagination is focused and unified around the game – indeed, the game may require both of us in order to function; but if we were both merely to visualise a ball, there would be little that our imaginings would have in common. The idea that artworks offer us a kind of unified, rule-bound way to make believe (including as a group) is a central tenet of Kendall Walton's highly influential *Mimesis as Make-Believe*. Ever since the publication of that book, the notion of play-acting or make-believe has had an important place in philosophical discussions of art and aesthetics. This is certainly not restricted to theatre: Walton's view is meant to extend to paintings and novels as well as to photos and films. This is not the occasion to enter into the details of Walton's theory. Readers should note that Walton's notion of 'make-believe', although it begins with examples of the children's games like the bear-stump game (the example is his), has a broader application. Hence, for Walton, anyone looking at any picture is engaging in make-believe.[52]

Setting aside Walton's specific use of the term 'make-believe' in his general theory of the arts, then, it seems to me that 'make-believe', in its everyday use, gives an emphasis on *action* as a response to what is imagined, which doesn't quite get the audience's response right. When we see the actor playing Oedipus appear on the stage, we're not meant to take part or get involved. Indeed, the standard notion of make-believe looks like a better description of what the actor is doing than what the audience is doing. That would suggest that the audience is perhaps *watching* a kind of make-believe; but, because they play no part in the action, their imaginary participation doesn't seem best characterised as make-believe or play-acting. Nonetheless, what is useful about this term (in relation to *mimesis* and theatre) is that it reminds us of the sense in which, at a typical theatrical performance, we're all 'in on it'. I am reluctant to characterise an audience as 'playing a game' at the theatre; but it is certainly involved in a kind of group pretence – even if that pretence does not require acting or responding in the manner suggested by the term 'make-believe'.

The relationship between imagination and imitation

We began this chapter with Plato, noticing that theatre looks to require two different kinds of *mimesis*: imitation and imagination.[53] On the one hand, things on stage look like their real-life counterparts. On the other hand, theatre requires pretence, imagination of various kinds, perhaps make-believe. Although they are clearly distinct, we can see that these two broad kinds of *mimesis* are related to one another in a number of ways. It might be, for example, that (say) dressing up the actor to look more like a Greek warrior (imitation) makes it easier for the audience to pretend that they are watching Agamemnon (imagination). Or, going back to the actor's *mimesis*, it might be that pretending to be Agamemnon (imagination) makes you look more like a Greek warrior (imitation). And sometimes, of course, a failure of imitation (a poor accent from an actor, an error in the scenery) makes it harder to engage imaginatively with a performance: poor imitation can undermine imagination.

It might be tempting to conclude from examples of this kind that the more successful the imitation, the more useful it will be as a guide to the imagination. Thus, for example, if the Chorus of Henry V had more space, more men and more horses at his disposal, then he wouldn't have had to go on stage and beg the audience for its indulgence.

I would like to warn against this view. First of all, as the discussion of Plato and Aristotle suggested, theatrical imitation doesn't merely seek to reproduce the appearance of everyday life: there's more to imitating a story than imitating exactly what it would look like if it really happened. Second, even if (following Plato) the purpose of imitation were to reproduce the appearance of everyday life, it's not clear that the more successfully it achieved this goal, the better it would aid our imagination. In his essay on the hobby-horse, Gombrich notes that for the 'hobby-horse' (a broomstick, or a simple horse's head attached to a stick) to become a horse in the imagination of the child, it is not necessary for the broomstick to look very much like a horse at all.[54] Indeed, it is likely that if the broomstick or toy horse were too much like a real horse, then it would ruin the imaginary game. Real horses, after all, are often too large or bad-tempered to be ridden by small children.[55] The same might be said, more generally, for the cavalry of *Henry V*: hundreds of real horses moving across an enormous stage would arguably ruin the effect that the Chorus seeks to produce. The key factor, Gombrich suggests, is not successful imitation but *interest*; it's got to be worth engaging with. We will go a long way with our imaginations – turning the stage into France and England, or the word 'barn' into a barn – if we think there's something in it for us. And whether we are interested or not has as much to do with the subject matter (i.e. what is being imitated) as the likeness.

Theatrical mimesis: *a case study*

Up to this point, I have been keen to keep these two *mimesis* families apart. But I would like to end by suggesting that the way that they interact on the stage (complex as it is) must be a central, perhaps even unique feature of theatrical performance. To do so, I shall consider a case-study: Gloucester on the cliffs of Dover.

In Act IV Scene VI of *King Lear*, the blind Gloucester is led by his son, Edgar, who is disguised as the madman, Poor Tom. Gloucester wants to kill himself, but Edgar devises a scheme to cure him of his suicidal thoughts. He tells Gloucester that he is leading him up a steep slope to the cliffs of Dover; in fact, they are in a flat field. Standing at what Gloucester thinks is the very edge of the cliff, Edgar, as Poor Tom, tells him:

> How fearful
> And dizzy 'tis to cast one's eyes so low.
> The crows and choughs that wing the midway air
> Show scarce so gross as beetles. Half-way down
> Hangs one that gathers samphire, dreadful trade!
> Methinks he seems no bigger than his head.
> The fishermen, that walk upon the beach,
> Appear like mice, and yon tall anchoring barque
> Diminished to her cock; her cock, a buoy
> Almost too small for sight. The murmuring surge,
> That on th'unnumbered idle pebbles chafes,
> Cannot be heard so high. I'll look no more,
> Lest my brain turn and the deficient sight
> Topple down headlong.[56]

Now that we have analysed the term, we are in a position to appreciate the varieties of *mimesis* used in a performance of this scene. As for imitation: the actors may be dressed to look like their characters (Gloucester's eyes may really look damaged, having been 'plucked out' on stage); Edgar is dressed up as a beggar; Edgar himself is impersonating a mad man (and there are hints in his conversation with his father that he isn't very good at it). More generally, the scene is part of a longer story, an action that, in Aristotle's terms, is being imitated before us. As for imagination: certainly, we are to imagine that we are in Dover, hence that the characters have travelled some distance and that certain other facts hold. But we are also to imagine the flat field and hence the difference between where they 'really' are and where Gloucester thinks they are. Sensory and propositional imagination are required, then, to fill in the gaps in the story and the scene itself. But as we listen to Edgar's powerful and imaginative description of the edge of the cliff, we also imagine the cliff-face and the vertigo felt by Gloucester as he waits to jump. We are, therefore, in three places at once: at a performance, with two actors on a simple stage; in a field in Dover, with Edgar and his blind father; at the edge of the cliffs of Dover, with Gloucester and a madman called Poor Tom.

Watching this scene (if suitably immersed), we do not congratulate ourselves for the complex interplay of imitation and imagination – and I am not suggesting that we should. Indeed, what's more remarkable is that, immersed in the action, we don't stop to think about it, because we are engrossed in the *mimesis*. It is not my aim in this book to make a case for theatre, as something unique or highly valuable. But it strikes me that no other artistic medium could provoke complex relations of *mimesis* that we find in a performance of this scene: a novel would erase the actors, with their impersonations and resemblances; a painting, as well as removing the actors, would leave out the features of the plot that enliven our imagination; even film, which has so many similarities with theatre, would lessen the role of imagination – it would probably take us straight to the field, obscuring the three-way relation between stage, field and cliff.

Conclusion

As we've seen, the single word, *mimesis*, unlocks very different families of concepts – imitation and imagination – each of which, in turn, reveals different and interrelated notions. Plato takes imitation to be copying the appearance of the everyday; but for Aristotle, it includes omitting details and even getting things wrong for the sake of poetic effect. As for imagination, we noted the difference between actors and audience; and between creative, gap-filling, sensory, propositional and make-believe imagination. I have suggested that these families of notions interact in a particular way on stage. But with all the different senses of *mimesis* in mind, we can see why it's not merely a feature of theatre, but also of other kinds of artistic and non-artistic activity. Far from meaning the simplistic copying of everyday life, *mimesis*, taken as a whole, looks to be a feature of everyday life, perhaps an important feature.[57]

Further Reading

Plato's *The Republic* and Aristotle's *Poetics* remain the key historical texts for the discussion of theatre and *mimesis*. For a sample of relevant discussions of *mimesis* and *The Republic*, see Nehamas (1982) and (1988); Burnyeat (1999); Halliwell (2002: 37–147); Moss (2007); Cain (2012). On Plato and the theatre: Barish (1981: Ch. 1) offers an overview of Plato's arguments against theatre, while Puchner (2010: Ch. 1) attempts to salvage Plato's reputation as a dramatist of sorts; Rokem (2010: Ch. 1) has a challenging reading of Plato's *Symposium*, in which Socrates discourses with playwrights. Santas (2006) and Ferrari (2007) are helpful general collections on *The Republic*. On *mimesis* in the *Poetics*, see Halliwell (1986: 109–137) and Woodruff (1992); on the *Poetics* in general see Halliwell

(1986), Heath (1996) and the collection of essays in Rorty (1992). See Halliwell (2002) and Huhn (2004) for more detailed and historically sensitive accounts of the concept of mimesis in the ancient world and in the eighteenth century, respectively. For a general account of theatre and *mimesis*, see 'Mimesis' in Woodruff (2008). Walton (1990) remains the central text on *mimesis* in contemporary analytic philosophy, although its focus extends well beyond theatre.

Notes

1 The best summary of the meanings and uses of *mimesis* in Greek writing is found in Halliwell (1986). My categories and examples, broadly speaking, follow his. See Halliwell (1986: 111–5).

2 Note that play-acting and imagination are not quite the same; we shall come to the difference shortly, but for the moment I would like to keep this as a general category, distinct from imitation.

3 References to Plato's *The Republic* give standard section references rather than page numbers; all translations are from the edition listed in the bibliography. It is a well-known conundrum that the discussions of *mimesis* in Books 2 and 3 license some (although not many) kinds of imitations (see e.g. *The Republic* 395c), whereas Book 10 opens with Socrates and Glaucon agreeing that *all* imitative poetry was banned. Some take this as evidence of inconsistency; Nehamas (1988) and Moss (2007) suggest solutions.

4 *The Republic* 393b. See also Plato's *Ion*, in which Socrates discusses poetry with a rhapsode.

5 *The Republic* 394b; but I seem to recall the part of 'narrator' being an important and coveted role in primary school Christmas plays.

6 Broadly speaking, Socrates is concerned with the former in *The Republic*, Book 10 and the latter in *The Republic*, Books 2 and 3. Both are referred to as *mimesis* and he does not distinguish them explicitly.

7 *The Republic* 597b. Speakers' names added for ease of reference.

8 There are other criticisms, too, some of which are explored in Chapter 5.

9 The question of what kind of imitation is being appealed to in the relationship between this world and the world of forms is complicated and has to be set aside. Halliwell (1986: 109-137) has some discussion.

10 See, e.g., Barish (1981: 8); Moss (2007)

11 See Nehamas (1988), Burnyeat (1999: 249–255) and Woodruff (2008: 130–5), from whom the following examples are developed.

12 Barish (1981) raises the question of just what the equivalent of the form of the couch is, in the case of theatrical *mimesis*. For the painter, the three parts are painted-couch/couch/form-of-couch. But theatre looks to imitate action, and forms, being unchanging, are unlikely to be actions (Barish 1981: 6–8). In a sense, Moss (2007) provides a speculative answer, claiming that the 'appearances' imitated by poetry should be understood as 'false appearances' or things-as-they-appear-to-be-but-in-fact-aren't. Poetry imitates what virtue appears to be and in fact isn't: namely, they present it as something shifting and varied, when in fact it is simple and unchanging.

13 Puchner (2010) has recently made a case for reinterpreting Plato as a dramatist, reforming the theatre of his day.

14 We can make room, of course, for 'false' stories that contain deeper truths; the point is that Plato's Socrates, if we take him at face value, doesn't seem to. O'Connor (2007) gives a reading of *The Republic*, looking closely at how it interprets and reworks some of the poetry it criticises. For an analysis of *The Republic*'s final myth, see Halliwell (2007).

15 *The Republic* 389b, 414b–415c.

16 See Lear (2006).

17 Nails (2002: 324–6).

18 Rokem (2010: Ch. 1).

19 Barish (1981: 11).
20 See e.g. Nehamas (1982); Belfiore (1984).
21 This is one of many conventional interpretations of Plato, presented in this chapter, which is challenged in Thakkar (2013). (In fact, at this point in his helpful notes to my manuscript, he wrote: 'I just think this is totally, heinously false.')
22 *The Republic* 604c.
23 *The Republic* 598b-c; also 599.
24 Nehamas (1988: 220). Socrates' use of an analogy between a painting and a mirror serves to emphasise this reading – see Cain (2012). But see Halliwell (2002: Ch. 4) for an alternative reading of the mirror analogy in the context of Plato's writings on visual art.
25 Unity of place is often claimed, falsely, to be a feature of Greek tragedy. Even Aeschylus writes a play in which the setting shifts from Delphi to Athens.
26 Lessing (1962: Section 56, p. 162).
27 However, for an argument that theatre was considered verisimilar see Nehamas (1988: 222–225).
28 Nietzsche's view of ancient tragedy, as we see in Chapter 3, emphasised the musical and poetic elements far above the imitative.
29 Quoted and discussed in Lessing (1962: Sections 84–5).
30 Hegel (1993: 48).
31 For those who treat Plato's dialogues as a kind of 'theatre' or 'drama' – as discussed above – Plato does take theatre seriously by writing his dialogues in conformity with his own philosophy and hence creating a kind of theatre or drama that does bring us closer to the forms.
32 It is generally but not universally accepted that Aristotle is responding to Plato in the *Poetics*; there is no explicit reference to Plato. Note that to say Aristotle is responding to Plato is not to say that he is responding to any particular Plato *text*. And, even if one denies that Aristotle has Plato in mind at all, one can still develop a response to Plato based on the *Poetics*. This last point is acknowledged even by those who seek to deny any other connection. See Woodruff (1992) and Woodruff (2008: 113). At the other end of the spectrum, some critics have entertained the idea that Plato's *The Republic* is itself a response to his young pupil, Aristotle. See Janko (1992), Halliwell (1986: 1) and see also Barish (1981: 7).
33 *Poetics* 49b. References to Aristotle's *Poetics* give traditional line references rather than page numbers; quotations are from the translation listed in the bibliography.
34 *Poetics* 51b.
35 As Woodruff (1992) notes, in claiming that tragedies express or present universals, Aristotle is not saying that they *imitate* universals. Instead, a tragedy presents universals by imitating (particular) *actions*. It is precisely the relationship between the actions and the universals that is so difficult to determine, as I argue in Chapter 2.
36 Of course, Aristotle's universals are *not* Plato's forms. Indeed, Aristotle explicitly criticises Plato's view. See Fine (1993).
37 *Poetics* 51a.
38 *Poetics* 51a.
39 *Poetics* 60b.
40 See *The Republic* 376e on stories as either 'true or false'; and, e.g., *The Republic* 377–9 on censuring the poets for getting the facts wrong.
41 Aristotle has more to say about this, which we discuss in the analysis of history plays in Chapter 3.
42 *The Republic* 395c. Or see *The Republic* 398a for the perfect actor, who would be immediately expelled from the city. We discuss his fears about the immorality of actors in Chapter 5.
43 The example is adapted from Woodruff (2008: 123).
44 The audience may need to have practical knowledge of certain conventions; and certain kinds of training may help them appreciate a performance on a deeper level.
45 Hume's *Treatise*, 266, quoted and discussed in Lamarque and Olsen (1994: 246).
46 *Henry* V, Prologue, lines 15–31.
47 For similar and related distinctions, see Sartre (2004: 8) on conceiving as opposed to imagining. See also Lamarque and Olsen (1994) Ch. 9 and Lopes (2003).

48 By calling this kind of imagination 'sensory', I do not wish to obscure significant differences between actually seeing the horses and having an imaginary visual image of the horses. Sartre (2004), for example, takes great pains to highlight such differences.

49 One could (visually) imagine years passing, but it would require the assistance of a certain kind of (authorial) imagination to do so. Take, for example, the middle section of Woolf's *To the Lighthouse*.

50 *Poetics* 48b.

51 Gendler (2003) gives examples and discusses empirical evidence.

52 See especially Walton (1990: 11–69). Indeed, Walton uses (and freely admits to using) many familiar words in an unfamiliar, technical sense, including 'fiction' (and 'fictional'), 'prop', 'representation'. Music, for example, counts as a prop. We discuss his view as it relates to art and emotion in Chapter 6.

53 That these two kinds of *mimesis* are analytically distinct is uncontroversial. Woodruff (2008) posits a unifying structure to *mimesis* in general, which appeals to the 'natural effect' of the original object (although I note, in passing, that I am sceptical as to whether all original objects could be said to have a 'natural effect' in this sense); Belfiore (1984) argues for a unified account of *mimesis* in Plato's *The Republic*.

54 Gombrich (1978: 8).

55 Sartre (2004: 28), makes a similar point about a stage impressionist, impersonating Maurice Chevalier: the more we look for particular resemblances, the *harder* it is to imagine the impressionist as Chevalier.

56 *Lear*, V.4.11–23.

57 Walton (1990: 7), Woodruff (2008: 124) and others certainly take this view of *mimesis*.

3 Truth and Illusion

Antonin Artaud's provocative collection of essays, *The Theatre and its Double*, is a call to arms for those who care about theatre. 'Life itself is in decline', he announces in the opening lines;[1] but the theatre, which could be a source of significance and vitality, has been stifled and suppressed: 'we have for too long been told theatre is all lies and illusion.'[2] Certainly, the claim that theatre is bound up with untruth, with falsehood and illusion, is long-standing: one ancient source reports that the very first tragedian, Thespis, was called a liar by Solon, the renowned Athenian lawmaker, for making things seem other than they are.[3] In a sense, Plato's complaints (which we explored in the previous chapter) are a version of this. But even without Plato's metaphysical commitments, the idea that theatre is somehow mendacious or illusory has echoed through the ages.

In the Preface, I pointed to the long-running antagonism between philosophy and theatre. We will look at a number of tensions between philosophy and theatre during the course of this study, but perhaps the most significant centres on the questions of truth. To put it provisionally: philosophers have always characterised themselves as truth-seekers, whereas – it is often claimed – theatre requires a certain kind of falsity or illusion. By way of a response, defenders of theatre have often claimed that plays, for all their apparent falsity or illusion, can somehow teach us about the world. This claim also goes back a long way: Gorgias the sophist, for example, claimed that tragedy is a form of poetry in which 'the deceived is wiser than the undeceived'.[4] Dramatists have frequently claimed that their works contain truths, even if such claims have been treated with scepticism.[5] The aim of this chapter is to investigate the claim that theatre rests upon falsity and illusion, and to examine the response that plays can, in fact, teach us about the world. There are, as we shall see, a number of different and apparently contradictory claims made about the relationship between theatre and truth; an important part of my task, therefore, is to try to disentangle them.

Content and form

Artaud's remark about 'lies and illusion' reminds us that, even at first glance, there are two completely different ways in which theatre might be said to be untruthful (or truthful): the first is through content; the second is through form.[6] As for content ('lies'): theatre might be untruthful (or truthful) because it somehow makes false (or true) claims about how the world is.[7] As for style ('illusion'): theatre might be untruthful because, in order to function, it depends upon some kind of illusion on the part of the audience. These things are separate and independent of one another. The focus in the case of content is on whether or not the play makes true or false claims (we will discuss what this might mean); this has nothing to do with the state of the audience. The focus, in the case of form, is on what state is required of the audience in order for the play to get going at all; this is independent of what the play is about, what it claims about the world, what statements it makes and so on.

One could therefore imagine different complaints focusing on the different elements. One way of thinking about Plato, for example, is that he complains about the content of plays being false, whereas their mode of presentation in the theatre making their false content seem true: poets don't really know about carpentry, but when they write plays about carpenters we take their claims seriously. The reverse seems to be the case in the following aphorism from Kierkegaard's *Either/Or*, in which the character referred to as 'A' writes:

> A fire broke out backstage in a theatre. The clown came out to warn the public; they thought it was a joke and applauded. He repeated it; the acclaim was even greater. I think that's just how the world will come to an end: to general applause from wits who believe it's a joke.[8]

In terms of content, what the clown is saying is perfectly true. But the form, the context of theatre is one in which he cannot be believed. What is 'false' about theatre here is not that it makes false claims seem true, but that it shuts out the possibility of recognising what is true and what is false. This, I am suggesting, is a criticism aimed at the form of theatre, not at the false claims made by individual plays. I propose, therefore, to consider separately the questions of how truth relates to the content and to the form of theatre.

Truth and content

When we watch things, we tend to learn from them. Sometimes we learn about the particular things themselves; sometimes we generalise. So if I watch a cat chasing a bird, I learn about that cat and that bird, perhaps also about cats and birds, perhaps predators and prey. For these sorts of reasons, the idea that we learn from theatrical performances in that sense isn't particularly controversial. What's more, when I watch *Hamlet*, I certainly learn plenty about *Hamlet* (the work of art) – about the characters, the plot and so on. It is also true that plays draw our attention to certain things or stimulate our reflection. I'll be thinking about different things, having seen *Hamlet*, than I would have done otherwise. Sometimes we are guided by the performance to think in a particular direction – about a certain historical event or theme or problem. If these kinds of thinking and reflecting – and the conclusions we sometimes draw from them – could be understood as a kind of 'learning from theatre', then that too seems uncontroversial. But those who claim that the theatre can teach us seem to be offering something more than these three kinds of cases can offer. Theatre (perhaps as art or literature more generally) is meant to offer us something special: more – or perhaps: more concentrated – than what we get in everyday watching; going beyond merely knowing about the artwork and beyond simply stimulating our thoughts. The point is not that these kinds of learning aren't important; it's that I don't think that anybody would deny that they are available to us at the theatre – and those who claim that theatre can be a vehicle for knowledge seem to think it can offer something more. To be clear: I'm not suggesting that we learn one thing, or one kind of thing, from theatrical performances: the thought is, rather, that there are lots of different ways that we might think we can learn. The question is: in what way or ways does that occur?

One obvious place to look is at what gets said. Writing about *Hamlet*, Bertrand Russell claims that 'the propositions in the play are false because there was no such man'.[9] There is something that seems right about Russell's remark. The play is a work of fiction – it is made up. And in *Hamlet*, as in most other works of fiction, there are propositions – claims about how the world is – that are false. Hence, for example, Bernardo tells Francisco that the clock has just struck twelve, which is very unlikely to be true in any modern production.[10] That is the sense in which what Russell says seems to be right. But there is also a sense in which Russell's remark seems to miss the point, at least as far as we're concerned. We do often feel as though we have learned something from a play – and it's not clear that what we have learned corresponds to anything that any particular character says. If plays are just strings of false propositions, then what or how do we learn from them? Conversely, if we leave the theatre having learned something about the world, then surely there must be a kind of truth presented to us on stage, at least some of the time? To answer these questions, it will help to think about what gets said explicitly at the performance as well as what may be implied.

Even with regard to explicit statements, Russell's claim requires serious qualification. First of all, there's a great deal more to *Hamlet* than 'propositions' (regardless of whether the propositions are true or false). First, of course, there are sentences that are not propositions. So, for example, neither the opening line ('Who's there?') nor the closing line ('Go, bid the soldiers shoot.') is a proposition: they don't make claims about how the world is and they couldn't be 'true' or 'false'. There's no reason why a play need contain any propositions at all – plenty don't.[11] Second, a play is more than just a series of sentences, whether or not they are propositions, and whether or not those propositions are true. Some plays have no words at all.[12] But even in conventional theatre, actions speak as loudly as words. Philosophers who have written about truth and literature have tended to focus on novels and poems – presumably because these artworks are (typically) a matter of words alone. In theatre, words are only part of the experience.

Finally, however, although many of the explicit propositions uttered in *Hamlet* are indeed false, there's no reason why some of them shouldn't be true. Plays often contain statements about the world that are true.[13] Here are three kinds. First, historical claims: when Horatio describes the state of Rome before the death of Caesar, he is drawing on a description from Plutarch.[14] As it happens, what he claims about Rome is probably false: the dead, we may suppose, did not arise from their graves; but there is no particular reason why we couldn't imagine Horatio saying true things about Caesar's Rome. Second, simple, factual statements: when Gertrude says 'there is a willow grows askant the brook',[15] it may be that, somewhere out there in the real world, there *is* a willow that grows askant a brook – hence, that particular claim is perfectly true. Third, what I call 'words of wisdom': Polonius tells Laertes that 'loan oft loses both itself and friend'.[16] Similarly, *Oedipus Tyrannus* notoriously ends with the 'words of wisdom': 'we should call no one happy, until he has crossed the border of life without enduring pain'.[17] This kind of general claim looks true (or, if one disagrees with these examples, one could at least imagine an equivalent). All in all, the fact that there is no such person as Hamlet, Gertrude or Horatio does not entail that *every* claim that they make about the world is false. Indeed, one could imagine a play in which many more true claims are made than in *Hamlet*.[18]

Can any of these true propositions help us to understand what we learn from plays? In the first two cases, clearly not. As to historical claims, we do not go to *Hamlet* to learn about Ancient Rome.[19] Second, suppose it's true that a willow grows askant a brook; Gertrude goes on to say that Ophelia drowned in that brook, a claim that (if we follow Russell) we must suppose is false, because there was no such person as Ophelia. In the context of watching the play, we do not distinguish in any way between these two claims, even although one is true and one is false; it makes no difference to us; it has no connection (I would suggest) with whatever it is that we think we learn from plays like Hamlet.[20]

That leaves 'words of wisdom'. The kinds of 'truths' expressed here look rather more like what we might want to learn from *Hamlet*. In the case of plays like *Hamlet* in particular, these are the sorts of phrases that get quoted independently of their dramatic context. Of course, even if one holds that some of the 'words of wisdom' uttered during the course of a play are true, there may well be many that are false. It doesn't seem right to say that what is learnt from the plays is achieved by the spectator sifting through the various 'words of wisdom' and accepting all the ones that she finds plausible. To put the point another way: if one were to go through the text of *Hamlet*, locate all the 'words of wisdom' with which one happened to agree, isolate them, and them get someone to read them out on stage to an audience, our intuition, I suspect, would be that this would be nothing like the 'learning' experience we talk about when having gone to see a performance of *Hamlet*. This suggests that 'words of wisdom' can't be all there is to it.

This consideration of 'words of wisdom' has been a matter of explicit statements in the text of plays. But, to state the obvious, words of wisdom, even when they appear explicitly in plays, are often woven into the action. They are not best understood as isolated statements by the playwright, in which he discloses his general views about the world. That is one reason why isolating the true words of wisdom from *Hamlet* and reading them out on stage would completely fail to have the right effect. Similarly, the claim that we shouldn't say that someone is happy until she has died without pain is hard to separate from the story of Oedipus himself. Putting this thought together with what we said earlier about the non-propositional content of a play, we have an incentive to move away from looking for truths in the explicit language of the play, and look instead for implicit truths.

Implicit truths

In a typical performance, a great deal is *implied*, rather than stated explicitly. If the explicit propositions uttered on stage are of no use to us (on their own), then perhaps we should turn to what is implied. Within what is implied, it might be helpful to distinguish between the specific (or particular) claims and general (or universal) claims.[21] Ibsen's *Ghosts*, for example, implies the particular claim that Captain Alving had syphilis, although this is never stated outright. It also implies the general claim that (contemporary) society systematically disadvantages women.

When people talk about learning from theatre, one common suggestion is that they are learning from implied, universal claims.[22] This thought is expressed by Aristotle, and I focus on his view, although he is by no means the only one.[23] Aristotle, recall, argued that tragedy presents universals to its audience. In presenting universals (what 'would happen'), plays can teach their audiences about the world. Aristotle's claim about universals has nothing to do with whether the explicit statements made by particular actors are true or false. Tragedy is an imitation of *action* (including verbal and non-verbal elements) and it is via the action that universals are made apparent to the audience. The play distils universal features of the everyday and then presents them on stage, such that what the audience sees is a presentation of what types of people do in types of situations. Hence the presentation of universal truths (about types of people in types of situations) is perfectly consistent with a fictional story, featuring completely made-up characters, who utter no truthful statements whatsoever; the universal truths must be implicit, not explicit.

When he wants to explain what he means by poetry expressing universals, Aristotle states that it shows us 'the kind of speech or action which is consonant with a person of a given kind in accordance with probability or necessity'.[24] Two interesting problems immediately arise from this account. First of all, what kinds of speech and action accord with probability and necessity? Second, whatever they are, how do plays show them? To put the point another way: if we want to know whether, say, *Oedipus Tyrannus* presents the kind of thing that would happen, then we need to ask two questions: first, what kinds of things happen? Second, what kind of thing does *Oedipus Tyrannus* present?

The first question – just what are the kinds of thing that happen? – is obviously not just a question for the theatre. But I stress it in order to distinguish between the (purported) message or claim made by a particular play and the truth of that claim. Even if we accept that plays are able to put alleged 'universals' on show, there's still a vast debate to be had about what kinds of things are in fact universal. Aristotle clearly thought both that certain types of people behaved in certain recognisable ways and that people's characters were relatively consistent over time. Plays – to express universals – should therefore depict people who correspond to type and who do so consistently.[25] This view has been a popular one: thus, fairly strict limits have, in the past, been placed on which characteristics were appropriate for which character types;[26] or actors and actresses could specialise in being a particular character type, known in nineteenth-century England and America as 'lines of business'.[27] Some of these 'types' look false or dated now, such as Aristotle's claim that it is inappropriate for women to display certain types of courage, or Lessing's view that women couldn't be viciously or cold-bloodedly murderous, although they could be murderous as a result of jealousy or some other passion.[28] And August Strindberg wrote, in the preface to his play *Miss Julie*, that the very idea of character as playwrights had hitherto conceived of it was completely false. People change their minds, act irrationally and behave inconsistently; strictly speaking, then, there's really no such thing as 'character'. If that's your view, then it will certainly change your notion of which universals might be on display.[29] There's a big difference between the communication of some universal truth and the confirmation of a particular prejudice or social attitude.

Even if one were agreed on what counts as a 'universal truth', we should be concerned with the second question – namely, how are such things communicated on the stage? Just what is universal about *Oedipus*? For one thing (as we saw in the previous chapter), we should avoid the temptation to equate what's universal ('what would happen') with 'what happens most often' or 'what happens every day'. *Oedipus Tyrannus* does not, thankfully, depict an everyday event, nor does it depict that event in a way that makes it look like an everyday event. Discovering that you've murdered your father and married your mother is hardly typical in that sense – and there don't seem to be any universal rules for how people behave in such conditions. Indeed, part of the fascination with the play lies exactly in the fact that the audience gets to watch the spectacularly unusual and horrifying event unfold before their eyes. But Aristotle obviously thinks that certain elements of that play may be universalised. Perhaps the play depicts a universal claim about how a person like Oedipus would probably or necessarily behave in such circumstances: someone concerned with his own status, who identifies himself with the prosperity of Thebes under his guidance, whose pride derives from his ability to solve problems, who would hunt relentlessly for whoever had polluted the city. Perhaps we could accept that such a person with such a history might tend to act in the ways that he does. Hence, in this sense, the play might offer the kind of thing that would happen.[30]

The trouble is that the more we include the specific details of the story (Oedipus' character, the riddle, the swollen foot), the less we end up with something that looks like a universal – like something that presents a *kind* of person or a type of situation. If the play just tells us what Oedipus *himself* would do in his particular circumstances, then we're left with very little that's universal. On the other hand, the more we try to generalise (the play shows us that 'a good man, acting in accordance with his best judgement, acts in a way that leads, unforeseeably though with astonishing ease, to his own destruction'.[31]), the more we end with ineffective slogans and platitudes that fail to capture the subtleties of the play and, often enough, happen to be non-universal or even false.

Furthermore, once we generalise away from the specifics of the story, we face the problem of different and perhaps inconsistent universals. Does *Oedipus Tyrannus* tell us the story of a proud man, or of a relentless truth-seeker, or both? Does it say that what happens to such a type is that he always comes to no good, or that he *probably* comes to no good? Does it tell us that we should try to accept our fate or that it doesn't matter whether or not we try to accept our fate? If it tells us something universal about humans, is it that knowing the truth about ourselves would ruin us, or is it that we all secretly want to kill our fathers and marry our mothers (and that this knowledge could be therapeutic)?

All in all, it's not very clear which *kind of thing* or *kind of person* or *general truth* a complex play like *Oedipus* or *Hamlet* can be said to depict. To put the point another way: we said that the universal claims are not uttered explicitly, but rather are implied by the action; the problem that we are facing here is that it's difficult (which is not to say impossible) to say just *what* is being implied.

By highlighting the difficulty of pinning down which universals are implied by a theatrical performance, I do not wish to suggest that *no* universals are implied or that nobody learns from theatre in this way. But our discussion of Aristotle's view raises a significant concern. As we have seen, hunting for explicit formulations of universal propositions that are (supposedly) implied in plays is a difficult business. If it's open to the individual spectator to derive certain implications into one universal proposition or another, then we are no longer talking about a straight-forward instance of 'learning' from true propositions (implicitly) expressed in the play; instead, we are talking about a kind of interaction between spectator and performance, in which the spectator develops or reflects upon her own views in relation to the play. There is nothing wrong with this, and indeed it may be an important part of what we enjoy about and take from good theatre. But this is not best characterised as 'learning truths' from a performance. If it is a kind of learning, then it's not clear that anything in the performance itself needs to amount to a truth, implicit or otherwise; all that's required is a certain kind of provocation or stimulation to thought. I don't suppose anyone would deny that theatre is able to offer that.

Non-propositional learning: learning how and learning that

Particular plays may convey certain messages – taken to be true by some spectators – either via what is uttered or via what is implied. In both cases, we have been talking about a play communicating to a spectator the claim that something is the case (a claim that may or may not be true). Philosophers often distinguish between knowing *that* something is the case (e.g. I know that a bicycle has two wheels) and knowing *how* to do something (e.g. I know how to ride a bicycle). On a standard view, knowing how differs from knowing that in at least two ways: first, knowing how does not consist in the knowledge of any particular proposition; second, knowing how manifests itself in having a particular capacity to act in certain ways.[32] Correspondingly, we might look to learning in two different ways: learning that something is the case, compared with learning how to do something. After all, we often learn *how* to do certain things without learning facts at all. Ancient rhetoricians were convinced that the best method of learning how to deliver an excellent speech was to watch other excellent speakers and to imitate and practice accordingly; this wouldn't involve any statements of fact about how best to deliver a speech – indeed, most writers on the subject agreed that trying to write down clearly articulated truths about delivery would be pointless. Finally, note that learning how needn't have any verbal content at all: I might learn how to drill a hole in a wall just by watching and repeating – neither the action nor the learning requires words; nor would I necessarily be able to express what I have learnt in words. This is helpful, because it takes us away from needing to look for verbally expressed (or implied) 'truths' to account for our learning – and summaries of the 'messages' from particular plays are notoriously weak (what one writer has nicely called the 'poverty of propositional paraphrase'[33]). So might what we learn from theatre be a matter of learning *how*, not learning *that*?[34]

For the moment, though, note that if the first feature of knowing/ learning how (that it is not propositional) was helpful, the second looks to be more problematic – namely, the commitment to 'knowing how' as an activity. The typical cases of learning how involve some kind of activity in response to something: riding a bike, drilling a hole in the wall, delivering a better, more powerful speech. It's not clear what the equivalent of this activity would be in the case of theatre. Audiences at plays are, to the dismay of some critics (such as Nietzsche or Rousseau), distinctly inactive; they are not obviously practising anything, during or after the performance.[35] The second, related point has to do with the evidence that something has been learned. It is perfectly true that those who have learned how to do something cannot always articulate in words what or how they have learned. But there is still little doubt *that* they have learned something. Abilities, like delivering a speech well or using new philosophical terminology and techniques, may not be reducible to lists of facts; but they can be demonstrated. Theatre audiences do not leave with any obvious new skill or ability.

Illusion

The other kind of worry that we noted at the start of this chapter was focused on the form of theatre, not on the content. This worry was focused on the concept of theatrical illusion. The association between theatre and (some form of) illusion is long-standing, although there have also been dissident voices.[36] But the question of what the illusion is and the related question of whether the audience is in some sense deceived by the illusion have proved highly contentious. Thus the focus of our discussion will be twofold: (1) What kind(s) of illusion do we find in theatre? (2) Does this kind of illusion require that audiences are deceived in some way? We will look at both of these questions in relation to different kinds of illusion. Before doing so, however, a word about their connection.

One reason why some might object to the very idea that theatre requires illusion is the thought, expressed by Dr Johnson amongst others, that theatre audiences are not deceived by what they see.[37] If illusion implies the state of being deceived by something and theatre audiences are not deceived, then they can be under no illusion. Some critics have suggested that the term 'illusion', when applied to the theatre (or to other kinds of art) is nothing more than a useful misnomer: thus, for Sparshott, it is 'a shockingly bad description' but 'an uncommonly useful label' and hence what is called 'illusion' is 'no more an illusion than German measles is measles or Vienna steak steak'.[38] If Sparshott's remarks may be taken to apply to 'illusion' at the theatre, then we might hope for reconciliation: no, theatre audiences are not *really* under any illusions, because they are not really deceived; but they do experience something analogous to an illusion, something for which 'illusion' is an adequate metaphor.

Unfortunately, however, things are not that simple. To agree on this account of theatrical illusion, we would have to agree on two claims: first, that theatre audiences are not deceived; second, that illusion implies deception. Neither is uncontroversial. As to the first, we have already noted Gorgias' remark that theatre audiences are deceived. Stendhal claims that a spectator may achieve (very brief) moments of 'perfect illusion', in which she believes that what is merely imitated on stage is really taking place; for him, then, the audience certainly is deceived (albeit momentarily) and, what's more, plays achieve their best effects just when spectators are subject to perfect illusion.[39] As to the second, although illusion can deceive, there are clear cases in which it does not. Driving down a familiar stretch of road on a hot day, I see a mirage for the tenth time; I am not deceived in the slightest, but for all that the mirage is still an illusion. So being the victim of the mirage illusion does not entail having the false belief that there's water on the road. So we can't agree, without further discussion, that theatre audiences aren't under illusions because they aren't deceived: for one thing, some people think audiences are deceived; for another, victims of illusions don't always entertain false beliefs about what they are seeing. Discussion of theatre and illusion requires a more detailed analysis of the kinds of illusion that may be present at the theatre, as well as the relation between each type of illusion and deception on the part of the audience.

Optical illusion

The Fraser Spiral (see figure) is an optical illusion: it is carefully constructed in such a way that it looks spiral; but, in fact, it is a series of
discrete, concentric circles, which do not touch each other. To begin
with, let us note some of the features of this illusion. First, the illusion is
not total — it is not, say, a very (or maximally) realistic dream. The latter
is the kind of 'illusion' suggested when philosophers speak of the 'argument from illusion', which begins by imagining someone (say) *completely*
under the illusion (i.e. very convincingly dreaming) that she is in front of
the Taj Mahal.[40] It is a stipulated feature of the totalising illusion that
'one cannot tell from the phenomenology of one's awareness' whether or
not it is an illusion.[41] But the Fraser Spiral is not like that. It is clearly
distinguishable from a real spiral, because you can follow any individual
circle with a pencil and see that you are going round in a circle, not
spiralling into the centre. Indeed, one could go further: optical illusions
are often found in books for children, and it is often part of the fun of
optical illusions that the person under the illusion can show that the
picture on the page is not as it appears to be. Illusions like these may also
play a significant part in visual art: hence, a talented sketch artist can
make the white of the blank page in one part of the picture look brighter
than the same white page in another part of the picture.[42]

A second feature of the Fraser Spiral has been alluded to already, but let
us be more explicit in this case. As an optical illusion, the Fraser Spiral
is 'belief-independent': it *looks* like a spiral to me, even once I know that
it is not a spiral. As I look at the Fraser Spiral, I am still experiencing
an illusion — even though I don't have any false beliefs about it at all.

Illusion is therefore compatible with an absence of false beliefs (about
the illusion). Another way to put this would be to say that the victim
of the illusion need not be deceived: hence, spectators may be 'victims of
illusion', even although they know the truth about what they are seeing.
Of course, that doesn't mean that there is *no* connection between illusion
and false belief. It's just that a necessary condition for X being an illusion
cannot be the existence of a false belief exactly when I look at X.

If we all agree that optical illusions are illusions, then an obvious
question to ask would be: 'are there optical illusions at the theatre?' The
answer is that sometimes there are, notably as a feature of set design. From
the perspective of the audience member, the 'room' on stage can look a certain way (say, symmetric); on closer inspection, it turns out to be completely
different (say, asymmetric). But, of course, plenty of theatre does not
make use of optical illusions in set design, so it wouldn't be right to say
that optical illusions are a systematic or fundamental feature of theatre.
The most we can say is that they may well be employed and (from the
perspective of the audience) it can be hard to tell.

General sensory illusion

Perhaps the Fraser Spiral and other optical illusions just form a subset of
an 'enriched' or broader kind of sensory illusion, which is a much more
widespread feature of theatre?[43] In designing a set as, say, a living room,
it seems that the set designer has to decide whether to make the 'room'
with materials that are as they seem to be (the 'room' seems to be and in
fact is made of plaster, bricks, etc.) or which are not as they seem to be
(the room seems to be made of plaster, bricks, etc., but is in fact made of
cardboard, canvas, etc.). A typical set may well make use of at least *some*
scenery that is not what it appears to be; so, if the latter is a kind of
illusion, then it seems that illusion is at least a common feature of theatre.
I call this 'set-design illusion', but it could be a feature of props and of
the actors' costumes, too. (A 'live' example might be the well-established
although now unfashionable practice of dressing up children to look like
adults, and then placing them at the back of the stage to make it look
further away.) The key point is that (unlike some other illusions that we'll
discuss) these illusions, if they are such, could arise from a static view or
snapshot of the stage and actors: we are talking about the materials of the
set and costumes, perhaps the make-up, lighting and so on.

It is important not to exaggerate the use and effectiveness of this kind
of illusion. Often sets, costumes, lighting and sounds are aids to imagination
rather than attempts to fool an audience. A man sitting on a simple, wooden
chair and wearing a paper crown does not produce the illusion that we are
looking at a king, seated on a throne in full, splendid regalia; what we see

are conventions that we are able to 'read off'. The aim of creating a set that resembles as closely as possible what it represents is a relatively new phenomenon in the history of theatre, although many theatregoers now take it for granted. The existence of conventional representation, such as the wooden chair and paper crown, has led some to argue that convention accounts for all of what we see at the theatre, hence that there is no illusion at all of this kind. Sensible theatregoers (people who understand what theatre is) know full well that what they see is a representation, so it's not a matter of illusion but one of convention.[44]

However, convention isn't all there is to it: sometimes (following the set-design example) spectators are genuinely tricked into thinking that a wall is made of brick, when it is not, and so on. In Thomas Mann's novel *Confessions of Felix Krull, Confidence Man*, Krull, the trickster narrator, recalls a for-mative childhood trip to the theatre. During the performance, he becomes enamoured with the dashing young actor, Müller-Rosé; but, meeting him in the dressing-room afterwards, Krull realises that (amongst other things) Müller-Rosé is ugly, smelly, spotty and coarse, and that his beautiful chestnut hair was merely a wig which, now removed, reveals him to be a redhead.[45] Müller-Rosé's hair looked chestnut but is in fact red. Krull, who believed that Müller-Rosé's hair was chestnut, had a false belief. It looks very much like the use of make-up, wigs, perhaps also lighting, very often, even typically, causes spectators to hold false beliefs. The same goes for set-design.

Now, as we've already seen, there's more to an illusion than the pro-duction of false belief; and some illusions function without producing false belief at all. But it's clear from this brief discussion that set-design can lead to things seeming to be other than they are, hence to deception and false belief on the part of the audience. All of this, taken together, seems adequate for the conclusion that this kind of illusion may well be a common feature of theatrical performances. Even so, does this mean that illusion (of this kind) is always present at the theatre? The answer, of course, is no. We have already seen how theatre can function perfectly well without scenery, without props, without elaborate make-up and costume design. Recall Peter Brook's set of minimal conditions for an act of theatre (the 'bare stage'): clearly, the kind of illusion under discussion here would not be necessary for such a performance. But we should notice that the set-design illusions occur relatively frequently, when one includes all the features of the set, the props and the costumes; and sometimes it can be very hard to know whether or not they are being employed.

The illusionist's illusion (magician)

A third kind of illusion may be associated with the theatre – namely, the illusions of the so-called 'illusionist', or stage magician. The illusionist, let us call him 'Houdini', *may* during the course of his performance make use of optical illusions and set designs of the kind we have already discussed. But he may not; and he certainly doesn't have to. Consider the following case: Houdini is bound tightly in chains and handcuffs, standing on the edge of a tank of water; his stage assistant kisses him goodbye (for he might really drown) and we see him thrown into the tank; a curtain is lowered, so that we no longer see him; a few minutes later he emerges, triumphant, freed from the chains. For the audience member, let us suppose, it looks as though Houdini has somehow wriggled himself free from his chains, using nothing but his body.[46] In fact, when the assistant kissed him, she passed him a key in her lips which, when the curtain went down, he used to unlock his chains. This example is not a visual illusion like the Fraser Spiral or like the 'brick wall'. In a very general sense, of course, things are not as they seem to be. But there is no trick *object* (the cardboard that looks like brick, the circles that look like a spiral); the trick was in the action, the concealment, the sleight of hand.

Although we have seen reason to doubt the use of deception or false belief as a criterion for theatrical illusion, note that Houdini's trick – the one that I just outlined – is connected with false belief in a different way. Most importantly, it is not obviously belief-independent: if I know full well that Houdini has just been given the key, then I won't be taken in by the illusion. I may admire his skill, but that is a different matter. Indeed, one can work backwards and say that if the illusion has worked on me then I probably have some false beliefs: that Houdini did not have a key, that the kiss was innocent, and so on. This helps explain other kinds of responses to the illusionist: when I nervously watch Houdini sawing his assistant in half, I probably don't *really* (and falsely) believe that he is subjecting her to a horrible, violent death. Still, even if I don't falsely believe that she is being sawn in half, I am likely to be (falsely) believing something else. Perhaps her legs are not where I believe them to be, and what I believe to be her legs are the legs of a different assistant. Thus, for both the handcuffs and the sawing tricks, if I know exactly how the trick works then illusion will simply fail. This is not so for the Fraser Spiral.

Do we find Houdini-type illusions at the theatre? Illusionists' shows are themselves a type of theatre, so in one sense the answer is obviously yes. But do we find them in more conventional, dramatic theatre? Certainly, on some occasions we find exactly that: Charlotte performs some in Act III of *The Cherry Orchard*. More generally, there are frequent examples of the audience being made to believe that something has happened, when in fact it has not. So it can look to the audience as if, say, one character has slapped another, when in fact she has not. This may be less impressive, but it is structurally equivalent to Houdini's handcuffs illusion: the audience really believes that something has taken place; but if they knew what was going on, the action would not necessarily have the same effect. Just as Houdini creates tricks to convince the audience that something is happening, when in fact it is not, so actors learn and practise plenty of methods by which they can fool their audiences; and, often enough, the spectator who recognises such a trick sees this as a mark of poor acting, just as the spectator at Houdini's show may be disappointed if she figures out what the kiss was for. Note that to say that the stage slap may be equivalent to Houdini's handcuffs trick is not to say, first, that there's no difference between the two. There is: Houdini's audience have come to see him in order to be awe-struck by his illusions, whereas the stage 'slap' is part of a dramatic performance with a different set of criteria for success (whatever they are). Second, this is not to say, of course, that every stage 'slap' is or ought to be trying to fool the audience into thinking that it is real: sometimes the slap is real; other times it might be obviously fake, for comic or for aesthetic purposes. But examples of this kind are not particularly hard to find and one can understand why they have been associated with theatre.

In the case of the stage 'slap', the actors behave in such a way that the audience thinks that something has taken place when, in fact, it hasn't. One can, of course, imagine an equivalent false belief, which doesn't exactly relate to an action. Recall the young Krull, who believed that Müller-Rosé, the actor, had chestnut hair. Krull visits Müller-Rosé not because he likes chestnut hair, but because he is so impressed by Müller-Rosé's personality. Müller-Rosé is loved by the audience, male and female, and he receives rapturous applause – applause directed at him, not at his character (even if it is in virtue of his character). It is not merely Müller-Rosé's hair colour, then, that turns out to be illusory. Müller-Rosé's 'dashingness', his heart-stealing prowess turns out to be a product of the stage, of lighting, make-up and distance. The contrast between Müller-Rosé's attractiveness on stage and his unattractiveness in the dressing room is what particularly fascinates Krull: Müller-Rosé is the repulsive little worm, who, each night, is transformed into a butterfly by the tricks of the stage.

To reiterate: Krull has not mistaken the character (as a whole) for the actor. He doesn't think that Müller-Rosé is the attaché (whose character he was playing). But just as it isn't possible to tell (as a spectator) whether Müller-Rosé's hair is his real hair, so, from watching the whole performance, it isn't possible to tell whether Müller-Rosé's charm is a function of the stage or a function of the actor (or both). Of course, this needn't just apply to charm: one might imagine getting a false impression of how frail an actor is. The person who asks, after a performance, 'do you think the actor really is so frail?', has not misunderstood the nature of theatre. Indeed, she has recognised that theatre tends to present actors in such a way that they (i.e. the actors) seem to be what they are not. As with the Houdini case, it seems at least possible that, had Krull gone to see the performance knowing Müller-Rosé's off-stage character and appearance, he wouldn't have found him so attractive when he was on the stage; similarly with the actor's frailty.

Krull, as we have seen, does not believe that Müller-Rosé is an attaché. But sometimes we do unthinkingly transfer the qualities of the characters to the actors who play them, without necessarily realising it. For some philosophers I have corresponded with while developing this chapter, the idea that we can be seriously confused about what 'belongs' to the actor and what to the character after a performance is simply unthinkable. But consider the following anecdote, reported by the playwright Michael Frayn:

> I once saw a performance of *The Elephant Man* at the National Theatre where one of the cast collapsed on stage. [...] Nicky [Henson, another member of the cast] told me afterwards that a doctor who happened to be in the audience [...] had at once gone backstage to help. After examining the patient he diagnosed not a heart attack but simple hyperventilation – then turned to Nicky and asked him with courteous professional deference if he agreed. Nicky looked around to see if there was a second doctor standing behind him. There was not. The second opinion was himself, or rather the character he had been playing on stage, who happened to be a doctor and whom he evidently embodied offstage still, even in the eyes of a real doctor.[47]

What this anecdote tells us is, of course, open to interpretation. Clearly, in the heat of the moment, the (real) doctor got a little confused; in general, once the performance is brought to an end, we do not take the actors to have the knowledge of the professionals they portray. It's unlikely, furthermore, that the doctor mistook the actor for the *Victorian* doctor he was playing on stage, or a doctor involved in the case of the Elephant Man, and so on. But this story might help to caution us against oversimplified dismissals of the power of theatrical illusion. After all, the doctor was not improvising along to the play, or suspending his disbelief, or taking some sort of fictional stance to the patient – that would have been wholly inappropriate to the gravity of the situation. Nor did the doctor lack a rudimentary understanding of how theatre works. Rather, he made a mistake, directly as a result of the theatrical performance. A mistake this pronounced may be rare – the exception, rather than the rule – but it should not be ignored, all the same.

It's likely that there will be types of theatre in which these sorts of illusions do not arise. Marionette theatre, for example, is unlikely to raise questions about the personality traits of the actors compared with the characters. But so far we have identified four types of illusion that it would be hardly surprising to find at a typical performance: optical illusions in the design of the stage; objects and materials that seem to be that which they are not; Houdini-type tricks, which make you think that actions have taken place, when in fact they have not; finally, actors whose qualities are sometimes employed and sometimes cleverly concealed for the sake of the performance. To say that not a single one of these is a necessary condition for theatre is to miss the point. When you go to the theatre, any or all of them may well be in play. To say that you can't believe your eyes is not to say that your eyes are always deceiving you; it's to say that they aren't reliable.

Under the spell

Although we have enumerated a number of different illusions that may be in play at a performance, it is notable that when philosophers (and dramaturges) write about theatre and illusion they often appear to have something else in mind – something that I want to characterise as being 'under the spell' of the theatre. This is the kind of trance-like or dream-like state that occurs as the spectator is absorbed in the action taking place on stage. Indeed, it seems to be the comparison with the dream that comes up most often. The spectator under the spell is watching intently, engrossed in the performance; the spectator not under the spell is thinking about what she will do once the performance is over, and checking her watch to see when that will be.

In each of the previous examples of illusion, I've suggested that they can be, perhaps often are, a feature of a typical theatrical performance. But being 'under the spell' seems to be a much more central feature of theatre. Indeed, it is a perfectly common and intelligible complaint about a performance that, for whatever reason (be it the poor acting, the miserable script, the nearby spectator talking on her phone) one simply could not get lost in the play or the spell kept on being broken – what Coleridge nicely calls being 'disentranced'.[48] We have seen why speaking of theatre in terms of 'necessary conditions' is a hard task, but a performance that does not in any way demand or produce the need to go 'under the spell' is at least a non-typical kind of theatre.[49] This accounts for the number of writers who are interested in techniques for maintaining theatrical illusion (in this sense) as well as those who are keen to warn against certain pitfalls. Needless to say, there has been plenty of disagreement: the discussions about the 'unities' of time and place (especially in France, but also elsewhere) were often associated with a concern for shattering the illusion: would an audience simply be unable to engage with a play that depicted the passing of several months within just a few hours? Is the use of advanced rhetorical technique, word-plays and poetic skill an impediment to illusion?[50] Are the rules for maintaining the spell different in comedy and tragedy?[51] And the debates between symbolist and naturalist theatre at the turn of the previous century often focused on what would maintain or disrupt illusion. Thus, on the naturalist side, Ibsen could write to the director of *An Enemy of the People*, demanding that the staging should not disturb 'the illusion that everything is real and that one is sitting and watching something that is actually taking place in real life'; Bruisov the symbolist could argue, in contrast, that 'the more lifelike the sound [of crickets chirping in a performance of *Uncle Vanya*], the less convincing the illusion'.[52] These (often heated) debates testify to the significance of this kind of illusion in theatre.

The claim that going under the spell is central to theatre must be qualified in two ways. First, as many writers on the subject have noted, it is not a binary matter of either being or not being under the spell. Stendhal and Coleridge (for example) are clear that one drifts in and out of this state to varying degrees during the course of a performance. Second, it is not necessarily the case that the more effective the illusion, the better the play. I've said that plays are unsuccessful (or, if successful, highly unusual) if they do not produce a certain quantity of illusion of this kind; but that doesn't mean that the more, the better. Breaking the spell, or manipulating its intensity, may well be part of a successful performance. Thus, for example, Lessing notes that tragedy depends far more heavily on illusion than comedy: breaking the spell can be a good way of making people laugh, but a bad way of making them cry.[53] For Coleridge, some modes of breaking the spell may be very effective near the beginning of the action, but disruptive at its height (for others, vice versa).[54]

The spell of theatre is clearly distinct both from visual illusions (the Fraser Spiral, the 'brick' wall) and from Houdini-type illusions. Coleridge rightly says of the spectator under the spell that 'it is at all times within his power to see the thing as it really is'.[55] This does not hold for the other types of illusion discussed so far.

One question that we have about the spell phenomenon is whether the spectator under the spell genuinely (but mistakenly) believes that the imitated action is real. As we have seen, the presence or absence of deception is not necessarily a helpful way of establishing whether or not the spell counts as an illusion; but because the discussion of illusion often veils a discussion of false belief, it is appropriate to say something about their relationship.

The main point to make is that it's difficult to tell what the spectator does and does not believe.[56] After all, how could we settle it? A standard (although not flawless) way to find out what someone believes is to ask her; but asking someone who is under the spell is going to break the spell. Another way (again, hardly perfect) of finding out what people believe is to look at their behaviour. Do people watching plays behave as if the plays are real? Unfortunately, the behaviour of spectators who are highly absorbed in what they are watching (especially those who weep during tragedies, or, equivalently, look scared during horror films) is far from uncontroversial and it has been the subject of much philosophical discussion, some of which we explore in Chapter 6. We can't go into the details here, but clearly there isn't an unambiguous answer. Indeed, much of the discussion seems to *begin* with the thought that people can't believe that what they're seeing is real (and hence to draw conclusions about the meaning of their behaviour) or, instead, to begin with the thought that people can't cry unless they think something is real (and hence to draw conclusions about their beliefs). A last option, favoured by Plato and Augustine – and not without contemporary advocates – is to conclude that audiences are temporarily insane.

A final strategy might be to point to the contribution of the spectator. Given that we can snap ourselves out of the spell, one could argue that it requires a kind of consent, cooperation or even active involvement and, hence, that the spectator is not deceived. How we describe the 'voluntary contribution' from the spectator may vary: Coleridge, for example, describes the 'temporary half-faith, which the spectator encourages in himself and supports by a voluntary contribution on his own part'.[57] (And elsewhere, of course, he speaks of the 'willing suspension of disbelief'.) Although he disagrees with the details of Coleridge's formation, McCollom defines theatrical illusion specifically in terms of 'the spectator's [...] participation in a dramatic action'.[58] But we can't simply move from the voluntary contribution of the spectator to the lack of false belief on her part. It would be perfectly consistent to hold that we contribute to our own false beliefs. Tied to the mast and screaming to be released, Odysseus believes (falsely, one assumes) that visiting the sirens is a pretty good plan; and there's a fairly intuitive sense in which Odysseus has contributed to this false belief. Of course, although he contributed to it, Odysseus can't obviously snap himself out of his false belief once it is in place; but to say (with Coleridge) that it's always within the power of the spectator to break the spell does not mean to say that the spell, when in place, is not a false belief. In any case, one could consistently claim that the spectator contributes to her false belief and that there are moments when she cannot snap herself out of it; in effect, this is Stendhal's view.[59]

We should set aside the question of whether the entranced spectator falsely believes. Instead, even if the spell is or causes a kind of false belief, the false belief doesn't last longer than the performance itself. Compare this with those generated by the other kinds of illusions that we have discussed: Houdini's audience, for example, will be as confused after the performance as they were during it; Krull was surprised by what he saw in the dressing room, long after the performance was done. It is true that certain psychological effects of the spell may endure past the final bow; but even if being under the spell means 'believing it's all real', we can all agree that nobody does so once the curtain goes down.[60] Indeed, Rousseau at one point complains that whatever beneficial moral effect is produced by theatre (if indeed there be any) 'lasts no longer than the illusion which produced it'.[61] In the Prologue to *Wallenstein*, Schiller asks the audience to be thankful that the muse, although she does 'create illusion', goes on 'in honesty' to 'Reveal the trick she plays, and not pretend/ That what she brings us is the stuff of truth'.[62] Even if the spell does produce moments of false belief, the fact that these come to an end with the performance suggests that Schiller is right to call the illusion an honest one.

Although they are different, the types of illusion that we've discussed may have an impact upon each other. Clearly, there are occasions when the visual and Houdini-type illusions go wrong and the mistake breaks the spell: if, say, a part of the set collapses; if we see the fake blood capsule before it explodes; if an actor is really hurt in a stage fight. But this is by no means the only way that these kinds of illusions may be related. Indeed, one might think that complicated but highly impressive Houdini illusions could also have the effect of breaking the spell – namely, if the audience is thinking 'how on earth did they do that?' instead of being engrossed in the play. In a recent production of *Danton's Death*, Danton was guillotined in such a realistic way that all the audience could think about was how such a stunt was performed. The distinction between different types of illusion can also help us to be clearer about which kinds of illusions we are referring to when we talk about theatre and illusion. Brecht, for example, is often considered to be 'anti-illusion' when it comes to the theatre: we look at his ideas in more detail in Chapter 7. In that chapter, I cite a description of a Brecht performance, in which what looks like a solid marble proscenium arch turns out, with a change of lighting, to be made of a transparent gauze. The effect is supposed, in part, to prevent the spectators from falling under what I'm calling the 'spell'; but note that Brecht is happy to use an illusion of one kind (the gauze that appears to be marble) in order to undermine an illusion of another kind (the spell).

The term 'theatrical illusion' evidently does not refer to one phenomenon. We have found a number of different kinds of illusion that often do play a part in a theatrical performance. Sometimes this is clear to the spectator; sometimes not. Although being deceived is not a necessary condition for illusion, spectators can be and frequently are deceived by theatre.

Nietzsche: illusion as truth?

Our treatment of theatre and illusion has thus far been an investigation of which types of illusions there may be at a theatrical performance. Some, as we have seen, do seem to require deception or false belief on the part of the audience; others do not. However, it might be possible to argue that illusion has a more positive role in relation to truth – not merely 'honest', as Schiller puts it, but truthful. The philosopher who wrote most extensively about theatre and illusion, Friedrich Nietzsche, came to a version of this conclusion.

Nietzsche's first book, *The Birth of Tragedy*, is an account of the origins, nature and function of Greek (specifically, Attic) tragedy.[63] Following Schopenhauer, the young Nietzsche held that what we take to be 'the world' (people, things, time, space, causation) is itself nothing but an elaborate illusion created by a single, unified, metaphysical 'will'.[64] For Schopenhauer, the reality of the will and the unreality of (what we mistakenly take to be) the real world of people and things has a number of devastating consequences. Chief among them is our everyday experience of desire. We want certain things, and we erroneously think that when we get these things we will be satisfied. But, since the world just is will (or desire), all that happens when we get what we want is that we want something else. Alternatively, if we do not get what we want, we are unhappy in our frustrated desire. The combination of these two thoughts is overpowering: first, none of what we think matters is real (our family or friends, our history or identity, our goals or achievements); second, to make matters worse, humans are systematically set up to be unhappy, to be suspended between being bored with what we have and being unhappy with what we don't have. Schopenhauer does not advocate suicide as an escape from 'the suffering of the world', but he clearly takes some comfort in the thought that the systematic roller-coaster of human suffering ends with death; certainly, it would be hard to take Schopenhauer's philosophy seriously without coming to the conclusion that we're better off dead than alive.[65]

Nietzsche's account of ancient tragedy combines his knowledge of the Greek world with his interest in Schopenhauer's philosophy. What Greek tragedy offered the Greeks, he thought, was an insight into (basically Schopenhauerian and very unpleasant) truths about the world and the place of humans within it. On occasion, to be sure, these truths could be expressed in the form of words uttered during the course of the performance. The chorus of *Oedipus at Colonus* is able, for example, to express the thought that the best thing for humans is not to be born at all (followed closely by dying very young).[66] These basic truths could also find expression in elements of the plot: Oedipus (in *Oedipus Tyrannus*) learns that his apparently stable, comprehensible and benevolent world is in fact appallingly brutal and in some sense fated to bring him misery.[67] Nonetheless, the truths expressed in ancient tragedy are not primarily located in the text and in the plot – and it has been, Nietzsche thinks, a mistake of the modern world (more or less following Aristotle) to seek them there. To understand what the truths are and how they are expressed, we must understand the nature of tragic illusion.

Nietzsche posits two forces at work in Greek tragedy, which he names after the gods Apollo and Dionysus. Apollo represents the drawing of (and respecting) distinct boundaries between individuals. Dionysus represents the loss of individuality and the transgression of boundaries. The tendencies that go by the labels 'Apollo' and 'Dionysus' are found, of course, in the gods who bear those names. But they are expressed in real-world activities (Apollo in dreaming; Dionysus in drunkenness and orgy) and also in characteristic forms of art (Apollo in epic poetry; Dionysus in choral dance and lyric poetry). Thus in epic poetry we learn about (but are separate from) the stories of Odysseus and his men; his adventures take place in a different time and in different locations. This is Apollinian in at least two ways: first, the listener learns about and is distinct from the different characters described in the epic; second, the listener is not himself imaginatively involved in what is described – he does not imagine himself as part of the story. Choral dance is Dionysian, Nietzsche supposes, in that the participant gets lost in the crowd and in the present moment, with no sense of separation and no notion of there being a 'himself' apart from others – what Nietzsche calls a 'complete self-forgetting'.[68]

Along with their differing activities and art forms, Apollo and Dionysus are connected with different states of mind.[69] In the case of Apollo, the characteristic state of mind is the illusion of the dreamer (although Nietzsche suggests that it is the dreamer who *knows* he is dreaming[70]). This is something like what I have described (above) as being 'under the spell': Nietzsche speaks of illusion, but also of 'semblance' (*Schein*). In the case of Dionysus, the characteristic state of mind is intoxication (*Rausch*).[71] The Apollinian Homer-listener is in a dream-like state of illusion; the Dionysiac participant in the drunken, choral dance loses himself in the crowd. Note that both states of mind are, in turn, unlike the experience of the average Greek, going about his day-to-day business – both take him away from the (for Nietzsche and Schopenhauer, illusory) everyday world. To that extent, both Apollinian and Dionysian art forms already offer a 'truer' experience than that of the average Greek citizen, who thinks that what he experiences is real: the epic presents a realm of illusion that the listener knows to be illusory (unlike the everyday realm of illusion, which he does not recognise as such); the intoxicated choral dancer escapes from the (false) idea that each of us is a separate, unique individual.

Greek tragedy combines the characteristic art forms and states of mind associated with Apollo and Dionysus. Dionysus is represented in the intoxicating song and dance of the tragic chorus, whereas Apollo is found in the actors and the plot, which, dreamlike, represent the actions of other people in other places. In combining the illusions and intoxications of the different art forms, tragedy also combines and expresses their characteristic kinds of truth. *Summary*

It has been a great mistake, Nietzsche thinks (made by Aristotle, among others), to look only at the Apollinian elements – notably the plot, the characters, the illusion – and to ignore the significance of the chorus. Ignoring the song and dance in favour of the plot and character has been made that much easier, of course, because our principle way of accessing Greek tragedy is through the surviving play texts, which preserve details of the Apollinian elements but not the Dionysian. What the Dionysian offers, with its intoxicated song and dance, is a kind of insight into metaphysical reality. We *really are* all one being ('Will'), not individuated beings with different goals; so the intoxicated, Dionysian mind is (in a sense) confronted with an important truth, albeit one that it could not express very coherently in words. Hence it is no surprise that the Dionysian state of mind – intoxicated self-forgetting – has a certain dominance over the dream-like, Apollinian illusion in Nietzsche's account of Greek tragedy. This accords well with the centrality of the god Dionysus to the festivals at which Greek tragedies were performed. The trouble is that the truths revealed by intoxication are hard to bear: if you really came to understand that everything apparently important to you is in fact completely insignificant, you might wish to give up on living. Hence, Nietzsche suggests, the knowledge acquired by the Dionysian man is repulsive to him. The function of the Apollinian illusion is to keep that knowledge at a sufficient distance, such that it does not destroy him completely: '[Dionysian] knowledge kills action; action requires one to be shrouded in a veil of [Apollinian] illusion'.[72]

The Greek spectator, then, identifies primarily with the dancers in the chorus, in their intoxication and self-forgetting. The veil of illusion provided by the plot and characters at the tragedy are sufficient to prevent the participants (actors, chorus, spectators) from accepting the truths to the extent that they end their existence. Although the horror, dissolution and destruction presented on stage and felt by the tragic chorus are *really* a feature of all human existence, the illusion that they are primarily happening to someone else – someone called 'Oedipus' or 'Agamemnon' – is sufficient to make them bearable. The Apollinian illusion (in the context of the overwhelmingly Dionysian tragedy) has the function, then, of bringing the Greek as close as possible to the truth, without permitting him to be consumed by it. It is a kind of heat shield, which enables him to immerse himself that much deeper in the fire of truth.

Nietzsche's account of ancient tragedy was mocked in its own day, especially in philological circles. Certainly, he was willing to take interpretative leaps that were not supported by the kind of historical evidence that his contemporaries expected. We needn't enter into philological debates about the origins of tragedy, but can quickly appreciate some complications and peculiar results of Nietzsche's account. First, of course, the apparent dependence on Schopenhauerian metaphysics is controversial and the appeal to Schopenhauer would subsequently be a source of some embarrassment to Nietzsche, who made it his task to criticise and oppose a wide range of Schopenhauerian claims. Whereas *The Birth of Tragedy* encourages the thought that this world is merely a dream or illusion, the later Nietzsche criticised precisely this view. From our point of view, although Schopenhauer's philosophy is insightful and stimulating, his central, metaphysical views are no longer taken seriously. Second, Nietzsche is offering an account of *ancient* tragedy, not of tragedy in general, let alone all theatrical performance. The Greeks were able to achieve their balance of truth, illusion and intoxication only in the context of a religious festival that is unknowable to us now; Greek dance and music – central Dionysian elements – are also largely unknowable. Indeed, Nietzsche thinks, true tragedy quickly became unknowable to the Greeks themselves, once they were under the influence of Socrates and Plato.[73] So even if we were to accept his account of ancient tragedy, it would add little to our modern understanding of theatrical experience, which (he insists) would be completely alien to the Greeks.[74] Finally, one cannot understand *The Birth of Tragedy* apart from the young Nietzsche's infatuation with Richard Wagner, including with the composer's views about art and society.[75] The final sections of *The Birth of Tragedy* call for a reinvigoration of ancient tragedy, pioneered by Wagnerian music-drama. This serves to underline the point that a central interest of Nietzsche's was the *musical* element of ancient tragedy, which (he felt) was lacking on the modern stage.

Conclusion

Theatre has never been too far from questions about truth and illusion. In both cases, what look like unitary notions turn out to reveal a cluster of different ideas, some of which we have had a chance to explore. Although we learn from theatre in lots of ways, and plays may in some sense contain or express truths, we did not find a particular or special way in which we learn from theatre – either in terms of learning that certain facts hold about the world, or in learning some new technique or skill. As for illusions, we noted that many different kinds of theatrical phenomena may go under the name 'illusion', that some of them suggest an audience that is deceived, whereas others do not. Finally, in Nietzsche's *The Birth of Tragedy* we find a vision of Greek tragedy that combines various kinds of illusion with the drive to understand and cope with what Nietzsche takes to be a truth about our existence. It also shows the place that a challenging account of theatre may have within a complex philosophical account of human culture.

Further Reading

Philosophical discussions of truth and fiction or truth and literature tend to focus on novels or poems rather than plays (or to treat play texts as independent works of dramatic literature). Walton (1990) and Lamarque and Olsen (1994) are weighty and influential tomes, not for the faint-hearted; for a helpful discussion of poetry and knowledge, see Geuss (2005: 184–219). On theatre and illusion, see Hamilton (1982), who argues – contrary to what I have suggested in this chapter – that theatrical 'illusions' are not deceptive and are not really illusions at all. Nietzsche's *The Birth of Tragedy*, for all its idiosyncrasies, remains important and interesting; Geuss (1999) offers a helpful introduction to a difficult but rewarding text.

Notes

1 Artaud (2010: 3).
2 Artaud (2010: 54).
3 See Barish (1981: 1).
4 Fragment 23, quoted in Halliwell (1986: 13).
5 See Puchner (2010: 75). Puchner also speaks of modernist playwrights using theatre as a 'laboratory of truth' (p. 119).
6 I'm not suggesting that there is a firm, self-evident or watertight distinction between content and form; the point is just to distinguish between two types of accusation concerning theatre and falsehood.
7 The notion of a 'lie' suggests not just making false claims, but *knowingly* making false claims in order to deceive. This seems wrong, so I won't pursue it further here: I take it that the untruths uttered on stage are meant to be 'lies' because the playwright and actors know that what they say is false, but they have to say it in order for the play to function. However, as we shall discuss in the following, the actors do not expect to be believed, to 'get away with it'. 'Lying', therefore, seems inappropriate – I shall speak instead of 'untruth'.
8 Kierkegaard (1992: 49).
9 Quoted in Lamarque and Olsen (1994: 53). Russell had a general view concerning propositions about non-existent entities (like Hamlet or the present King of France) – namely, that statements about such entities were *false*, rather than, as Strawson argued, neither-true-nor-false. Russell's is not an undisputed view, but I shall not challenge it here.
10 *Hamlet*, 1.1.5. (Citations from *Hamlet* refer to the edition listed in the bibliography.) Elizabethan productions typically began in the afternoon, so it's unlikely to have been true for them either.
11 Beckett's *Rockaby* might be one contender. Francesco Cangiullo's *Detonation*, which has no words at all, is a clear case.
12 Such as Francesco Cangiullo's *Detonation*.
13 This is a modest claim, with which most philosophers agree; there is disagreement about if and how such statements are 'asserted' by the author or actor (see e.g. Beardsley [1981: 421] on 'assertion in the fullest sense'). I do not mean to suggest that any of the truths described in the following paragraphs are sincerely uttered by the author or actor. See Urmson (1976); Lamarque and Olsen (1994), Chapter 3.
14 1.1.111–9; Plutarch's 'Life of Julius Caesar'.
15 4.7.164.

16 1.3.75.

17 *Oedipus Tyrannus*, lines 1529–30, in Sophocles (2003) p. 107.

18 Walton (1990: 79) goes further in holding that an author could write a work of fiction in which *every* sentence is true. Currie 'What is fiction?' offers a helpful exploration of some problem cases.

19 I am suggesting that historical truth/falsity makes little difference to us in plays like *Hamlet*; but for a certain class of plays, namely history plays, I'll argue (in Chapter 4) that it does make a difference. As we'll see, this is more than just a question of whether the history play's *propositions* are true.

20 Not only does it make no difference; it may be, as some have argued, that asking whether a statement in a play or novel is true or false is inappropriate or somehow misses the point. See Gale (1971).

21 Obviously, this distinction holds equally for explicit claims, discussed above. Horatio's statements about Rome are particular; Polonius' 'words of wisdom' are general or universal.

22 Artaud himself, with whom I began this chapter, writes (in defence of his 'theatre of cruelty') that 'we are not free and the sky can still fall on our heads. And above all else, theatre is made to teach us this'. See Artaud (2010: 57).

23 Hence, for example, when psychoanalytic models were applied to literature, they were said to 'reveal' the universal features of the characters and explain their real motives and actions. For Freud on Hamlet, see Freud (1961: 265); see also Jones (1949). Many other kinds of literary analysis claim to uncover latent or concealed claims.

24 *Poetics* 51b.

25 *Poetics* 54a. For Lessing, Aristotle's point is that, although there are inconsistent people, they don't make for very good characters in plays. See Lessing (1962: Section 34, pp. 98–9).

26 This formed part of the French concept of *les bienséances* – roughly a notion of the decorum appropriate to the stage.

27 Booth (1995: 330).

28 Lessing (1961: Section 30, p. 84).

29 In Strindberg's case, he thought *Miss Julie* did present to its audience universal truths – rather unpleasant, misogynistic ones about how women can never be as good as men. But it didn't do this through fixed character types.

30 See, e.g. Frede (1992). Frede argues that Aristotle posits pleasure in tragic imitation because of the recognition that certain types of people do certain types of things.

31 This is taken from Shelley (2003: 185). We discuss the context of his claim in Chapter 6.

32 These two features are identified as standard in the literature by Snowdon (2004), although he goes on to criticise this account.

33 Jacobson (1997: 198).

34 This has proved a popular idea, especially among those who claim that theatre teaches us how to be moral – claims that we explore in more detail in Chapter 5. Take, for example, Palmer's claim that the artwork 'gets us to see something and not merely to know' that something is the case. See Palmer (1992: 193).

35 This is not true for all plays, of course – and some modern theatre practitioners have attempted to train audiences to develop certain skills. See e.g. Boal (1995), who prefers to speak of 'spectactors' than 'spectators'.

36 Brecht, Nietzsche, Stendhal, Coleridge, Lessing, Rousseau and Boucicault are some of the writers on theatre who have taken it as evident that illusion is involved in theatrical performance in some way. Hamilton (1982) argues against this, although he largely assumes that illusion implies deception – an assumption we have reason to challenge.

37 See Fogle (1960).

38 Sparshott (1952). Sparshott is talking about illusion as applied to art in general.

39 Stendhal (1962).

40 See e.g. Reynolds (2000).

41 Dancy (1995: 421).

42 See Gombrich (2002: 190).

43 Taking 'fake' set designs to be an extension of optical illusions follows the structure of Hamilton (1982: 41), who considers and eventually rejects this formation as an instance of illusion.

44 This is one of the claims of Hamilton (1982).
45 T. Mann, *Bekenntnisse des Hochstaplers Felix Krull* (Fischer Taschenbuch Verlag: Frankfurt am Main, 2007), p. 32.
46 There may also be cases, as there were with Houdini, in which the 'illusionist' really does *do* something highly difficult or unusual and the audience believes truly that he has done it and admires this feat; in the context of the illusionist's performance (as opposed to the official, record-breaking attempt), not knowing what is real and what is not adds to the pleasure.
47 Frayn (2010: xi).
48 Quoted in Fogle (1960: 35).
49 See Chapter 1. If stand-up comedy is a kind of theatre, then that might be one candidate.
50 Stendhal (1962), Fogle (1960: 40) and McCollom (1947: 185–6) discuss these phenomena.
51 Lessing (1962: Section 42, p. 28) argues that they are: tragedy relies much more on the spell than comedy; breaking the spell can have comic effects.
52 Ibsen quoted in Booth (1995: 299); Bruisov (2001: 74).
53 Lessing (1962: Section 42, p. 128).
54 See Fogle (1960: 34).
55 Quoted in Fogle (1960: 36).
56 Brinker (1977: 191–6) agrees that asking spectators whether they really believed is pointless. Note that, unlike me, he uses 'under the spell' to indicate those moments when the spectator really believes in the action.
57 Quoted in Fogle (1960: 36).
58 McCollom (1947: 184).
59 See Chapter 6.
60 Hence, to take a standard (but non-theatrical) example, I might fear stepping into the shower after seeing *Psycho*; more generally, I might feel sad or emotionally drained after seeing a tragedy. But this is not a matter of entertaining false beliefs. Gendler (2003) discusses this phenomenon. The doctor-spectator at *The Elephant Man,* discussed above, does not (as I argued) believe *everything* he saw on stage – he carries over one rather major illusion.
61 Rousseau (2004: 268).
62 Schiller (1979: 169).
63 Although we think of Nietzsche as a philosopher, he was also professor of classical philology with relatively little formal philosophical training.
64 Or rather, *The Birth of Tragedy* is best explicated in the light of Schopenhauer's views. Nietzsche had already expressed severe reservations about Schopenhauer's metaphysics and some commentators take *The Birth of Tragedy* to be intelligible apart from any commitment to Schopenhauer. See Janaway (1998), in which Nietzsche's remarks are reprinted and discussed. References to *The Birth of Tragedy* (henceforth: BT) will give the section and, where appropriate, the page number in the listed translation.
65 See 'Additional Remarks on the Suffering of the World' and 'On Suicide' in Schopenhauer (2000). Schopenhauer's view of death is more complicated than I've suggested: individuals die, but they never *really* existed in the first place; the will, which creates (the illusion of) individuals, is unchanging and eternal. For Schopenhauer's own, rather different account of tragedy, see the third book of his *The World as Will and Representation.*
66 Sophocles (2006: 97); for Nietzsche's view of the significance of this thought, see the discussion of the story of Silenus at BT 3.
67 Schopenhauer, of course, does not have a monopoly on thoughts of this kind; but one can see how they are easily subsumable under his metaphysical framework.
68 BT 1, p. 17.
69 BT 2, p. 19.
70 BT 4.
71 The connection between Dionysus and intoxication is clear enough, in that he was the god of wine. '*Schein*' (illusion, semblance) means 'illusion', but is also related to light (i.e. 'shining'). Hence the connection with Apollo, god of the sun.
72 BT 7, p. 40.

73 Nietzsche is not so much referring to the specific arguments of Plato and Socrates, which we looked at in the previous chapter (though they may have played their part); instead, he means the Socratic method in general, with its heavy emphasis on a particular kind of rationality.
74 BT 8, p. 42.
75 Like his infatuation with Schopenhauer, Nietzsche's infatuation with Wagner weakened as he got older and he became highly critical of Wagner. But both Wagner and Schopenhauer remained significant influences on his thinking.

4 History in the Making: Theatre and the Past

Herodotus of Helicarnassus here presents his research so that human events do not fade with time.[1]

With this sentence, Herodotus, also known as the 'father of history', begins his account of the war between the Greeks and the Persians. The Greek armies, vastly outnumbered, triumph over the invading forces of the East; their victory makes possible the Athenian civilisation, including its philosophy, its theatre and, of course, Herodotus' work itself. So just like philosophy and theatre, history (as we now know it) can claim to have its origins in the Greek world. And, in that Greek world, Herodotus, the first historian, is known to have interacted with the philosophers and the playwrights. It is thought, for example, that he was a friend of Sophocles, the tragedian; and certainly Herodotus' history, just like Socrates' philosophy, is mocked in the comedies of Aristophanes. But before Herodotus wrote his history – probably while he was still a child – the tragedian, Aeschylus, put on a play about the very same Persian war.

Aeschylus had actually fought in the Persian war, in the great Greek victory at the Battle of Marathon; but he chose to write his tragedy about the Battle of Salamis and from the Persian perspective.[2] Set at the court of the Persian king, *The Persians* features a messenger's speech, describing the battle:

> The shores of Salamis, and all the neighbouring coasts,
> Are strewn with bodies miserably done to death. […]
> Our bows and arrows were no help; there, overwhelmed
> By crashing prows, we watched a nation sink and die.[3]

Performed just eight years after the battle itself, the messenger's speech is the earliest surviving account of Salamis – earlier than, and different from, the account left to us by Herodotus. It would have been performed in front of an Athenian audience who knew all too well the cost of war; many of them would have fought in the very battle described on stage; all of them would have lived through it. Behind the spectators, ruined

Athenian buildings would have provided a strong reminder – if one was needed – of the cost of the war. Many modern readers have found *The Persians* boastful – a play written by the victors for a victorious and jubilant audience. There is no doubt, though, that Aeschylus does not shy away from describing the horrors of war.

Regardless of how we interpret it, Aeschylus, the first playwright whose works survive, wrote the first history play – a play depicting a historical event, using historical characters;[4] and, as it happens, the battle he wrote about was also described by the first historian in the Western tradition.[5] Tragedies based on recent historical events, events within living memory, were certainly a rarity in the ancient world; far more common were those depicting familiar myths. Indeed, *The Persians* is the only surviving non-mythic tragedy from the golden age of Greek theatre.[6] But history plays have continued to be written – by Shakespeare, Pushkin and Ibsen, to name but a few – and they have continued to be popular.

As I have said, a natural focus for the relationship between philosophy and theatre is the question of the extent to which (and how) theatre can put the world on the stage. We have looked at this question for theatre in general, in terms of *mimesis* and truth; but history plays are a special case, because they explicitly look to connect what is going on in front of the audience with something that really happened. As such, they form an obvious point of interest for philosophers interested in the relationship between theatre and truth in general, not to mention theatre and the philosophy of history. Wherever history plays have appeared, it has been natural enough for spectators to ask about the relationship between what they are seeing and the events that they claim to depict. This chapter looks at philosophical approaches to this question.

To begin with, let us imagine that we go to see a performance of a history play – say, Shakespeare's *Julius Caesar* – and that, once the performance is over, our theatregoing companion asks us: 'I wonder if it happened like that?' This is the question I shall use to guide us in our inquiry. A few comments about the question itself: First, the question is comparative, not merely historical. Our companion wants to know something about the relationship between the performance and the past. She isn't asking only about the historical event, so it won't do to hand her a history book. Second, she is not – or not just – asking about the truth-values of the propositions as they appear in the text of the play. We have just seen a performance, with actors in costumes, with scenery – with words, to be sure, but words with emphasis and intonation. So *how* things were said might be just as important as what was said. Finally, we should keep the question of how accurate it is separate from how successful it is as a literary or theatrical enterprise. Note that it would be perfectly possible to think that historically accurate plays are better *as plays*, but we can remain silent on that matter.

Now that we have our guiding question, the chapter proceeds as follows: first, I give some defining features of a history play. Second, with this in mind, we can look at some possible answers to the question.

What is a history play?

As we have seen, the notion of a play that depicts real historical events goes back to the very beginning of theatre as we know it. In relation to Aeschylus' play, I have already mentioned two criteria that are important, but certainly not exhaustive: the play uses proper names, which refer to real people and real places, and the play depicts real events.

As to the first – the use of proper names – it is true that plays like *Julius Caesar* refer to real people and real places (Atossa, Mary Stuart, Richard of York, St Albans). Of course, *referring* to somebody or something is not the same as saying something true about them. If I say 'Julius Caesar was not a Roman' then I am saying something false; but I am saying something false *about Caesar* in virtue of using his name to refer to him. So the reference to real people and places in history plays is independent of whether what is said about them is true (and independent of whether what they do on stage is what they really did). But the use of proper names referring to real historical people or places is not all it takes to be a history play. After all, *Hamlet* (at least sometimes) does that – Horatio, for example, speaks of Rome. It isn't enough, then, just to use a historical name. Nor is using historical figures as characters a distinctive feature of history plays: plenty of playwrights depict meetings between famous people that never took place, or that imaginatively fill in the details of real meetings.[7] Note, too, that it would be far too strong to say that history plays use *only* real people and real places: that is false, at least for the major historical playwrights of the Western canon, who are perfectly happy to make up characters when it suits them.

Second, history plays depict events that really happened: Brutus did stab Caesar. Other examples might be: a battle, a particular period or occasion in a famous person's life, a meeting between historical figures. To say that the event 'took place' is certainly not to say that it took place in just the way depicted on stage, that everything happened in this way, or that every scene has a real, historical counterpart (indeed, I shall be arguing against precisely this view). Thus, defining history plays in terms of 'events that really happened' does not give us an answer to our guiding question. Our companion, we may safely assume, knows full well that Caesar was stabbed by Brutus: she wants to know if it happened *like that* (i.e. in relation to the performance we just saw). Historical playwrights make up characters, meetings and conversations – including supernatural ones (as in *The Persians* or *Julius Caesar*); all we are saying (here) is that they do so in the process of depicting something that happened: the defeat of the Persians at Salamis, the murder of Caesar. This is perfectly true, but as a definition of a history play, it still leaves a great deal to be desired, because it covers all sorts of plays that we wouldn't think of as 'history plays'. Many playwrights use stories, perhaps from newspapers or from their own experience, as a basis for their fictional writing. Georg Büchner's unfinished *Woyzeck*, for example, was inspired by a story in a newspaper; but it is clearly an imaginative, fictionalised account of the events and we wouldn't call it a history play. Others use legends or religious stories, which may or may not have a basis in truth: for example, the Greek tragedies, based on Homeric myths, or the mediaeval miracle plays, based on stories in the Bible. The line between myth and history can be hard to draw; hence Nietzsche's remark that 'it is the fate of every myth to creep gradually into the narrow confines of an allegedly historical reality'.[8] Nonetheless, mythical and religious plays are not normally considered history plays.

A third feature of the history play is that the events depicted by history plays must be more than just 'real'; they must be public. Suppose *The Glass Menagerie*, which Tennessee Williams describes as a 'memory play', depicts real events from his past; even so, it is not a history play, because those events are known only to Williams (and a few others).[9] We do not have independent access to them, or independent reason to believe that they took place. Thus, the spectator at the history play typically knows that it is a history play, and this has a certain influence on how she understands what she sees.[10]

Furthermore, the history play requires something of its author: a responsible engagement with the sources. Suppose *Julius Caesar* was written after Shakespeare had heard only the barest details of Caesar's death; by pure coincidence, he happened to get much of it right. Knowing this, we would be reluctant, I think, to call it a history play.[11] As it happens, we know that Shakespeare did engage closely with his sources, especially Plutarch, perhaps Suetonius and others. Pushkin and Büchner also work closely with source materials: Pushkin was, in fact, an accomplished historian; we shall discuss Büchner presently. To take a more recent example: Michael Frayn published, together with the play text of his history play, *Democracy*, a detailed account of his sources, which gives an idea of the amount of research that can go into a history play.[12] To think that the playwright has engaged carefully with the sources and that the play depicts a real event does not equate to thinking that all of the words uttered by historical characters were in fact uttered by the corresponding characters; in fact, it seems consistent with some history plays to think that *none* of the historical figures said what the characters are depicted as saying.[13]

Finally, we must distinguish the history play from the counterfactual play. Suppose someone writes a play about the conspiracy against Caesar, an event that took place, refers to real people, is public; suppose, too, that she works closely with ancient sources and modern histories; and suppose, finally, that in the climactic scene, Caesar fights off Casca and escapes to join Mark Antony before Cassius, Brutus and the others can lay a finger on him. There is no reason why such a play might not be a great success as a work of literature; but it is not a history play. We should add, then, that history plays do not alter the significant historical facts. It is clear that the category of 'significant historical facts' is loose; but it is also clear that, for the plays to be history plays, Caesar must die at the hands of the conspirators, Henry V must win at Agincourt, Robespierre must turn on Danton and Desmoulins, the Persians must lose at Salamis, and Boris Godunov must be crowned as Tsar.

These, I take it, are the central features of the history play. Plenty of plays take a stricter approach to historical accuracy – and we shall discuss some of the possibilities in what follows. So now that we have an idea of what they are, we can turn back to our guiding question, following the performance of *Julius Caesar*: did it happen like that? Answers to this question, I would suggest, could take roughly three forms: it's the wrong (or inappropriate) question; yes; no. I shall look at them in that order.

The wrong question?

Is there something wrong with asking whether the real event happened like the performance? Aristotle, as we have seen, wrote that drama (as a species of poetry) must treat universals, not historical particulars. In Aristotle's terms, history can tell us what has happened, but theatre can tell us what would happen (which is also the realm of philosophy). Telling us what would happen – teaching us about universals – is, he suggests, much more important than just telling us what happened to happen on one occasion. So, for example, Herodotus the historian may tell us about the Battle of Salamis; but Aeschylus the tragedian (and Plato, the philosopher) can tell us universals about, for instance, human conflict and weakness. For him, then, theatre just isn't history and it ought not to be. Of course, as he points out, sometimes things that have happened – historical events – can be the kinds of things that do in general happen. But here the playwright's role is to turn the historical event into something poetic and universal; the aim is certainly not to give the audience an accurate understanding of whatever happened to take place.[14] The question, then, should be not 'did it happen like this?' but the rather clumsier '*would* it happen like this (necessarily or for the most part)?' On a common reading, Aristotle is interested in what types of people do in types of situations.[15]

We've already explored one problem with Aristotle's claim about theatre: namely, that it's difficult to say just which universals are being presented in any one play (see Chapter 2). But even supposing that theatre does present universals: how, in that case, does history fail to do so? After all, if the story of Oedipus can tell us about 'what would happen', then why can't the story of Xerxes or Leonidas? When Aristotle criticises history, he singles out Herodotus.[16] By way of comparison, then, here is the famous moment in Herodotus' history when Xerxes surveys his vast army:

> As he looked out over the whole Hellespont, whose water was completely hidden by all his ships, and at the shores and plains of Abydos, now so full of people, Xerxes congratulated himself for being so blessed. But then he suddenly burst into tears and wept. [...] 'I was suddenly overcome by pity as I considered the brevity of human life, since not one of all these people here will be alive one hundred years from now.[17]

If a play can offer us universals about human life (and we have seen reasons to doubt that this is the case), then it is far from clear why histories like this cannot.[18] To put the point another way: the passage just quoted would have its effect (whatever that is) whether or not I treat it as a historical account or a fictional one.[19]

There is also a second, much more contemporary line of objection to the question as it currently stands. This goes as follows: that we are asking about the connection between fiction and history; but (according to this line of argument) these are in fact much the same thing. Shakespeare offers one narrative; other sources offer other narratives; there is either no truth about what 'really happened,' or, if there is, it is necessarily distorted by the mode in which we present it.[20] It is certainly true that ways of writing about history have a great effect on how it is received and understood, and there is a great deal more to be said about the claims made along these lines; but I will not pursue the radical thought that there is no distinction between fiction and history, because I share the common view that this conclusion has not been firmly established.[21]

Finally, some philosophers have argued that, far from being the same thing, the distinction between fiction and history is so severe that one should refrain from treating them as potentially encoding the same kinds of information. *Julius Caesar* uses historical material for inspiration, but it is a work of fiction. The definition of 'fiction' in question matters little: the historical claims have not been properly 'asserted'; the performance was just a game of make-believe or a special social practice. In any case, the fictional nature of the performance renders insignificant the connection with historical truth. If you want to know about history, read a history book; don't watch plays. Defenders of this last view, if they are not mad, are not suggesting that there is no connection between *Julius Caesar* and the historical events that inspired it, and that it depicts. Nor would they say that there is no route, as it were, between the fictional claims of *Julius Caesar* and the factual claims of the historian. What they are suggesting, I take it, is that the interesting and important features of *Julius Caesar* are best understood in terms of its essence as fiction.[22] It ought to be construed as a work of fiction, not as a work of history. A variant of this would be to say much the same thing about *literature* and history: given its status as a literary work, *Julius Caesar* must not be construed as 'a piece of reportive or fact-stating discourse,' in which scenes are included 'to establish certain propositions as true in the mind of the reader'; indeed, say some, our literary appreciation depends upon not construing it in this way.[23] The question of the play's connection with the death of the historical figure is peripheral (which is not to say unanswerable), and ought to be recognised as such.

I do not wish to challenge these views of fictionality (or literature) in general. But I do want to reject using a firm distinction between history and fiction (or literature) to conclude that we shouldn't bother asking about the connection between *Julius Caesar* and the events it depicts. Looking at what a history play is – a focused, engaged depiction of real events, which assume responsible engagement with the sources on the part of the playwright and independent, historical knowledge on the part of the spectator – it seems a perfectly reasonable thing to ask.

History Plays As History

Sticking to *Julius Caesar* for the moment (we will look at other kinds of history play in the following), one answer to our guiding question – did it happen like that? – might, of course, be 'yes'. For a long time, Shakespeare's history plays have been thought to have considerable value as educational tools. We force children to sit through them, not just because we want them to learn about Shakespeare but also, perhaps, because we want them to learn about Rome. Georg II, Duke of Saxe-Meiningen, put on Shakespeare's Roman plays with the explicit intention of giving the audience a historical education. Often known as the 'first modern director', Georg had studied something very unmodern, namely archaeology; and he used recent archaeological discoveries to inform his productions.[24] Now, as we have seen, history plays are not necessarily accurate in terms of the words spoken by the characters and sometimes in terms of the events depicted on stage. For Georg II, this was no problem: he 'corrected' them: moving Caesar's death from the Capitol (where Shakespeare has it) back to the Curia of Pompey.

It's pretty clear that people can learn something about Rome from *Julius Caesar* – indeed, I doubt that anyone would really deny that – but there's a difference between learning something from the play (say, that Brutus and Cassius fought against Octavian) and answering yes to the question 'did it really happen like that?' After all, one can learn plenty from counterfactual history plays, or simply from plays that feature historical figures, but that doesn't mean that what is depicted really took place in the way that is shown on stage.

A more philosophically advanced account of how history plays depict history was developed by the philosopher Georg Lukács, in his book *The Historical Novel*. A full explanation of Lukács' claims would require a background in the Marxist theory that Lukács assumes, but that is not typically known by a twenty-first-century reader. Nonetheless, even for our purposes, Lukács' approach can be instructive. Lukács begins not with what historians do, but with what playwrights do. More accurately, he looks at the form of historical drama and asks what it is good at. He identifies certain features of historical drama, and then, having done so, asks which kinds of history are suitable to be presented in this way.

To begin with, he claims, historical plays are very effective at presenting conflicts or collisions.[25] This might be a personal decision for a particular character, or a conflict between different characters. Two further points here. First, the conflicts and collisions suitable for dramatic portrayal are brief and focused. Plays are much shorter than, say, novels or epic poems. They are not so good at depicting slow development over time, either character development or political and social development. What they can offer, very effectively, is moments of decision and conflict, in which, for instance, a character must choose between two significant options. Lukács clearly connects drama with the portrayal of political revolutions, although he is careful not to limit historical drama to the portrayal of revolution.[26] Something like the French Revolution would provide good material for a drama; but the so-called 'industrial revolution' – relatively speaking, a slower, more gradual development of technology over a longer period of time – would not be so suitable. Second, a conflict between two characters often represents a much broader conflict between certain ways of life or ethical codes.[27]

Lukács has in mind Hegel's famous reading of Sophocles' *Antigone*.[28] Antigone's dead brother, Polyneices, has been publically disgraced; his body has been left to rot in the open, deprived of important burial rites. The King, Creon, forbids anyone from performing the burial rites on Polyneices. Antigone disobeys and, ultimately, dies for it. For Hegel, the conflict between Creon and Antigone displays the unfolding of a deep tension within a Greek ethical life that had seemed harmonious, natural and necessary to its members. Antigone and Creon embody different commitments within this apparently harmonious ethical life: Creon is associated with man-made law (i.e. human rather than divine *and* male rather than female), warfare and the affairs of the *polis*; Antigone is associated with the Greek conception of femininity, divine law and duties of the family – and the codes of practice relating to the burial of family members, which, of course, powerfully combine these latter two. The circumstances arising from the plot reveal that the ethical commitments of Creon and Antigone, far from being harmonious currents within a unified Greek society, can turn ferociously antagonistic. Both Creon and Antigone are acting ethically by the standards of their community and yet both are ultimately shown to be in the wrong. On Hegel's historical account, it is Creon's codes of ethics which (temporarily) prevail over those of Antigone, as the Greek form of life progresses towards a Roman emphasis on a man-made (and male) legal order at the heart of society.

There is a great deal more to Hegel's account and to the interpretative challenges associated with it. As to the former, he has an argument to the effect that the sister–brother relationship is uniquely placed to draw out the conflict in Greek life, especially from the sister's point of view; as to the latter, some interpreters prefer to see Hegel not as giving a historical analysis of the Greeks as they in fact were, but rather of the idealised Greeks imagined by Hegel's contemporaries.[29] But we do not have to investigate Hegel's reading too closely to acknowledge that the dramatic collision between Creon and Antigone is more than just an argument about the individual preferences of two people. However we interpret their conflict, we can acknowledge that Antigone and other plays can explore collisions between ideas, ways of life and ethical codes by staging them in conflicts between individual characters. The extra step, suggested by Hegel and reflected in Lukács, is that plays like *Antigone* display with clarity the breakdown and transition of one form of life to another.

Lukács' second claim is that historical dramas typically put the principal or most important historical figures on stage as the main characters. Here (as elsewhere), Lukács is comparing theatre with the novel. In a historical novel, he claims, the most important historical figures appear as minor characters, whereas the main characters in the historical novel are very often fictional.[30] So, for example, *War and Peace* features Napoleon and the Tsar as fleeting, minor characters, whereas Pierre and Prince Andrei are major (fictional) characters. Thus, although *War and Peace* is a historical novel, a play of *War and Peace* wouldn't be a history play. Therefore, we would be surprised to find someone reading *War and Peace* and asking: 'Did it happen like that?' The historical novel uses historical events, or simply a certain historical context, as the backdrop to the fictional story it wants to tell.[31] *Julius Caesar*, of course, is not the story of Caesar and Brutus set against the backdrop of turbulent times in the history of

Rome: Caesar and Brutus *are* the turbulent times in the history of Rome; historical events and historical figures are the central subject of the play. The historical novel and the historical drama are therefore formally very different kinds of stories, with no straight route from one to the other: if *King Lear* were rewritten as a novel, Lukács claims, it would have Edgar as the main character and Lear as a minor character, instead of the other way around.

If we put these strands together, we reach the idea that historical theatre can present moments of intense conflict, set at a particular moment in time, with different characters embodying different elements of the conflict. Lukács' point is, in part, that this mode of presentation is effective only for certain historical periods, not for others. In support of his claims, Lukács can point to a number of historical dramas that depict just the brief, decisive moments of conflict that he is talking about. To refer back to some examples we have already discussed: Shakespeare's *Julius Caesar* depicts not only a decisive time in the lives of Caesar, Brutus and so on; it also depicts a significant, volatile and brief period in the history of Rome (and arguably, by extension, the history of the Western world). The brief period in which Caesar is assassinated is perfect for theatrical representation, because it has the right combination of important historical figures and brief, decisive conflicts. The characters embody the conflict and transition between the old and the new Roman order. One could make similar points about *Danton's Death*, Shakespeare's plays about the Wars of the Roses, Pushkin's *Boris Godunov* (a favourite but lesser known example of Lukács), or Ibsen's *Emperor and Galilean*. In each case, the plays are set in turbulent, changing times.[32]

Lukács' theory of what makes a historical drama successful (as history) is therefore that it accurately portrays the collisions and conflicts of the time through the collisions and conflicts of its main characters. In a restricted sense, then, he would say that what was going on in Rome when Caesar died is accurately portrayed in Shakespeare's play, but not in the sense, perhaps, that our theatregoing companion meant when she asked her question. This contrasts his approach to history in theatre with that embodied by Georg II (who insisted on factual accuracy). An example of this may be found in his attitude towards anachronisms. Clearly, on Georg II's approach, historical anachronisms would be an embarrassment: it's not acceptable to show a historical character on stage using a piece of technology that wasn't available to the historical figure in question. Hence Georg II corrected Shakespeare's 'mistakes'. For Lukács, such anachronisms are unproblematic: because history plays are supposed to represent conflict and collision, they are not measured by how historically accurate they are with reference to factual details: 'in drama, historical authenticity means the inner historical truth of the collision'.[33] Indeed, he explicitly praises Shakespeare as better history (i.e. better at representing specific historical conflicts) than Schiller, even though Schiller is more historically accurate.[34] The key distinction, therefore, is that which he draws between 'historicism' (i.e. getting the historical facts right) and what he calls 'real historical fidelity', which for him involves the appropriate expression of the historical collision of social forces.[35] Inspired by Lukács' argument, for example, Agnes Heller defends the anachronistic chiming clock in *Julius Caesar*, on the grounds that it adds to the drama of the play in a way that aids our *historical* understanding of Rome – this even though there could have been no chiming clock at the time.[36]

Given the brief account of Lukács' theory, it hardly seems appropriate to offer objections as such. What I propose to offer, instead, are a few pointers towards some peculiar and controversial assumptions, features and results of his theory. These should be enough to highlight just where the major points of contention lie. To begin with, Lukács isn't just interested in the historical period in which the play is set. He is also interested in the historical period in which the play is written.[37] Just as certain historical periods are more suitable for *setting* plays, so (he thinks) some historical periods are more suitable for *writing* plays. Drama's 'relatively short, intensive periods of flowering', then, are the lucky combination of appropriate setting and writing times.[38] It's not just that Shakespeare chose well in writing a history play about the end of republican Rome; it's that he had the good fortune to live in a time when writing plays was the appropriate literary genre. Other dramatists – the French tragedians, for example – were not so lucky.[39] Later literary authors, writing about the very same historical events, would write novels instead.[40] This prompts the question: which features of a period make it suitable for writing plays? The answer is similar to the answer he gives for the suitability of a time for setting plays: it's a matter of periods of brief, intense historical conflict and upheaval. A successful historical play will be the result of a kind of resonance – a set of relevantly similar conflicts – between the time of the author and the time in which the play is set. Speaking of Shakespeare's Roman plays, Lukács says: '[Shakespeare] was able to adapt from Plutarch's history those features which the two periods had in common. [...] The generalised form of the drama reveals the features which the two ages hold objectively in common.'[41]

A challenging conclusion of Lukács' theory, then, is that a history play is just as much (if not more) about the time in which it was written as it is about the time in which it is set. There is a weak sense in which we can all agree about that: history books and history plays must relate their subject matter to their readership or audience – what the readers and audience members already know and assume is a crucial factor in what to include and omit. But Lukács is saying something more than that: it's not just a question of having to 'inject the spirit of his period into the ancient world', of the playwright explaining and making intelligible the past event to an audience with less than perfect knowledge of it, by forcing them to appear in some sense similar. Rather, it's the playwright picking out and highlighting features of her own society and social conditions, which happen to correspond objectively to those of some past time, and dramatising those on stage.[42]

This produces the third somewhat counterintuitive conclusion from Lukács' work. Because history plays explore the author's time as much as the time in which they are set, and because their goal is to dramatise the conflicts that both times have in common, there is no special reason why any of the events depicted on stage need to have happened and, perhaps even more strange, there is no particular reason why *any* of the characters need to have real, historical counterparts. Take *King Lear*, for example, which is based on a dubious chronicle about a (probably legendary) king called 'Leir'. The play is set in a historical period characterised by sudden change, conflict and upheaval. The fact that (for all we know) none of these people ever existed doesn't make the play bad *as a history play*, as long as the conflicts and collisions depicted in the play resonate appropriately with the conflicts in Shakespeare's day.[43] Clearly, if history plays can feature nothing but legendary characters and fictional plots, then we have come a long way from our initial conception of a history play, the typical features of which were given at the start. These included (at least some) significant characters who correspond to real, historical figures, and a certain minimal commitment to depicting events that really happened.

Against history plays as history

The final answer would, of course, be no: it didn't happen like that. This, I'll be suggesting, is the right answer to give. But in fact, I want to suggest, there are two different ways of interpreting the question: hence, there are two different questions, each of which should be answered 'no', but for different reasons. To understand why this is, it might be helpful to distinguish between two different uses of the word 'history': first, when we say, for example, that there has been violence throughout human history, we use 'history' to refer to past events or a process of (usually, although not always) human development across time. The violence was a feature of past, human societies, hence of our history. But we also talk about 'history' in a completely different sense, as a kind of academic or intellectual discipline. This discipline is (now) paradigmatically undertaken by academics or intellectuals – it might involve writing books, studying sources, making arguments based on the evidence, and so on. As a matter of fact, the word 'history' comes from the Greek word ἱστορία (historia), which means research or investigation, suggesting 'history' in the second of these two senses. This is the word that is translated as 'research' in the Herodotus sentence quoted at the start. Hence, when students come to university to study 'history', they are in fact studying history in both of these senses. They are studying the past; but, perhaps more importantly, they are studying the means and methods used by historians to investigate and understand that past.

When philosophers speak of the 'philosophy of history', they are using a term that is also ambiguous, corresponding to the two different meanings of 'history'. First, one might have philosophical claims to make about human history, the chain of events or process of human development over time. Philosophers like Hegel and Marx, for example, have philosophical accounts of how and why humans have developed in the way that they have. This kind of philosophy of history is sometimes known as 'speculative philosophy of history'. Second, philosophers also have views about the practises and methods of historians: perhaps about how best to study the past, how (if at all) one can know what happened, how best to make arguments based on the evidence. This kind of philosophy is sometimes known as 'analytic philosophy of history'. It can also be called 'philosophy of historiography', to make it clear that its subject matter is what historians do (historiography – literally, the writing down of history) and to distinguish it from (speculative) philosophy about the nature of past events and their connection. In summary, then, the object for study for speculative philosophy of history is the events themselves; the subject matter of analytic philosophy of history is the work of historians – their methods, their books, and so on.

These two different notions of history suggest two slightly different questions about the relation between the performance of *Julius Caesar* and the events that took place in Rome:

1 The eyewitness question: Would it have looked (and sounded) like that? (History as events)
2 The history book question: How does my understanding of the event, having seen the play, compare with my understanding of the event if I were to read a history book? (History as discipline)

What may seem like a relatively fine distinction turns out to be significant. Thinking back to *The Persians*: should we compare Aeschylus' play with the Battle of Salamis itself, or (say) with Herodotus' historical account of the Battle of Salamis?[44] Is the audience member best understood as an eyewitness or as a history-book reader?

Let's take the eyewitness question first. We should begin by reminding ourselves that plays are not really very good at looking like the events that they depict (or looking like the fictional events that they depict would look like if those events were really to take place). We discussed this point in relation to Plato's arguments about *mimesis*, so we shan't dwell on it here. But even historical playwrights have been keenly aware of it: Pushkin notes in a draft preface to his history play, *Boris Godunov*, that theatre is the least verisimilar of all the arts; Shakespeare has The Chorus in *Henry V* beg the audience to fill in the obvious gaps: 'Think, when we talk of horses, that you see them/ Printing their proud hoofs i'th' receiving earth.'[45]

Technically, such thoughts would probably suffice for a 'no' to the eyewitness question. But we can adapt it a little. Our theatregoing companion knows, let us suppose, that Rome was bigger than the stage, and she knows that Caesar did not die in a theatre, with lots of people watching. (Strictly, the Curia of Pompey *was* in a theatre, at least part of a theatre complex – but the point is clear.) So we could perhaps interpret her more generously: imaginatively filling in some of the details (and imaginatively ignoring others), could it have looked and sounded like that to an eyewitness?

Again, though, the answer must be 'no.' This time, we need to say something about eyewitnesses and history. First, to make the most obvious point, no single eyewitness could have seen what we see during the course of the play: Brutus in private conversation with Cassius, Mark Antony speaking to Caesar's body, and so on. At least, then, the 'eyewitness' view would suggest that we, as eyewitnesses, mysteriously accompany the main events, without being seen or heard.[46] But this suggests a further problem: what are the main events? Eyewitnesses often don't have any idea what is going on in front of them. They are confused, disorientated and sometimes afraid for their lives. Theatre audiences at history plays are guided through the significant details, introduced to the important figures and told about the important events that take place 'out of sight'; they are offered a degree of understanding and insight that goes far beyond the level of the eyewitness. Hence, for example, *Henry V* begins with a conversation between two clergymen about Henry's character and development, which also sets up the meeting between Henry and the French ambassador. So when the ambassador suggests that Henry is young and wild, the audience has already been prompted to understand that Henry used to be like that, but is now a wise and considerate scholar (at least as far as the church is concerned).

Finally, note that theatre audiences don't merely know more than an eyewitness would happen to know: they know more than an eyewitness could possibly know, namely the future. For eyewitnesses to historical events, even very important ones, are not always as well informed as audiences in history plays. Xerxes, the Persian king, was an eyewitness to the battle of Salamis (the subject of Aeschylus' play); yet, crucially, he didn't know what the Greeks were up to until it was too late.[47] The history play is the telling, or retelling, of the familiar story.[48] Watching as Caesar goes to drink with the conspirators, we know exactly what is going to happen; Caesar and, one might suppose, the contemporary eyewitness, do not. Nothing could be further from retelling of the familiar than the experience of the eyewitness, living through uncertain, turbulent times. All of this suggests that history plays do not turn audience members into eyewitnesses.

Suppose, though, that it's not a matter of having the experience that a contemporary Roman eyewitness would have had; instead, it's a matter of the experience that the modern spectator would have if she were transported back in time to watch the events unfold. Of course, transporting the spectator – shoving her into the Delorean and setting the clock for 44 BC – wouldn't do at all. She does not, let us suppose, speak Latin or Greek; she wouldn't know where to go; she might not realise which one was Caesar, which Brutus. She needs a translator and a guide, who whispers the names of the people she sees, directs her gaze to the fateful moments, fills her in on some of the historical context and what has happened when she wasn't looking. If this is her experience of *Julius Caesar*, then we must see the playwright and company guiding her – a kind of invisible, Super-Virgil – through the streets of Rome. With their aid, we can understand why the spectator knows much more than those around her, including how events will unfold and some of what their significance will be for the next couple of millennia or so. Perhaps, in that case, she is a witness of sorts?

But with that, we have something that looks more like an answer to the second question than an answer to the first. For what is the Super-Virgil – the guide, the explainer, the translator (if necessary), the one who selects and emphasises the historical events for our benefit and understanding, the one who explains the differences between our time and the time in which the events took place – what is he, if not the historian? And, in as much as the spectator has been the receiver of this information, her question should be the second one: how does *Julius Caesar* compare with the work of a historian?

Of course, it may well be that *part* (though, as we shall see, certainly not all) of what the historian does is to give the reader some insight into what it might have been like to be there. Thus a recently published history of Europe, beginning in 1648, opens by explaining that 'a time-traveller from today arriving in the seventeenth century would find no aspect of everyday life more alien to modern experience [than seventeenth-century communications technology]'.[49] When Plutarch praises Thucydides – one historian praising another – he writes that Thucydides' goal is 'to make his auditor a spectator'. Hobbes, who translated Thucydides, cited approvingly this comment from Plutarch, adding that Thucydides 'setteth his reader in the assemblies of the people and in the senate, at their debating; in the streets, at their seditions; and in the field, at their battles'.[50] But putting the reader in among the assemblies *and doing nothing else* would hardly be good history. Presumably, what Hobbes and Plutarch mean is that the reader of Thucydides is given enough of the facts, context and background information, together with the words of Pericles and so on, to understand what was going on. Obviously, her understanding won't be the *same* as a contemporary spectator – as we have seen, in some ways she knows more, in others, less. That much is true for the reader of the history book and for the spectator at the history play. With that in mind, we turn to the second ('history book') question: to what extent does seeing the play compare with reading a history book (about the same events)?

Note, first, that the potential answers to the 'history book' question are different. Asking the eyewitness question, we were comparing (watching) the play with (watching) the event. Of course, the play could never be better than the event at looking like the event; nor, in fact, could it be nearly as good. It might have been like enough to the event that we could have answered 'yes' – although, as it happens, I have argued that we should answer 'no.' Turning to the history book question, matters are different. We are asked to compare what the spectator at the play gets (in terms of historical understanding) with what she might get from reading the history book. I'll say that her understanding is significantly worse; but note that (unlike with the eyewitness question) the answer could be that it is even *better*.

Might someone claim that the history play gives the spectator a better understanding than the history book? Yes; and someone has, although perhaps it is no surprise that the someone in question is the author of a history play. Writing about his play, *Danton's Death*, Georg Büchner claimed: 'The dramatist is in my view nothing other than a historian, but is superior to the latter in that he recreates history: instead of offering us a bare narrative, he transports us directly into the life of an age; he gives us characters instead of character portrayals; full-bodied figures instead of mere descriptions. His supreme task is to get as close as possible to history as it actually happened.'[51]

The context of this remark is, in part, a letter to his family in which the young Büchner is on the defensive about the play's foul language (by contemporary standards). His point is partly, therefore, that he can't be blamed for all the smut, because it was there in history and he was simply recreating it, like any good historical playwright. Büchner does not elaborate on why the playwright is better than the historian, but it's clear that the superiority is related to the play *as history*. It's not that the play is more fun, more worthwhile or (with Aristotle) more universal. A number of thoughts might motivate Büchner (or someone who argues to the same conclusion). Plays are more vivid than books. Perhaps they are easier to remember. Plays might (like diagrams, maps or dioramas) be better ways of explaining things than written prose. This is all very well, but being vivid and easy to remember – welcome though it undoubtedly is – is not the mark of a successful history book. The same goes for better explanation: it's welcome, of course, but if the information is there, it's there.

Büchner's defender might also want to elaborate on a difference between written and performed history. The actions that led to Caesar's death were just that: actions. Written history faces a kind of translation problem: it must turn movement and action into words on the page. Translations are never perfect, one might say. Certainly, the notion that the task of writing down the past is a peculiar one – one that may ulti-mately fail – has been much discussed. De Certeau writes, for example, that 'historiography (that is "history" and "writing") bears within its own name the paradox – almost an oxymoron – of a relation established between two antinomic terms'.[52] History plays, one might argue, do not face this translation problem. 'Stories are not lived but told,' wrote Louis Mink; but plays are lived.[53] History is action; plays are action, or, in Aristotle's phrase, imitations of action; books are, well, books. To say all this is not to say that (written) history is fiction, or that there's no truth about what happened in the past, or that any piece of writing about Julius Caesar is as valid or true as any other. All we are saying is that theatre (as history) doesn't obviously face the same problem that (written) historiography faces.

Indeed, looking to the way that Büchner wrote *Danton's Death,* it is possible that something (roughly) like this thought was on his mind (although just what was on his mind is not our focus here). *Danton's Death* is a history play about some of the key figures in the French Revolution – a play that, for whatever reason, has not achieved the same fame in the English-speaking world as it has elsewhere.[54] The play depicts the events leading up to the execution of Danton, Desmoulins and others at the hands of Robespierre. In addition to possessing all of the various features of the history play that we enumerated earlier, *Danton's Death* uses a great many historical speeches, cut and pasted directly from the sources. It has been estimated that one-sixth of the play is composed of direct or indirect quotation – a great deal of this is direct.[55]

So let us try to fill out Büchner's argument on his behalf. The historian, he would suggest, will tell you that Robespierre looked like this, that he said and did such-and-such; where there were speeches, he may provide the words for you to read on a page and where there were actions, he will describe them. But Robespierre was a person, not a collection of speeches and biographical details. A historical account of his life will never, no matter how accurate, bridge the gap between the word on the page and the human being who lived, breathed and was guillotined in 1794, having apparently shot himself in the face. Plays do not need to bridge the gap, because the gap does not exist. So a historical play featuring Robespierre will, Büchner suggests, always be better than its written equivalent. Of course, that won't be the case if the playwright makes up details about Robespierre. But if, like Büchner, the playwright uses the historical sources carefully – if she even has the historical characters giving speeches taken directly from the sources – then, he thinks, the result will be better *as history*, i.e. better when judged by the standards of what historians do.

Readers who know Büchner's play will know that in addition to quoting directly from the sources, he made up some of the characters (Marion) and that he also invented dialogue between real figures: most importantly, the final meeting between Danton and Robespierre (the conversation took place, but it is not known what was said). Because I am using his claims only as an example, this hardly matters here. One could just as easily consider a play in which more than one-sixth – perhaps even all of it – was direct historical quotation. In 1996, for example, the Tricycle Theatre in London used an edited transcript of the Nuremberg trials to stage a reenactment, *Nuremberg*, in which all of the words were taken directly from what was said in the trial itself.[56]

Two thoughts might seem to go against Büchner, although in fact they do not. First, one might complain that his play (or, perhaps, the play that takes his method to the extreme) doesn't tell us the whole story. The trouble with this, as a criticism of historical theatre, is that it also applies to any other kind of historiography. History books leave out an enormous amount of detail. A history book about the French Revolution, for example, could justifiably tell its reader about the France of Louis XIV and Louis XV by way of explaining Louis XVI's France; it could also compare the monarchies of contemporary France, England and Russia; it might discuss the French Enlightenment theories in which some of the key participants were steeped, not to mention the biographies of Robespierre and Danton, or those of the King and Queen. And we have not even begun to talk about the events of the revolution itself – the storming of the Bastille or the flight to Varennes or the Battle of Valmy. It is clear that not every detail will find its way into even a detailed, expansive volume on the revolution. To be selective, to omit certain facts or discussions, does not make you a bad historian; indeed, a good historian knows what to leave out as well as what to include. This is just as true for the historical playwright as for the conventional historian, and so it cannot be a reason for rejecting the former in favour of the latter.

Second, one could point out that historical theatre doesn't merely report facts. This is certainly true: historical theatre is not merely a report of a set of facts about the past. Those facts are interpreted and a version of them is presented to the audience. As before, though, if this is a criticism, then it also applies to the history book. Historians do not merely reel off lists of facts. Hayden White's distinction between the narrative history and the 'annals' is helpful here: the annals merely record events as they happen, with no apparent connection between them: 'Year 1: X died; Year 2: Y died.' Although it is presumably a statement of facts, the annals is not a work of historiography – at least by modern, Western standards.[57] To become such, it would require a narrative structure, in which the events were in some way connected (did X's death have anything to do with Y's?). What's more, even a presentation of the facts can be deeply misleading. Suppose a child asked us who Julius Caesar was. Suppose we answered: 'Caesar was a Roman legal reformer and minor religious official, who wrote a book about rhetorical style; he was the nephew of the famous general, Marius, who had rescued Italy from German invasion.' What we would be saying would be perfectly true. But it wouldn't be a very good historical account of Caesar if that's all we said. So it's important to note that history plays aren't bad history just because they don't tell the full story and they don't merely report facts.

On further examination, though, Büchner's claims are found to struggle. For one thing, he is talking about 'character portrayals' in written and dramatic history. But even if we agree with him that theatre can do this better, we must note that character portrayal is only part, perhaps a small part, of historiography. It might be (for example) that a history of modern Europe could not responsibly avoid a portrayal of the character of Napoleon, even of Robespierre. But it might be equally compelled to describe the changing population densities, comparative living conditions, development of trade routes, political systems, changes in modes of transport, military technology and so on. None of these (important) features involves character portrayal, and there's no particular reason to think that character portrayal is more important than any of them in understanding the historical period in question. More decisively, there's no reason to think that theatre could claim to portray them better than written history, if indeed it can portray them at all.[58] (It is for similar reasons, I suggested above, that Lukács thinks that history plays are appropriate only for limited historical circumstances. Although note that 'character portrayal' in Lukács has a different function: not showing what Robespierre was like, but showing how he embodied certain historical conflicts.)

That was just to show that Büchner's claim, even if successful, must be restricted: it could work for historical events only in which character portrayal is central. But there are other reasons to think that it won't be successful. For one thing, Büchner's play may be accurate in that it presents the sources – historical speeches – in an unusually direct and faithful manner. However, as Collingwood and others have long argued, it is not the historian's role merely to present the sources to the reader.[59] There are a number of reasons why this incorrectly accounts for the work of the historian: first, some sources (pottery, ruins) are not presentable directly and in spoken form. Second, some sources are known to be unreliable, but there are interesting things to say about *why* they are unreliable, and how exactly they get it wrong. Büchner's direct quotation method, taken to its extreme, would limit the playwright to presenting just the accurate, reliable source material. But historians want to explain where certain myths come from and why certain false claims might have been given credence. These explanations are a crucial part of what it is to be a good historian. The historian must always interpret and analyse the sources, drawing certain conclusions and presenting them. All of which suggests that even if the character, Robespierre, uses the speeches of Robespierre (the historical figure), that doesn't make for good historiography. The historian might question the validity of the source, or compare it with differing accounts of what he said, and so on.

Second, even if Büchner presents the most historically accurate picture of what these characters were like, he cannot present rival interpretations and disputes about the facts; and he cannot, in the course of the play, flag up which parts of the story are his own fictional inventions (the character of Marion), which parts of the story really happened but are presented in more detail than is really known (Robespierre confronting Danton) and which are direct quotations from historical sources (Desmoulins' opening lines). This is not just a problem for Büchner's use of direct quotation. It is a problem for historical theatre in general. For although historians, like playwrights, cannot present the whole story, they can make it clear where there are disputes about certain facts, and they can then make a case for interpreting the evidence one way and not another. It is this that seems typically lacking from historical theatre. To take a different example, the problem with *Julius Caesar*, then, is not that it doesn't tell the whole story; it's that it presents each element in the story as equally sure-footed, as equally justified. It does not explain where the evidence is lacking, or where the historian is speculating. This is important, because weighing up the evidence – 'showing your working' – is a paradigmatic feature of historiography. It is not optional for historians whether they explain how secure their claims are. Writers of historical plays, of course, are free to provide explanatory material making the relevant distinctions – and, indeed, some do.[60] But such written material is nonetheless a supplement to the play itself. Even if all of the play text is taken from historical sources, as in the case of *Nuremberg* (discussed above), it is clearly possible to wonder whether certain artistic decisions reflect historical events or not. Hence, as it happens, one reviewer of *Nuremberg* noticed a black ste-nographer arriving on stage just when Goering 'explained' the differences between the races; it's not clear to a spectator whether this is a deliberate comment from the director by means of an obvious historical inaccuracy, an accurate representation of those who were present or just a powerful coincidence.[61]

Even so, we have left Büchner's principal claim untouched: namely, that there is a certain (if highly restricted) area – character portrayal – in which theatre can do historiography better than a historian. But our fur-ther considerations have given us reason to doubt even this. What is it that Büchner adds to Robespierre, which the (written) historian cannot offer? It is the 'full-bodied figure', living, breathing and speaking. The Robespierre we see on stage does not merely *say* the words; he says them in a particular manner, with particular emphasis. He is not merely dressed in the kind of clothes Robespierre wore: he is wearing a shirt of a *particular* colour. To 'complete' the full-bodied figure, in short, the playwright (director, actor) must make decisions about how to present him.

The problem here is that some of these decisions must be made about matters that simply cannot be known. We may know that Robespierre wore red, but was it *this* red? That his voice was high-pitched, but was it *this* pitch? It is not known, and yet a decision must (consciously or otherwise) be made. So it may be that precisely the necessity of filling in the unknowns is what makes Robespierre on stage more 'full-bodied'; but in that case, what we have is not better historiography at all. What we have is an imagined reconstruction that gives a false sense of certainty about what is and is not known. Of course, our theatregoing companion didn't for a moment think that the costume colours and vocal pitches at *Julius Caesar* corresponded to those of Caesar's Rome. She has more common sense than that. But sometimes it's not clear; and, more importantly, there's no way in principle of knowing (from the performance) what has been invented and what hasn't. Büchner was claiming, as a benefit, the effect of one of the very features which makes his play worse, not better, as history.

Conclusion

By way of conclusion let us return, briefly, to the two senses of history that we mentioned earlier: history as the events themselves and history as the academic study of the past. History plays provide a highly effective way of stimulating interest in both – they make us interested in what happened and often in how we can know and think about what hap-pened. But if we think that they offer us an eyewitness presentation of events then, as I hope to have shown, we are very much mistaken. And if we think that they function as successful replacements to written history, then we may have misunderstood the task of the historian in thinking about the past.

Further Reading

Relatively little has been written on philosophy and history plays. The discussion in Lukács (1983) is still highly interesting, although the intellectual ground has shifted and many of his reference points are likely to be unfamiliar to the contemporary reader. Heller (2002) treats Shakespeare as a 'philosopher of history'. Rokem (2000) focuses on post-war theatrical representations of the French Revolution and the Holocaust. I recommend Frayn's 'Postscript' to his history play, *Democracy*, which gives a playwright's perspective on constructing a piece of drama out of real, historical events. Some of the material from this chapter appears in Stern (2012).

Notes

1 Herodotus (2007: 3).
2 Some claim that Aeschylus fought at or witnessed Salamis; but this is not known for sure.
3 Aeschylus (1961: 130–1).
4 See below for more detail on what I take to be a 'history play'. The use of the term 'history play' in relation to Aeschylus is obviously anachronistic: not only would he not have used the term 'history play' – he would not have even known the word 'history' in that sense because, as we have seen, he was writing before Herodotus. Our subject here is not the history of the term or the appearance of the separate genre, which seems to have arisen in Renaissance England, but with the concept of representing the past on the stage. Nonetheless, many of our examples are explicitly 'history plays' and I assume that our guiding question is posed in the context of that tradition.
5 As it happens, the earliest description we have of the performance of a tragedy – also in Herodotus – features a play that depicts real and recent events. Phrynikos' *Fall of Miletus* reduces its audience to tears, the play is banned and its author is fined a thousand drachmas. See Herodotus, Book 6: 21 (2007: 435). For an extended reading of this anecdote, see Kottman (2008) Ch. 6.
6 Many of Aristophanes' comedies, such as *The Clouds* (which ridicules Socrates), have contemporary settings and depict real people; although one would not exactly class them as history plays, rather as fictions set in contemporary Greece.
7 Examples include: Johnson's *Hysteria*, Churchill's *Top Girls*, Frayn's *Copenhagen*.
8 BT 10, p. 53.
9 Williams (2000: 395, 400)
10 Anecdotally: at a recent performance of a history play, a professor of English Literature said to me: 'It's a history play, so I expect it's pretty much true.' A colleague, having been to see a history play, told me that if she'd discovered that certain historical characters were not at all as they were portrayed in the play, she would have 'written in to complain'.
11 Some have taken the opposite view in related discussions. Ryle (1933) argues, for example, that had the *Pickwick Papers* been true, unknown to its author, it would in fact be a biography. This strikes me as mistaken. 'Biography', like 'history' and 'history play', implies a certain engagement between the author and the sources.
12 Frayn (2010: 251–287).
13 This, for example, is likely to be the case for *The Persians* – how would Aeschylus have known what was said at the Persian court? Indeed, *The Persians* – written before the first history – may well fall foul of this criterion.

14 *Poetics* 51b.

15 *Poetics* 51b. For an interpretation in terms of 'types' see, e.g., Frede (1992).

16 Reference to Herodotus at 51b. Aristotle mentions Herodotus elsewhere, but never Thucydides.

17 Herodotus, Book 7, (2007: 45–6).

18 Some philosophers argue something stronger about history and universals: namely, that the study of history reveals (more or less) strict universal laws about human activity. I have not explored this thought, because that is not what Aristotle means by 'universals'; and, more importantly, the whole idea of strict laws of history seems implausible. But see Day (2008), especially Chapter 4, for introduction and analysis.

19 Walton (1990: 97) makes a similar point: 'Sophocles' portrayal of the Oedipus story may improve my understanding of matters of contemporary interest as much if I consider it apocryphal as it would if I thought it true.'

20 Versions of this view are offered in White (1980) and Barthes (1981), amongst others. White is often accused of confusing the latter two.

21 See Carroll (1990) for discussion.

22 Hence, for example: 'Fictionality has nothing to do with what is or is not real or true or factual; […] It is hoped that asking whether a given work is fiction or nonfiction […] will lead to a better understanding of what it is.' (Walton 1990: 102–3)

23 Lamarque and Olsen (1994: 280). In addition to being 'literature' as opposed to 'history', it is likely that *Julius Caesar* is also covered by 'the fictive mode' for Lamarque and Olsen, because undoubtedly, as with *War and Peace*, 'there is some undisputed fictional content.' (1994: 285)

24 See Booth (1995).

25 Lukács (1983: 89–91).

26 Lukács (1983: 97–99).

27 Lukács (1983: 93, 114, 117, 147).

28 See Hegel (1977: Sections 438–476).

29 For more on both of these points, see e.g. Pinkard (1996: 135–46) and Hoy (2009).

30 E.g. Lukács (1983: 103, 127).

31 There is obviously a great deal more to say about his view of the historical novel – characters in novels, as fictional creations, needn't be aligned with one side or other and the history may consequently be represented in a different way. I won't pursue this here, because our focus is on theatre.

32 The historical figures who count as the 'most important' for Lukács just are the ones who most concisely and effectively embody the relevant social conflicts. So they may not be the historical figures we normally think of as the most significant – and they certainly won't necessarily be the greatest or best. (1983: 123–6)

33 Lukács (1983: 150–1, 153).

34 Lukács (1983: 156).

35 Lukács (1983: 166).

36 Heller (2002: 317).

37 Elsewhere, Lukács argues that one's level of historical awareness is determined (in part) by the age in which one lives. Hence, *when* one is alive directly relates to the way in which one is able to understand history. See 'Class Consciousness' in Lukács (1971).

38 Lukács (1983: 108).

39 Lukács (1983: 95; see also 1983: 115).

40 Or, if they did write plays, the plays would be unsuccessful. Or, as Lukács suggests, if they were to write successful plays, those plays would be more novelistic than dramatic. The latter is his explanation for the success of Ibsen.

41 Lukács (1983: 155–6).

42 Lukács (1983: 156).

43 See the discussion of Schiller's *Don Carlos* (Lukács 1983: 165); Lukács can also treat *Romeo and Juliet* as a history play depicting Italy at the close of the Middle Ages (1983: 118).

44 A further point, of course, is that a play like *The Persians* is valuable as primary historical evidence for later historians; that is not our focus here.

45 *Henry V*, Prologue, Lines 26–7; Pushkin quoted in Carlson (1993: 241).

98   *From the World to the Stage*

46 A related question in film studies asks if viewers of films imagine themselves there at the events (or looking through the lens). See, e.g., Currie (1995: 171), who argues convincingly against this view.

47 *Persians*, lines 1007–1040 in Aeschylus (1961: 150).

48 The idea that historical discourse requires knowing more than an informed contemporary is a central claim in Danto (1965); Mink (1970) offers a similar analysis of story-telling in general.

49 Blanning (2007: 3).

50 Hobbes (1822: vi). Hobbes also gives the Plutarch quotation. I'm grateful to my colleague, Marcus Giaquinto, for directing my attention to this quotation.

51 From a letter to his family, July 28, 1835; see Büchner (1993: 201).

52 De Certeau (1988: xxvii).

53 Mink (1970: 557).

54 Rokem (2000) explores this lack of success, with respect to its reception in America.

55 For a detailed analysis of Büchner's use of sources, see Büchner (2006: 485–498). Note, of course, that the play was written in German and the speeches were made in French, so the words are translated.

56 See Norton-Taylor (1997).

57 White (1980) certainly wouldn't disagree with this statement; but he argues that, in not being placed in a conventional narrative, the annals has certain virtues that are overlooked by modern-day readers.

58 Several modern playwrights, Brecht among them, have tried to solve this problem. We discuss some of his ideas in Chapter 7.

59 See 'Historical Evidence' in Collingwood (1994).

60 See e.g. Frayn (2010: 251–87).

61 Paul Taylor, 'Theatre Nuremberg: The War Crimes Trial', the *Independent*, 10th May, 1996. Taylor takes it to be the former.

Part II

FROM THE STAGE TO THE WORLD

5 A School of Morals?

The *Encyclopaedia* or, to give it its full alternative title, *The Systematic Dictionary of the Arts, Sciences and Crafts*, stands as the greatest monument to the French Enlightenment. It is a systemised, catalogued summary of human knowledge, guided by reason, which stretches in its completed form to a colossal 20,000,000 words. The Encyclopaedia boasted a number of well-known contributors, including Voltaire, Rousseau, Montesquieu, Diderot and D'Alembert. Of these, Voltaire, Rousseau and Diderot were, amongst other things, philosophers and playwrights. Voltaire's plays, although now virtually unknown to English-speaking audiences, were enormously successful in his time – and were praised to the skies, not least by Voltaire himself. Rousseau was better known as a writer of operas (both music and libretti), but he was also a moderately successful playwright, as was Diderot.[1]

Given this star-studded setting, the huge public spat over the ethics of the theatre that followed the publication of an article in the *Encyclopaedia* in 1757 is surprising.[2] For one thing, the author of the catalyst article was D'Alembert – not a playwright, but primarily a mathematician and philosopher (also, for some time, a coeditor of the project, with Diderot). For another thing, the article concerned had ostensibly nothing at all to do with theatre – its subject was Geneva, 'situated on two hills at the end of the lake which today bears its name but which was formerly called Lake Leman'.[3] The final surprise was who took issue with this article and chose to register his objections the following year, in no uncertain terms: none other than the playwright, philosopher and erstwhile *Encyclopaedia* contributor, J-J. Rousseau. What had irked Rousseau the most, as a proud citizen of Geneva, was the suggestion, so brief one would scarcely notice it, that Geneva might benefit from the construction of a theatre, albeit strictly regulated to avoid moral corruption:

> in this way, Geneva would have the theatre and morals and would enjoy the advantages of both; the theatrical performances would form the taste of the citizens and would give them a fineness of tact, a delicacy of sentiments, which is very difficult to acquire without the help of theatrical performances.[4]

That is, although D'Alembert acknowledges that the Genevans are in some respects two hundred years ahead (of educated, late eighteenth-century Parisians) when it comes to morals, there's something lacking that could be provided by the theatre. As he later put it, the theatre is 'a school of morals and virtue. [...] It is morality put into action, it is precepts reduced to examples'.[5] As well as benefiting from an improvement in moral sentiment, the theatre at Geneva would provide the city with 'decent pleasures' – that is, well-earned amusement and entertainment.

The two claims that D'Alembert makes for theatre – that it entertains, and that it can be moral – can and have been made either separately or together in defence of theatre. Certainly, they go back as far as Horace's claim for poetry in general, that it should be useful and pleasant (*'utile et dulce'*). We shall look at each in turn.

Pleasure and entertainment

First, a word about the difference between pleasure and entertainment. For our purposes, distinguishing between three ideas is helpful: first, pleasure as a sensation; second, pleasure in general; last, entertainment. First, for some, pleasure is best understood as a kind of bodily sensation, perhaps as an opposite to pain; this, roughly speaking, is the view that Aristotle presents in his *Nichomachean Ethics*.[6] Pain, following this line of argument, is the feeling that we get when something is going wrong with the body – it is an indication that the body is being hurt, damaged or over-exerted in some way. So when I put my hand into very hot water, the pain I feel is an indication that the body is being harmed. Correspondingly, pleasure is the sensation that we get when we are doing something that is naturally good for us: warming my cold hands by the fire. Although it might cover some of what we call pleasurable, this view can't be all there is to it. For one thing, it can't easily explain why, for example, some food gives us more pleasure than other food. Sadly, the food that is most pleasurable to eat isn't always the food that gives us the best nourishment. But even among foods that are equally nourishing, it's normal to get more pleasure from one than the other. So if I prefer my eggs boiled, rather than poached, the difference in pleasure isn't reducible to a difference in how nourishing they are. Furthermore, there are things in which we take pleasure that don't look natural at all (but that don't look perverse or unnatural either).

Second, then, we speak about taking pleasure from activities, where it's clear that this is neither a bodily sensation nor a natural improvement. Writing poetry, playing music or watching sport may be pleasurable, but it seems reasonable to say that this pleasure is neither a bodily sensation nor related to the satisfying of some natural need (music and poetry aren't natural, that is, in any obvious way). Broadly speaking, we are talking about things that 'please us', which is not the same as giving us a particular bodily sensation. Indeed, some activities in which we take pleasure might be thought to be precisely the opposite of natural, bodily pleasure – i.e. they might be harmful, even painful.

This brings us to entertainment, which, I suggest, has two features. First, an entertainment is something the specific and primary purpose of which is to bring pleasure to those involved (usually in the second sense, above). One might take pleasure (in the second sense) in all sorts of things that have some completely different purpose. If I enjoy my walk to work, the walk is a pleasure but not an entertainment. Note, however, that an entertainment need not (and probably doesn't) bring pleasure to all concerned: people who organise or perform at 'entertainments' may find them unpleasant and tiresome, and may just do so for the money; a sporting event may be pleasurable for the crowd, but that's probably not how the players on the losing team would describe it. Second, an entertainment is something that has been organised, planned or structured; it has something non-spontaneous about it. So although the unplanned, unprompted stroll after dinner might have pleasure as its object, it isn't an entertainment; but the organised walking-tour is. Theatre looks pleasurable in the second sense, but not the first; therefore, when I speak of 'pleasure', I mean this second sense of pleasure, unless otherwise stated. (Of course, not everybody finds theatre pleasurable and, sadly, not every performance is pleasurable.) And it looks very much like an entertainment, as defined.

In fact, Rousseau's argument is against theatre as entertainment, but not as pleasure. He notes that humans have a short life span and therefore that our time is precious. In the context of such a brief life, we must make use of those moments that we have: 'every useless amusement is an evil.'[7] To this, Rousseau adds that going to the theatre must necessarily replace some other activity; he considers the duties of 'a father, a son, a husband, a citizen' more natural and therefore more fulfilling than the artificial pleasures of the theatre. Man's natural pleasures 'are born of his labours, his relations, and his needs'.[8] Theatre is bad, because unnatural – that is, presumably, unrelated to man's labours, relations and needs. Looking back to our distinction between pleasure as sensation and pleasure in general, it's clear that Rousseau doesn't object to pleasure as a sensation, nor to taking pleasure in certain things. Rousseau is not therefore objecting to pleasure as such, but rather to entertainment as such. Pleasure can and should accompany duty; so, when there's duty to be done, why create useless amusements and diversions?

Actually, Rousseau's attack on theatre (as entertainment) is a little more complicated than that: a pleasurable but inherently useless entertainment (like theatre) might indirectly be useful and advantageous, if all the people who attend it would otherwise be doing much more unpleasant things like stealing, flattering and fornicating. But if they would otherwise be engaging in useful, natural activities, then entertainment becomes suspicious.[9] This is hardly a defence of theatre that any sympathiser would welcome and seems more a rhetorical device than a serious claim. It's also hard to escape the conclusion that this is a comparison between fornicating Parisians and hard-working citizens of Geneva – or at least between Rousseau's idealised conception of the two. D'Alembert's perfectly reasonable response to Rousseau on the brevity (and misfortune) of human life is: well, then why not have a little fun?[10] However, the key point for Rousseau is obviously that theatre is *unnatural* – hence it's not useful, just mere entertainment.

As we saw above, one can distinguish different kinds of pleasure – specifically the natural, bodily sensation can be distinguished from simply taking pleasure in a variety of different things. Rousseau evidently thinks that pleasure should be connected with *natural* activity and hence that pleasure deriving from artificial (i.e. non-natural) activity is somehow inappropriate.[11] Pleasure ought to be natural: natural pleasure is good because natural; and artificial pleasure is bad because non-natural.

There are at least two ways to respond to Rousseau on this point. The first is to argue that theatre is in fact natural (whether by Rousseau's or another standard). The second is to argue that using nature as a criterion for which pleasures are and aren't acceptable is deeply suspicious. First, then, one could point out that theatre brings people together, stirs their emotions and (sometimes) gives them pleasure – and, in doing so, satisfies some natural inclinations (just as in religion, sport, and so on). Theatre, for example, moves people; and people, in general, as D'Alembert remarks, need and like to be moved.[12] This, as I suggested above, seems rather tenuous. Another line might be that the mimetic element of theatre (discussed in Chapter 1) is somehow naturally pleasurable: it's a natural desire to imitate, copy, enact the doings of others around us; indeed, Aristotle suggests this in the *Poetics*.[13] Second, and more convincingly, one could question the notion of 'nature' as a good criterion for making judgements about whether things are good or bad, useful or useless. One should always ask, first, how one can possibly *know* what is natural and what is not? Is this a matter of what animals do, what humans used to do a long time ago, or what you think humans *would* ideally do, if not interfered with in various ways? Each answer is unsatisfactory, for any number of reasons.[14] We might wonder, contra Rousseau, whether being a 'citizen' is all that natural – or what 'natural' means if it is. Note that this objection also counts against the first response to Rousseau: if we don't know what's natural and what isn't, then we can't defend theatre on the grounds that it's natural. Second, one should ask why it matters whether something is natural or not. Presumably, by most standards, antibiotics and life-saving surgery are unnatural; but nobody seems to be crying to get rid of them. As so often, the appeal to nature is a thin veil for whatever bigotry the author happens to have inherited or taken on. In Rousseau's letter, this becomes particularly clear when he comes to discuss women. In defending his claims that a married woman should keep away from all men other than her husband, that women belong at home with children, that 'there are no good morals for women outside of a withdrawn and domestic life', Rousseau simply appeals to nature: 'Nature wanted it so, and it would be a crime to stifle its voice'.[15]

The school of morals

D'Alembert was neither the first nor the last to take the view that the theatre could be not merely entertaining, but also a school of morals. Unsurprisingly, this claim was often made by playwrights – among them Lessing, Schiller, Racine and Voltaire.[16] (That said, it was by no means a universal view among playwrights – towards the end of his career, Goethe, for example, denies that theatre has a beneficial moral effect on the audience.[17]) When we assess moral defences of theatre, it's helpful to bear in mind that they are often directed towards Christian criticisms. The conflict between the theatre and the church has a long history – about as long as the history of the church itself. And it has only really ceased as both have ceased to be taken seriously as venues for public moral learning. This was not so in the past. For the early Christian church, Greek theatre was objectionable because pagan; but, even worse, it was part of a festival for Dionysus, a particularly unchristian deity, who symbolised, amongst other things, intoxication, subversion and orgy. There were also other standard church criticisms of theatre, besides its pagan origins: its allegedly inherent use of illusion and deception, which were seen to contradict Jesus' demands for truth; its effect on the emotions of the audience, taking their minds away from God. In as much as the church was (and is) an actively political organisation, theatre also represented an inherent political threat, for reasons discussed in Chapter 7.

Of course, as with music, painting, sculpture, war, politics and everything else, the Church was happy to make use, for its own purposes, of those things it openly and vociferously opposed.[18] Hence we find early Christian tragedies, Jesuit didactic theatre, medieval pageant plays and so on. Nonetheless, the Christian message on theatre has for the most part been overwhelmingly negative and the claims of the playwrights (and philosophers defending them) to be presenting a school of morals should be seen in that light. Hence Racine, although claiming that Greek theatre was also a school of morals, implicitly defends *Phèdre* on Christian grounds. In this play, he says, thinking about an act is punished as harshly as carrying it out would be; this connects his play to the specifically Christian doctrine preached by Jesus in the Sermon on the Mount, according to which thinking about a sin is as bad as committing it.[19] Still, if criticisms of the theatre were often Christian-inspired, one can put many of them in non-Christian terms. And nobody did this better than Rousseau, when he came to answer D'Alembert's proposal for a theatre in Geneva: 'Theatre and morals! This would really be something to see, so much the more so as it would be the first time.'[20]

We shall look at the typical moral defences of theatre and how Rousseau (and others) attacked them. The specifics may vary, but the same points frequently reoccur, and they come down to what I'll call 'immediacy', 'emotion' and 'justice'.

Immediacy

Of course, one can always teach abstract moral codes, but actually *seeing* good and evil deeds before your very eyes has a much clearer and more powerful effect. In this regard, Schiller's early speech 'On Theatre Considered as a Moral Institution' (1784) is typical.[21] It's all very well to tell people, as for example in the Bible, to respect and honour their parents; but show them the scene from *King Lear*,

> when his white hair streams in the wind and he tells the raging elements how unnatural his Regan has been, when his furious pain finally pours out from him with those terrible words: 'I have given you all!' – How detestable does ingratitude seem to us then? How solemnly we promise respect and filial love![22]

Schiller's suggestion is that the direct witnessing of good and evil that theatre offers to its audiences gives them an alternative to a prescriptive, theoretical morality. If this claim seems a little overblown, then we should admit that humans learn a great deal by example, not merely by sets of rules. However, the claim that theatre teaches us about morality in a kind of immediate way stumbles against two kinds of objection: one worry is how we recognise these kinds of moral messages; the other is whether, even if we could, that would do any good.

As to the first, we should also note the recurrence of a problem we've already seen in another context: the problem of generalising from theatrical examples. As we saw when discussing Aristotle's claims about theatre and universals, trying to spell out just what the general claim is from a specific narrative looks difficult, perhaps impossible. Plenty of people, one supposes, watch *Lear* without taking home any message about how children ought to behave towards their parents. But even if, say, Schiller is right that watching Lear sends home a message about the importance of filial loyalty, one question *Lear* asks (I would suggest) is how far filial loyalty may be stretched – at what point (if any) does a father's behaviour become unreasonable and intolerable? One wonders, for example, what Schiller would make of Hebbel's *Agnes Bernauer*, in which Albrecht's father disinherits Albrecht and then quietly arranges for the murder of Albrecht's innocent wife. Modern debates about the relation between art and morality also stumble upon these straightforward, interpretative problems: hence, two philosophers will offer different accounts of the role of idleness in *The Cherry Orchard*.[23] If the message is ambiguous, then the alleged moral effect is at least diluted. Worse still (as Rousseau suggests), individual spectators will probably find confirmed in an ambiguous narrative whichever morals they took in with them in the first place; if so, the possibility for a real moral confrontation is limited.[24] What's more, I take it that we don't typically think that the best plays are those with clear, unambiguous morals; it's probably part of what we think is appealing about *The Cherry Orchard* that it provokes this kind of discussion.

Suppose that a play does communicate something unambiguous about right and wrong. Defenders of the school of morals nonetheless stumble across a further problem, namely that theatre doesn't ask us to *do* anything in response. That is, in the most general sense, theatre doesn't ask that we change in any way. Defenders of the theatre claim that it is better than being told a moral principle, because it directly shows the terrible effects of immorality. However, all the audience is required to do is to sit there and privately condemn what's going on. They are not required to act in any way. In Schiller's Lear example, we may *promise* to honour our parents – but do we ever actually fulfil such promises? For Rousseau, this is not merely a limitation on the effectiveness of theatre as a tool of moral instruction – it actually makes its effect *immoral*:

> In giving our tears to these fictions, we have satisfied all the rights of humanity without having to give anything more of ourselves; whereas unfortunate people in person would require attention from us, relief, consolation, and work, which would involve us in their pains.[25]

By setting plays in distant times and places (as French tragedians always did, and many playwrights have done and still do), theatre actually makes morality more *distant* – something for far-off people in far-off places, nothing to do with the audience when they leave the theatre. Furthermore, condemning the immorality of *other people* has never been something that we find difficult – especially when those 'other people' are fictional characters, played by actors. The difficulty comes in applying these thoughts to ourselves – but theatre enables us to forget this obligation and to feel smug about how moral we are.[26]

Emotion

Plutarch tells the story of a murderous tyrant, Alexander of Pherae, who has killed many men, but who weeps at the sufferings of the characters at a tragedy and walks out of the theatre: 'he was ashamed that his citizens should see him, who never pitied any man that he murdered, weep at the sufferings of Hecuba and Andromache'.[27] We shall look at theatre and emotion in detail in a separate chapter. However, the connection between them is often given a definite moral angle, which deserves a mention here. Abstract moral theory presents itself to reason, to the intellect. But the theatre makes you *feel* the terrible effects of evil (and the wondrous effects of good). Alexander of Pherae may have been told, one supposes, that forcing others to suffer was wrong; but the presentation of the suffering Trojans at the theatre produced an emotional response that he could not ignore. This can be taken further by defenders of the theatre, to suggest that repeated watching of plays can *train* one's feelings, so that one becomes more sensitive to the effects of good and evil in everyday life. The point of this is to distinguish between theatre and, say, a moralistic fable. At the end of Aesop's fable *The Boy Who Cried Wolf*, one learns the principle that one shouldn't lie, because liars aren't believed even when they tell the truth. Few have claimed that good theatre could or should leave the audience better able to recite moral principles, or a moral of the story. But many have thought that theatre can be particularly effective in stimulating certain emotional responses and understanding the emotional responses of others.

Perhaps surprisingly given its quaint and optimistic ring, the idea that narrative artworks have a special or privileged role in moral, emotional development has seen a strong revival in the last few decades – often combined with claims that fall roughly under the 'immediacy' bracket discussed above. Views of this kind have been advanced by a number of philosophers, primarily in relation to novels, but also poems and plays. Typical, in this context, would be Cora Diamond's claim that 'poetry [...] helps develop the heart's capacities that are the basis for the moral life by deepening our emotional life and our understanding of it'.[28]

Behind the view that theatre trains our moral, emotional responses, there often lies a view both about the emotions themselves and about the way they are connected with morality. For some philosophers, particularly in the Aristotelian tradition, a moral person is characterised by her appropriate emotional responses. Hence, if theatre can train us to respond appropriately to the world, then it would make us more moral; and it might do so without pretending to communicate any easily verbalised moral principles. Adherence to such a view will depend upon how seriously you take the connection between being moral and having appropriate emotional responses to the world. For some, this is an appealing thought; for others it is a diversion. Worth mentioning, too, is that emotional response – viewed as something that clouds judgement and gets in the way of reason – has been taken to be dangerous by many, including Plato of course. If that's the attitude you have towards the emotions, then the idea that theatre stimulates emotions at all may be seen by some as a blemish; hence, for example, Tertullian complains that 'there is no spectacle without violent agitation of the soul'.[29]

Even assuming that being moral and being emotionally responsive are closely connected, one thing we ought to ask is whether our emotional responses to plays are all that much like our emotional responses to real life – hence whether theatre can be a useful training. We'll see in our separate discussion of theatre and emotions that some philosophers doubt whether this is the case. Without going into the details at this stage, it seems plausible that my attitude towards the characters appearing before me on the stage is and ought to be different from my attitude towards real people whom I meet on the street. As we have already said, characters on the stage are isolated from my own actions and there's not much more I can do for them than sit there and emote. What's more, the properties of at least some fictional characters are so different from those of real people that making close connections between the two just misses the point: their lives, their speeches, their actions are neat, limited and finite in a way that the lives of the living can never be, which might make our responses to fictional characters and our moral pronouncements about them artificially simple or at least substantially different.[30] If so, perhaps what I feel for Hamlet really ought not to have any effect whatsoever on what I feel for someone real. Certainly, we shouldn't assume that I should behave towards theatrical representations of events in the same way that I should behave towards their real-life equivalents.[31]

Even supposing that there is a close connection between my emotions as spectator and my emotions in everyday life, some have concerns about whether that connection should be all that positive. First, we might think that the person who cares a great deal for fictional characters ought to divert her attention back towards real people. When we look at the relationship between theatre and the emotions, I'll discuss my response to *Uncle Vanya* – feeling desperately sorry for Vanya and Sonya, wasting away their lives; but it might be that spending that kind of time and energy getting upset and worrying about fictional characters is a diversion or a waste: perhaps I should have been worrying about the countless real people more deserving of my attention. Second, even supposing that plays give some special emotional insight, there's a gap between gaining emotional insight into the lives of others and using that insight for good. As it happens, Alexander of Pherae wept for the Trojans and left the theatre – but one might imagine such a tyrant learning from the emotional insights of the great playwrights and using them to further his cruel ends.[32] In fact, Plutarch's story suggests that Alexander, far from learning to be more merciful, was concerned that the theatrical performance was making him appear weak. Alexander echoes Plato's concern that theatre makes us sympathetic to feelings that we pride ourselves for avoiding outside that context. For Plato, then, the emotions that we experience at the theatre certainly can have an effect on the way we feel when not in the theatre: but that, for him, was exactly the problem.[33] Emotional responses that we wouldn't experience or respect under everyday circumstances should not, he thought, be given some special status just because we feel them in response to plays. Hence Rousseau (familiar, of course, with Plato's criticisms) questions why we should risk emotional moral training at all – that is, why reason shouldn't be sufficient for loving virtue and hating vice.[34]

One further suspicion, already evident in Plato's writing: whereas modern philosophers have tended to focus on the novel and its effect on the individual reader, the typical spectator at the theatre is part of an audience and subject to a kind of group psychology. We feel things in a group, which we probably wouldn't feel on our own. This seems true both for what we find moving and for what we find funny. Philosophers in general, it is fair to say, have often been suspicious of 'the crowd': Chrysippus the Stoic is reported to have said, when asked if he was following the crowd to hear a speaker, that if he had wanted to follow the crowd he wouldn't have studied philosophy.[35] For Plato, the fact that we wouldn't feel such things on our own was reason to be suspicious of group emotions; hence, Martin Puchner has suggested that Plato's dialogues, read aloud to small groups of students, should be understood as an attempt to escape from the perils of the theatrical crowd.[36] Against Plato, of course, we could maintain that the mere fact that I wouldn't feel a certain way unless part of a group does not entail that that feeling is illegitimate. There are many things that we can achieve only as part of a group, and many things we dare to do only as part of a group. These achievements should not thereby be discounted. If I do or feel, as part of a group, something that I would avoid on my own, there's no reason to suppose that the latter judgement cancels out the former.

In summary, although nobody doubts the ability of the theatre to move us, we are a long way from thinking that being moved entails a lasting or significant moral effect at all – let alone a positive effect. And even if we did think that some plays could morally educate through the emotions, we would not have shown that all plays have such an effect, or that the plays we think are the best (as works of art) have such an effect.[37]

Justice

The final defence for the theatre as the school of morals is that it shows justice being done. Put simply: plays show virtue rewarded and vice punished. Hence they have considerable power over a world in which this so evidently fails to happen. What's more, the idea that your wrongdoing will later be punished is central to Christian theology and, subsequently, to the Kantian moral tradition.[38] Plays which show virtue rewarded and vice punished – 'poetic justice', as it came to be known – are therefore educating their audiences with regard to a central tenet of moral understanding, at least according to one highly influential worldview. Hence, the theatre is a better place to learn about the rewards of virtue and the horrors of vice – in Schiller's words: 'in its [theatre's] fearsome mirror, the vices are shown to be as ugly as virtue is shown to be lovable.'[39]

The first and most obvious objection to the claim of the theatre to show justice is that it simply doesn't. The failure to show virtue rewarded and vice punished can occur in two different ways: first, virtue is punished (or not rewarded), vice is rewarded (or unpunished); second, it's not clear who is or is not virtuous. There is a further division to be made in the second case between (1) plays that are ambiguous about who is virtuous and who isn't and (2) plays in which the question of virtue and vice simply doesn't arise.

First, then, we find candidates for successful plays in which vices go completely unpunished. One might think of *The Winter's Tale*, in which Leontes, in a fit of jealousy, attempts the murder of both his childhood friend and his daughter, and indirectly causes the death of his son and, so he thinks, his wife. In the end, his wife forgives him and they are reconciled. Elsewhere, we find virtuous people (perhaps with minor faults) punished severely. In Racine's *Phèdre* – which Racine defends explicitly on grounds of moral instruction – Hippolyte is cursed by his father and dies after being attacked by a sea-monster – a slimy, coiled, scaled, yellow, horned, bellowing bull-dragon; this, for the crime of loving someone he shouldn't. In *King Lear*, the vicious sisters Goneril and Regan certainly die; but then so does the virtuous Cordelia.[40]

Second, theatre can fail to show virtue rewarded and vice punished by not showing, with any clarity, who is virtuous and who is not. Büchner's *Danton's Death*, in which questions of virtue explicitly arise, might be said to fall into this category. And in Molière's *The Misanthrope*, the question of just who is virtuous and who is vicious proved one of the central problems of interpretation – an ambiguity that may have contributed to the play's continuing success.[41] The playwright Michael Frayn cites, with approval, Friedrich Hebbel's dictum: 'in a good play, everyone is right'; or, put the other way around, if it's clear that one side is right and the other side is wrong, then you've got a bad play.[42] Finally, as I suggested, for many of the best and most popular plays, notions of virtue and vice are hardly at the forefront; characters are all complex, often flawed in some way, and the conflict arises from character and circumstance. *Romeo and Juliet* is a well-known example of a play that lacks obviously virtuous or vicious characters (even although they all might make mistakes or get carried away); recall Johnson's complaint that Shakespeare 'carries his persons indifferently through right and wrong'.[43] Similarly, we can very seriously doubt first, whether, say, *Oedipus Tyrannus* is in fact best understood in terms of virtue and vice, and, second, whether this first point makes any difference to how we should understand its merits. Aristotle's claim for tragedy was that it represented the fall of someone greater than us – this certainly seems like a better description of the fate of Oedipus, Othello or Hippolytus than the claim that they are like naughty schoolboys punished for misbehaving. It should be noted, then, that trying to seek out virtue or vice in specific characters is often an extremely bad way of reading and interpreting plays. What's more, one might go further and argue that, in the case of tragedy in particular, the presentation of a morally satisfactory world-order – one in which the good are rewarded and the bad punished – simply cuts against the requirements of the art form: a tragic world just is a world in which suffering is unavoidable or incomprehensibly basic.[44]

However, as Rousseau argues, even assuming that plays really do show virtue rewarded and vice punished, there are a number of reasons to question the moral efficacy of theatre. First, says Rousseau, they often do so in such an unbelievable way that people can't take this lesson seriously. Suppose we agree that, in *Phèdre*, Theseus acts rashly in cursing Hippolytus and that he gets punished accordingly by the death of the latter: even so, Rousseau might claim, the manner of punishment – the (notoriously) sudden appearance of the deadly sea monster – is so absurd that nobody in their right mind would be influenced by it.

Second, there's an age-old problem about vice being good fun to watch. As Rousseau notes, applause at the end of plays often goes to the wicked, entertaining characters rather than the virtuous ones, who can often seem boring.[45] This is a familiar problem in other areas of literature – such as in Milton's *Paradise Lost*, in which the author struggles (and fails) to avoid making Satan the fascinating if tragic hero of the tale. A useful example from prose fiction is *Fanny Hill*, the first pornographic novel in English: after a series of less-than-virtuous adventures, Fanny learns the pleasures of the mind and gets happily married; but the 'virtuous' ending to the book is hardly grounds for claiming that it was or should be read as a moral handbook; 'rewarding' the characters at the end isn't always successful in banishing the enjoyable impression of vice.[46] Many of the famous Shakespearean parts are those of villains of a sort, whether Richard III, Iago or Lady Macbeth. Although they come to no good in the end, this hardly cancels out the enjoyment and fascination that their evil doings produce. This is of course connected with the first point: if the punishments happen at the very end, in a contrived and unbelievable manner, then the overall effect may be the memory of the attractive, evil character.[47] One should not, incidentally, conclude from this that plays should show *only* virtuous characters. Lessing puts the objection well: it would not only lead to very bad plays, it would also make virtue seem such a commonplace that it's hardly worth striving for. He makes these comments having watched a play that suffers from an abundance of Christians desperately trying to get martyred. If everyone's doing it, it's not that impressive.[48]

There is one final criticism of the claim for justice, which turns the original and supposed advantage of theatre on its head. Suppose theatre can (and does) show virtue rewarded and vice punished; and suppose that real life does not. The suggested advantage of this was that theatre could school us about virtue, better than real-life examples. But there is a danger here. If theatregoers are led to believe that the world is such that good people are rewarded and bad people are punished – when in fact that isn't true – then they are less likely to want to change the world and transform it into a place where that really happens. There is a risk, then, that showing comforting stories in which the bad people always get what they deserve could really deceive us and make us think that we don't need to work to make things better. Relatedly, some philosophers have plausibly argued that confronting and engaging with immoral works – ones that certainly don't present virtue in a good or comfortable light – can itself offer an important ethical function, challenging us to develop our ethical outlooks and respond in new ways. Our moral views, after all, are not set in stone; there are prominent examples of plays (like Ibsen's *Ghosts*) that seemed at first to be scandalously immoral, but that could no longer provoke such an extreme reaction and may even seem to have lost their moral edge.[49]

The ethics of the actor

So far, we have considered some of the arguments for and against the theatre as a school of morals. In his proposal for the Geneva theatre, D'Alembert notes a concern that the people of Geneva have about the construction of a theatre: 'they fear, it is said, the taste for adornment, dissipation, and libertinism which the actors' troops disseminate among the youth.'[50] D'Alembert doesn't in fact deny that such fears are well grounded. Instead, he says, although this reputation is probably deserved, if we were to treat actors with more respect, then perhaps they would behave a little better.[51] One wonders whether actors would have been grateful for this defence. So far, we have considered two claims made on theatre's behalf – that it brings pleasure and that it can be morally instructive. In both cases, the arguments concern the effect that the plays have on the audience. But, as D'Alembert's remarks should serve to remind us, there is an equally long and well-established tradition, at least among critics of theatre, of targeting not the audience, but the actors. We are certainly not the first generation to accuse actors of being shallow, self-important, attention-seeking hypocrites, prone to histrionics, any more than we are the first to accuse philosophers of being useless, bearded, impractical dreamers.[52] We should recall, as noted in Chapter 1, that theatre is possible without actors, perhaps without human performers too. Not all theatrical performers impersonate, so criticisms relating to impersonation simply would not arise under those circumstances. Nonetheless, acting – in the sense of an actor playing a character – is familiar enough that concerns about the ethics of acting should find their place here.[53]

When D'Alembert speaks of the barbarous prejudice against actors, he might be looking to Greek sources for support. Plato (as we shall see) speaks of the dangers, for actors, of engaging in *mimesis*. Even Aristotle, for all his desire to defend theatre, acknowledges the vulgarity of acting and of performance in general.[54] His response to this is to downplay the actors' importance: tragedy is fundamentally a matter of plot and character – so it has its most significant effects when read. Thus in an important sense, it needn't be performed at all, and playwrights who rely on the 'spectacle' of theatre are inferior.[55] In fact, the Greek disdain for actors is, by later standards, relatively mild. Rousseau, feeling the need to excuse this mildness, suggests that because the Greek actors were respected citizens (as opposed to the Roman slaves or contemporary professionals), male (as opposed to contemporary mixed troupes), and taking part in a sacred festival (not an evening entertainment), there was less room for contempt. However, the Romans treated actors with disdain, not only by reputation, but also by law.[56] With the increased hostility from the church towards theatre in general, the lot of the actor hardly improved. A mediaeval English play specifically designates actors as agents of Satan, and some Tudor townsfolk were so fearful of the corruption brought in by actors that visiting troupes were quite often paid not to perform at all.[57] But for some of the more aggressive tirades against actors, D'Alembert could look much closer to home – no further, in fact, than his fellow *Encyclopaedia* editor, Denis Diderot. In *The Paradox of Acting*, Diderot claims to have great respect (in principle) for the profession of the actor; but, he goes on to say:

In society, unless they are buffoons, I find them polished, caustic, and cold; proud, light of behaviour, spendthrifts, self-interested; struck rather by our absurdities than touched by our misfortunes; [...] isolated, vagabonds, at the command of the great; little conduct, no friends, scarce any of those holy and tender ties which associate us in the pains and pleasures of another, who in turn shares our own.[58]

And then, of course, there's Rousseau, who summarises the reputation of actors as follows:

I see in general that the estate of the actor is one of license and bad morals; that the men are given to disorder; that the women lead a scandalous life; that both, avaricious and spendthrift at the same time, always overwhelmed by debts and spending money in torrents, are as little controlled in their dissipations as they are scrupulous about the means of providing for them. I see, moreover, that in every country their profession is one that dishonours, that those who exercise it, excommunicated or not, are everywhere despised.[59]

Rousseau's statement about the universal unpopularity of actors is a prelude to a claim that, in effect, well, there's no smoke without fire.[60] His remark about actresses leading scandalous lives should remind us that, whatever insults have been directed at actors, the same have always been directed at actresses, normally with the charge of sexual wantonness thrown in for good measure. Prynn the puritan's pithy remark – 'women actors, notorious whores' – is just the tip of the iceberg in this regard.[61] Even factoring in the miserable, ever-present sexism of so many of those who have shaped our thoughts, the abuse levelled at actresses is impressive, not to say surprising. One is reluctant to look for 'reasons' for this prejudice, in just the same way that one is reluctant to look for 'reasons' for anti-Semitism or racism, but those offered include: a simple failure to understand what a virtuous woman could possibly be doing outside the home; the tendency of the beautiful actress to become an object of desire for men and envy for women; and the idea that, in charging money for people to watch her, the actress puts herself on sale and is therefore a prostitute.[62] (Rousseau, incidentally, argues all three.) Because none of these amounts to a serious argument – however representative and damaging they have all proved to be – we won't pursue them any further here. However, we should note that the ability of theatre to subvert certain norms, including putting women on stage (in a context of extreme restrictions on what women were allowed to do) does have a political potential, which is discussed in Chapter 7.

Where one does find defences of the acting profession, they tend, like D'Alembert's, to be less than satisfactory from the actor's point of view.

So, for example, we find Pinciano claiming that actors are necessary for the theatre and so, because we like theatre, we might as well tolerate actors.[63] Unfortunately, considerations similar to these led to the claim that theatre would be better off without any actors at all. Lessing thought that actors are at their best in mediocre plays, that their artistic success is transitory, depending on the whims of the audience and that they are frequently better off masked; Kleist claims that marionettes would be more graceful; and then in the twentieth century, E. Gordon Craig developed the influential idea of the actor as an 'Über-Marionette', based on his view that acting, as mere impersonation, is not really an art.[64] The remainder of this chapter looks at the most common complaints made against actors and actresses.

Becoming what you pretend to be

As we saw in Chapter 1, Plato treats theatrical *mimesis* as comprising a third-person and a first-person component: the stage looks like something (from the audience's point of view); and the actors are pretending to be people whom they are not. We've already looked at Plato's objections to the former; he also has objections to the latter. In *The Republic*, Socrates is concerned that imitating someone, although at first it requires work, can increasingly become natural – so much so, that one can begin to take on characteristics of the person one is imitating.[65]

To understand Socrates' claim, it may help to recall (from Chapter 1) that one of the meanings of *mimesis* – the word here translated as 'imitation' – describes one person using another person as a kind of role-model or exemplar. Hence, in one of the examples we used in Chapter 1, the cheating wife who followed her cheating husband's example would have engaged in a kind of *mimesis*. Obviously, she isn't pretending to be her husband or trying to pass herself off as him. However, Plato is obviously positing a link between mimicking someone and treating them as a role-model: pretending to be an evil character has a tendency to lead one to use that person as a role-model, to take on some of the characteristics of that person.

This, of course, leaves room for imitating (i.e. pretending to be) good people and thus developing their good characteristics, which, Plato thinks, is possible in principle but extremely rare in contemporary tragedy and comedy: 'If [the guardians of the city] do imitate anything, then from their earliest childhood they should choose appropriate models to imitate – people who are brave, self-disciplined, god-fearing, free, that sort of thing.'[66] In other words: there's obviously nothing wrong with using other people as role-models – and, consequently, there's nothing wrong (in principle) with acting. You just have to use the right role-models and act the right parts. The trouble with theatre, of course, is that typically speaking, if the play is to be of any interest at all, there have to be *some* characters who are, to put it mildly, not the kind of people you'd want your children to grow up to be. And even if vice is punished on stage (which we've seen reason to doubt), the actor still has the experience of pretending to be somebody unworthy of imitation.

If Plato's proposed ban on imitating the bad sounds like the out-pourings of an elegant and tyrannical hysteric – as Plato's *The Republic* in general often does – then we should remind ourselves of the perceived importance of role-models to this day. Needless to say, the theatre is no longer the place to look for them; but athletes, film actors and other public figures are chastised for their failure to be 'role-models', to be appropriate people for children to imitate.[67] Furthermore, to continue the analogy with modern child-rearing, part of the concern with toy weapons or violent computer games is surely that it's not a good idea for children to imagine, to play at being violent. This is the modern equivalent of Plato's point: if you don't want people to be X, you shouldn't allow them to imaginatively pretend to be X.[68] A further comparison with modern debates might be the thought that 'playing' a hideous character – say, a historical serial-killer – inevitably invites (or even requires) the actor and perhaps the audience to sympathise with that character. Actors who are interviewed about playing certain roles are often asked about this.

Of course, one might well have objections to Plato's line. For one thing, it's not obvious that actors pretending to be certain characters really do take on such traits of these characters, or use them as role-models. Do we really find in old, experienced actors nothing but a cluster of contradictory and confusing personality traits, gleaned over time from all the characters they've played? What's more, because the parts played in theatre repertoires are not always simply 'good' or 'bad', the process of imitation might also be one of coming to understand another complex, human perspective – a more practical and hygienic equivalent of Atticus Finch's wise advice, namely that you never really know a man until you stand in his shoes and walk around in them. The very ability or capacity to pity someone – seen by many, including Rousseau, as a moral virtue – might be said to depend in some sense on imaginatively pretending to be them.[69] And perhaps, in response to the fears of sympathy with evil characters, one might think that such characters really do deserve sym-pathy, at least up to a point. Finally, one might argue exactly the oppo-site point to Plato and claim, following roughly Freudian lines, that the mimetic acting out of certain activities (or audience's watching them) might provide a kind of substitute satisfaction. In other words, imagina-tively pretending to X might be a way of *not* in fact doing X, rather than (as Plato would have it) an encouragement to X.

Deception and inauthenticity

Once he's finished setting out the general reputation of the actor, Rousseau gives his view of what being an actor actually consists in:

> What is the talent of the actor? It is the art of counterfeiting himself [...] of appearing different than he is, of becoming passionate in cold blood, of saying what he does not think as if he really did think it.[70]

There is no doubt, of course, that acting typically involves pretending to be somebody else. Then again, of course, it's hardly as though the actor expects to get away with it, against the audience's will. Somebody who pretends to be me in order to withdraw money from my bank account does not produce programme notes for the cashier, in which he details all the people from whom he has previously stolen money. Anticipating precisely this response, Rousseau admits that actors aren't actually deceiving people when they're on stage. But, he complains, they do learn the tools for deception, for seeming to be other than they are when they are off the stage; and by teaching actors to dissemble, and rewarding them when they do it well, we encourage them to make use of these skills in everyday situations.[71]

All things considered, actors probably don't learn useful tools for deception in everyday life (rather than tools for a highly restricted, minimal kind of play or impersonation in the peculiar setting of the theatre). But although I see no reason to take Rousseau very seriously here, I do think he points us in the direction of a more interesting discussion of theatre, deception and authenticity. Anybody familiar with the classical theatre repertoire will be aware of the importance that the twin notions of deception and authenticity have on the stage, as part of many theatre plots. Seeming to be what you're not – and the failure to discern that someone else is other than he seems – are among the most common themes of theatrical work. Think of the Shakespearean comedy, with all its dressing up and misrecognition; or of the tragedy in which the failure of the hero to recognise another (or himself) is what brings about his downfall. To name but a few well-known examples, this forms much of the subject matter of *Othello*, of *The Merchant of Venice*, of *The Misanthrope* and so on. In this context, it seems peculiar to attack theatre for something that it often addresses head on: the danger and perhaps also the necessity of seeming to be other than you are.

A second, and more sceptical, point should also be made with respect to the claim that acting encourages inauthenticity. The central notion for 'authenticity' is one according to which a person has a kind of genuine 'centre' or 'essence'. The authentic person is then someone who acts in accordance with this genuine centre or essence – who seems to be nothing other than he really, essentially is. This presents us with a static picture of human beings, according to which one is either being genuine (action corresponding to essence) or not. Needless to say, a full discussion of this idea is beyond the scope of this chapter, but a couple of broad concerns can be made clear. First, why can't it be part of somebody's 'essence' or 'authentic centre' to be different things to different people at different times? Second, can't the actor, in playing different roles in different contexts, be a very good indication of what we all do in one way or another? Anybody who, for example, has taught in a classroom will have an idea that teaching is very often a kind of acting. And people often talk about being different at work, and at home, and with their friends. These variations needn't be seen as a failure to be authentic; they might just be perfectly understandable adaptations to differing circumstances. Indeed, this thought has been taken further, by those who think that we are in some sense acting or performing *all the time* – that when we interact with other human beings, and perhaps even when we present ourselves to ourselves, we are acting or playing a part. Such 'role-playing' needn't be understood as deceptive or treacherous, but rather as a necessary and often benign function of human social interaction.[72]

Emotion or craft?

The claim to inauthenticity might be spelled out in a rather different way, without appealing, as Rousseau does, to the idea that the actor will, once the performance is done, go about using his special deception skills to steal your money and your dutiful, housebound wife. Diderot's *Paradox of Acting* is a reaction to a long tradition, traceable to Aristotle and to Horace, of viewing the art of the actor as that of being emotional in accordance with the part.[73] According to the view Diderot opposes, that is, the actor succeeds best when he *feels*, say, the wrath of Lear at his daughters' betrayal or the intoxicating passion of Romeo for Juliet. This makes the actor a person of extreme passion, of sensibility – someone who gets very emotional very easily. If that is the case then Rousseau is wrong to cast suspicion on the actor for getting emotional 'in cold blood'. If the actor really does feel the part, then it's not a question of pretending to be emotional, it's just a matter of getting emotional very easily.

For Diderot, this gets things exactly wrong. If actors were so emotionally fragile, they'd have trouble appearing every night, remembering their lines, and knowing where to stand. An actress who really felt the intense passion of Phèdre would have great difficulty remembering and reciting such beautiful poetry.[74] An actress who was sufficiently emotional to feel that distraught every night would frequently be so completely incapacitated by excesses of emotion that she wouldn't leave her dressing room at all. In fact, the successful actress is precisely the one who doesn't get emotional, who keeps under control at all times, and never lets herself go.

Diderot's remarks should also be understood as an attack on theatrical verisimilitude, which we discussed in relation to Plato (in Chapter 2). If actors really did 'feel' the parts they were playing, then they would perhaps look more realistic – more like ordinary people, in such circumstances, would look. But because the theatre is not at all verisimilar, this would hardly help matters. For example, he points out, death on the stage – quick, poignant and often beautiful – looks nothing like the slow, grubby, agonising deaths of real life.[75] Similarly with excesses of emotion: when one is really angry or passionate, one typically says very little.

Diderot is therefore making two separate and independent claims about, for instance, the actor playing an angry character on stage: (1) that the actor does not feel angry at all and (2) that the external signs that the actor makes to indicate anger do not look like anger as it really is in the world. For Diderot, we read emotions off actors by way of a kind of convention or symbolism: the audience knows that certain gestures (when performed by an actor on the stage) *indicate* anger, even although, on reflection, real, everyday anger looks nothing like that.

For our purposes, what's important about Diderot's argument is this: acting is not just an extension of everyday passions; it is, instead, a craft by which one learns to mimic certain outward signs of emotion, without inwardly feeling anything *at all*. After all, says Diderot, actors need to know where to stand and what to say; they need to react to new and unpredictable situations (e.g. another actor forgetting his lines); they must remember not just the script but certain emphases, phrasing and accentuation. In the depths of their 'passion', they must look in the right direction for the light, they must make the correct outward signs and gestures. In all of this, there can be no room for the supposed passion that is being portrayed. A passionate person would forget all of this. Hence the conclusion: 'it is we who feel; it is they [actors, but also playwrights] who watch, study, and give us the result.'[76] Acting is therefore inauthentic in this sense: that there is no correspondence between the emotions that the actor displays (or indicates by certain conventions) and the emotions that the actor feels. He is not what he seems to be.

Both of Diderot's claims seem extreme and are open to more moderate versions. As for the notion of emotional conventions, it seems more likely that actors exaggerate or caricature typical emotional reactions – rather like cartoon versions of surprise or fear. Hence, the 'symbols' or gestures that indicate some emotion are related to the everyday non-theatrical counterpart of that emotion. This leaves room for the stage version of the emotion to look very little like its counterpart, thus preserving Diderot's central claim. It also fits with Diderot's claim about actors studying us to learn about our emotional responses. If emotions were a matter of pure convention, then there would be no point studying us at all (except perhaps studying our responses to conventional emotion-symbols).

As for his second claim about actors feeling nothing: one might wonder, and some indeed have argued along these lines, whether there might be some interplay between putting on certain outward signs of fear, anger, etc., and then, in consequence, actually feeling them to a certain extent. There might not be such a sharp line, that is, between feeling the emotion and showing the outward signs of the emotion. So, for example, clenching your fists might actually make you feel angry. The extent to which one accepts this interplay relates to the point just made about Diderot's first claim. If the outward signs of emotion, as used by the actor, are not in fact the real things, but rather a matter of stage convention, then putting on those outward signs should have no effect at all. So looking afraid, on the stage, looking nothing like looking really afraid, will do nothing to trigger fear.[77]

Diderot's claims about acting, if accurate, have positive as well as negative implications – as he clearly acknowledges. For one thing, it makes space for acting as a genuine technical skill. Good actors aren't merely people who feel strongly and on cue – they study people's expressions, movements and voices and they must train and practice like a musician or an athlete. When an actress portrays a distressed mother, claims Diderot (perhaps hyperbolically), her cries are planned to the nearest twentieth of a quarter-tone.[78] Diderot's claims about actors are informed by his friendship with the famous English actor, David Garrick. Garrick, says Diderot, would practise different facial expressions, one after another, representing strong and contrasting emotions. All the while, he would feel nothing at all.[79] One is reminded of a musician practising scales. Diderot was writing as the social status of the actor, although still not respected (as Rousseau argues, above), was certainly better than it had been. Some actors (and even some actresses) were able not only to make a living, but even to become wealthy by their profession. Mme Clairon, mentioned in the *Paradox of Acting*, is one example. Garrick is another: not only was the word 'star' (meaning a successful actor) first used for him; he would subsequently have the honour of being buried in Westminster Abbey. Just fifty years earlier, in France, the police had, under cover of darkness, tossed the body of the celebrated actress Adrienne Lecouvreur into an unmarked pit.[80] The conception of acting as a craft was made all the more plausible once it was, relatively speaking, more profitable and more socially acceptable.

Second, if he's correct, Diderot makes Plato's case against acting a lot more difficult. If actors don't really feel, don't really sympathise with their characters; if, at the end of the performance, the deception is all on the side of the audience and the actor is only weary as a gymnast is weary, then it's hard to make the case that an actor playing an evil character is likely to turn evil. Of course, the actor will need to learn how to mimic the outward appearance of certain emotional states that relate to that character; but that's hardly the kind of imaginative sympathy that seems to have alarmed Plato.

Finally, far from fitting nicely together with Rousseau's attacks on the actor, if Diderot is correct about the actor's representation of emotion looking little like the real life equivalent, then he may be seen to answer Rousseau's concerns about deception and inauthenticity. For Diderot, that is, nothing happens on stage as it does in nature.[81] If so, actors pretending to be angry or in love in everyday situations (i.e. when not on the stage) would simply be laughed at, even although the same technical skills, on stage, bring the audience to tears:

> They are well enough on the stage [...], with their actions, their bearing, their intonations. They would make but a sorry figure in history; they would raise laughter in society. People would whisper to each other: 'Is this fellow mad? [...] In what world do people talk like this?'[82]

Where Diderot does criticise actors, it is for having the misfortune to possess the skills to please everyone. The actor, he claims, is rather like the courtier – someone who is allowed no autonomy, no say in what he does; instead, he must please those around him, and bend to their will. Where the courtier always has to think of the king, the actor always has to think of the poet and, of course, of the audience.[83] During the course of this process, the actor is allowed nothing of 'himself', no opinion, no personality, no independence.[84] Diderot was hardly the first to make this connection: Raphael Holinshed, the chronicler who provided the sources for a number of Shakespeare's plays, writes that Edward II (he of the notoriously unpleasant death) 'furnished his court with companies of jesters, ruffians, flattering parasites, musicians and other vile and naughty ribald, that the king might spend both days and nights in jesting, playing, banqueting and such other filthy and dishonourable exercises'.[85] The further suggestion, in Diderot's comparison with the courtier, is that the actor is a kind of useless flatterer, someone who has no real purpose other than to please the ruler (or the audience). Contrary to the claim (under 'deception and inauthenticity', above) that actors do what we all do anyway, this marks out the courtier and the actor as different from the rest of us. It's not that we don't 'act' in everyday life – it's that, when we do so, we are permitted 'to delight some and to weary others'.[86] If, by profession, one has to please, then the option of taking an independent route (which others may or may not like) is closed off.

If this is a criticism of the acting profession, then it is a much milder one than those of Plato and Rousseau (as Diderot no doubt would acknowledge). In combination, these claims about the actor amount to (1) that the purpose to which he is tied is, like that of the courtier, one of flattering and bringing pleasure and (2) that he has little room for independence beyond the pen of the poet and the whims of his audience; hence, like the courtier, he is a kind of puppet. As for (1), we should question whether the comparison with the courtier is really appropriate. The point about courtiers is that they are *useless* flatterers – and, even more, that they might be damaging to the ruler, by constantly telling him how good he is and how everything he does is right. This is not exactly the actor's role. As we've seen, the theatre does provide pleasure, but this is hardly an objection in itself, without some further background views; and, indeed, for many it is an advantage. Furthermore, many of the most famous and popular plays, although bringing pleasure of a certain kind, tell dark, unpleasant stories, which (to say the least) don't tell us flattering, unambiguously positive things about what it is to be human. There's no clear analogy with the courtier making the king feel good about himself. As for (2): not many of us, in our working lives, have complete independence in what we do. Whether it's the demands of a boss, of a company or institution, or even just of the market, complete freedom to offend or please whomever we like sounds like a far-off dream. And despite the frequent (and often unfavourable) comparisons made between the actor and the puppet (or marionette), a successful or lasting substitution seems a long way off.[87]

Conclusion

Even to pose questions about theatre and morals is to walk into a minefield of shifting moral belief and cultural practice; it is unlikely that we would get to a final message about theatre and morality, and it's unclear why we would want one. Theatrical performances don't happen in isolation – moral or otherwise – from our everyday experiences and our deep cultural attitudes. But many ambitious claims have been made about the ethics of theatre, from the rather grandiose defences of the school of morals, to Rousseau's savage attacks. We have now had a chance to look at some of the main lines of argument. For the reasons we have discussed, it is just as unlikely that theatre, taken as a whole, corrupts or improves: where the moral message of a play is clear (which, often, it isn't), that still leaves the question of whether an audience will approve of that message or be provoked into challenging it further – and, even if they approve, there's the question of whether their approval will translate into any meaningful change. As for the charges against actors, we have seen that many of these, on closer inspection, look unfair or rest on questionable premises.

Further Reading

For Plato's attack on the moral effects of theatre, see *The Republic* (and relevant further reading from Chapter 2, above). Rousseau's *Letter* still packs a powerful punch and addresses many of the better-known arguments both for and against the moral efficacy of theatre; Barish (1981) includes a chapter on Rousseau. Contemporary philosophical writing on art and morality (or literature and morality) has tended to leave theatre behind; but two collections – Levinson (2001) and Gardner & Bermúdez (2003) – are nonetheless useful. Gardner (2003) offers a comprehensive analysis of (unsuccessful) attempts to combine tragic drama with moral doctrine, especially in the German philosophical tradition. As for acting: Diderot's *The Paradox of Acting* remains highly engaging; his other writings on theatre are collected (in French) in Diderot (1936); Mason (1982) provides an accessible introduction to various aspects of Diderot's thought, including his aesthetics. Generally, Benedetti (2005) is an accessible introduction to various theoretical approaches to acting; and for a more challenging collection of essays on acting, see Zarrilli (1995).

Notes

1 Diderot's most important play, *The Head of the Family (Le Père de Famille)* would be performed in 1761.
2 This chapter uses texts from Rousseau, Schiller, Diderot – among others – to think about theatre and morals. The eighteenth century offers such a heated and richly rewarding set of debates on the subject – which are of sufficiently general application – that I feel this focus is warranted. But of course such debates neither began nor ended with the *Encyclopedia* – and Rousseau is clearly responding to a long tradition; for more, see the further reading.
3 D'Alembert (2004: 239).
4 D'Alembert (2004: 244).
5 D'Alembert (2004: 356–7).
6 Aristotle's view of pleasure is more complex than this would suggest: his remarks in Books VII and X of his *Nichomachean Ethics* have been taken by some to suggest not one but two 'theories' of pleasure.
7 Rousseau (2004: 262).
8 Rousseau (2004: 262).
9 Rousseau (2004: 293–4).
10 D'Alembert (2004: 354).
11 What matters to Rousseau is the connection (or lack of connection) between pleasure and nature; he is less concerned with whether or not pleasure is a bodily sensation. Nor is Rousseau being utilitarian: he doesn't think that pleasure is a good in itself.
12 D'Alembert (2004: 361).
13 *Poetics*, 48b.
14 E.g. animals do such a wide variety of things that no general rules emerge; 'humans a long time ago' leaves open the tricky question of *which* humans and at which time; and what humans ideally would do begins to look like a matter of dogma, rather than nature.

15 Rousseau (2004: 311–3). Rousseau associates arguments for male/female equality with city-dwellers – i.e. with those who know and understand nothing of 'nature', here understood as a kind of idyllic rural life.
16 Lessing (1962: Section 2); Voltaire quoted in Carlson (1993: 147); Racine (1991: 23); Schiller (1962).
17 In his *Nachlass zu Aristoteles Poetik*; for discussion see Carlson (1993: 182).
18 For the example of art and music, see Augustine's *Confessions* (X: 50, p. 208).
19 Matthew, Chapter 5, Verses 27–8.
20 Rousseau (2004: 299).
21 Schiller (1962: vol. 20, pp. 87–100). Translations are my own. The speech is reprinted under its original title as '*Was kann eine gute stehende Schaubühne eigentlich wirken?*' (What can a good repertory stage actually accomplish?). Note that this is an early speech and does not represent Schiller's later views – some argue that it may also have been tailored to fit the views of his particular audience. (See Sharpe 2007: 101.) Nonetheless, it is typical of contemporary moral defences of the theatre.
22 Schiller (1962: vol. 20, p. 93).
23 Carroll (2001: 147); Hamilton (2003: 38–9).
24 Rousseau (2004: 264). Strictly, this is an argument for why theatre can't improve morals; there are other reasons, he thinks, why it can damage them (pp. 292–3).
25 Rousseau (2004: 269); see also Diderot (1883: 56): 'A member of the audience is not excited to offer help, but only to grieve.'
26 Rousseau's objection may also count against some of the more recent versions of a moral account of theatre. Feagin (1983), whose view we explore in the next chapter, suggests that tragedy in particular helps us to test out our moral responses to the world – but, Rousseau might argue, a test that doesn't require us to do anything is no test at all. The same might be said for Woodruff's claim that theatre helps us to understand what we ought to do, even if we don't actually have to act on it (2008: 162–4): the failure to do what we know we ought to do is, often enough, a serious failing in itself.
27 From Plutarch's 'Life of Pelopidas' in Plutarch (2001: vol. 1, p. 403).
28 Diamond (1982: 31). Other defenders of this kind of view include Beardsmore (1971), Palmer (1992) and Nussbaum (1990), who has made this view highly influential; but in her case, this is particularly in regard to novels, which, she thinks, have a special status. Woodruff (2008) has recently offered a version of this view, specifically in relation to theatre.
29 Quoted in Carlson (1993: 28). Williams (1973: 207–229) offers a helpful discussion of the relationship between morality and the emotions. The anti-emotional stance of much of the philosophical tradition is something that Nietzsche was particularly good at locating and mocking. See 'Reason in philosophy' and 'Morality as Anti-nature' in his *Twilight of the Idols*.
30 See Vogler (2007).
31 See Jacobson (1997: 186).
32 See Hamilton (2003: 39–40) for discussion of both of these concerns.
33 *The Republic* 492b and 605c.
34 Rousseau (2004: 267).
35 Reported in Diogenes Laertius, *Lives of Eminent Philosophers*, Book VII, p. 291.
36 Puchner (2010: 3–35).
37 I have not ventured into a separate and popular discussion among philosophers of art, stemming in part from an offhand remark of Hume's, about whether moral 'defects' in works of art necessarily undermine them aesthetically. The answer is: no. But for discussion see Jacobson (1997) and Hamilton (2003).
38 For discussion, see Gardner (2003); Gardner argues that philosophers in the Kantian tradition failed (with good reason) to reconcile the demands of morality, as they saw it, with tragedy.
39 Schiller (1962), vol. 20, p. 93.
40 These remarks on virtue and vice in Shakespeare, Racine and others are in no way meant as criticisms of the plays. I simply point to problems with the strategy of defending them morally on the grounds of justice. If that strategy yields hopeless interpretations of great works of literature, then that is one more reason to abandon it.

41 Among the apologists for the character of the misanthrope is Rousseau. Historians suggest that this probably wasn't the attitude taken by Molière's audiences.

42 Frayn (2010: 137).

43 'Preface to Shakespeare' (1765), quoted in Gardner (2003: 239).

44 See Gardner (2003). Gardner also offers a critical analysis of some of Schiller's later and more philosophically complex attempts to reconcile tragedy and morality; these include the attempt to replace tragic fate with the demands of moral reasoning and, elsewhere, the view that tragedy presents its characters as capable of moral vocation, if not worthy of moral praise.

45 Rousseau (2004: 267).

46 On the 'moral' ending of *Fanny Hill*, see Haslanger (2011).

47 This is not meant to suggest that Shakespeare was *trying* to show virtue rewarded and vice punished although that claim, as a defence of theatre, was certainly available at the time – it was used by George Whetstone in 1578, in the preface to what would become the source play for Shakespeare's *Measure for Measure* (see Carlson 1993: 79).

48 Lessing (1962: Section 1, p. 7).

49 Jacobson (1997) develops this thought using the reception of Ibsen's *Ghosts*, amongst others.

50 D'Alembert (2004: 244).

51 D'Alembert (2004: 244).

52 The word 'hypocrite' comes, of course, from the Greek for actor, and 'histrionic' derives from the Etruscan word for the same; on philosophers, the best formulation probably belongs to Lord Macaulay: 'They promised what was impracticable; they despised what was practicable. They filled the world with long words and long beards; and they left it as wicked and as ignorant as they found it.'

53 For a fine-grained discussion of the relationship between performing and acting, see Kirby (1995).

54 *Poetics* 62a.

55 *Poetics* 62a. One doubts whether the same could possibly be said of comedy.

56 Rousseau (2004: 307).

57 Wiles (1995: 87); Thomson (1995: 178). Generally, see Barish (1981).

58 Diderot (1883: 62–3).

59 Rousseau (2004: 306).

60 Rousseau (2004: 307).

61 Quoted in Thomson (1995: 202).

62 On the second point: Samuel Pepys, for example, notes how many men 'hover about actresses' once they leave the stage – although it's clear from his diaries that he wasn't afraid of doing so himself. See, e.g. Thomson (1995: 208).

63 Quoted in Carlson (1993: 60).

64 Kleist (1978); Lessing (1962: Sections 25, 56); Craig (1911).

65 *The Republic* 395c.

66 *The Republic* 395c.

67 This condemnation certainly occurs, even if it's often nothing more than a thin pretext for envy, frustration and social conservatism.

68 See Nehamas (1988). I write as somebody who was never allowed to play with toy guns as a child, for precisely this reason.

69 See Barish (1981: 269–70).

70 Rousseau (2004: 309).

71 Rousseau (2004: 310). On the question of how (if at all) spectators are deceived by theatre, see Chapter 3 and Chapter 6.

72 Goffman (1956) is the classic statement of this kind of view.

73 Aristotle's *Poetics* 55a. Horace writes: 'If you wish me to weep, you must feel sorrow yourself.' (*Ars Poetica*, II, 102–3) Diderot is specifically responding to *Garrick, ou les Acteurs Anglais* by Sticotti.

74 Diderot (1883: 43–4).

75 Diderot (1883: 23).

76 Diderot (1883: 14).

77 See, for example, Lessing (1962: Section 3, p. 12); for accounts of the 'circle of effect' response to Diderot, see Carlson's helpful discussion of the reception of Diderot's work – Carlson (1993: 233–4).
78 Diderot (1883: 15).
79 Diderot (1883: 38). Benedetti (2005) notes that Garrick was perfectly happy to acknowledge that, on certain occasions, he suffered profoundly with his characters when on stage (p. 81).
80 Holland and Patterson (1995: 296).
81 Diderot (1883: 5).
82 Diderot (1883: 20).
83 Diderot (1883: 61).
84 Rousseau (2004: 310) also speaks of the actor annihilating himself in the course of his profession.
85 Thomson (1995: 173).
86 Diderot (1883: 61). The idea that actors (and courtiers) are not permitted to be displeasing may be a further cause for the comparison between actresses and prostitutes.
87 As in Kleist (1978), Diderot (1883: 61), Lessing (1962: Section 4).

6   Emotions

I leave the performance of *Uncle Vanya* with a peculiar mixture of emotions. Undoubtedly, they are imprecise, fleeting and indefinite. But I may be able to say something about them, without fear of gross inaccuracy. I pity Vanya and Sonya; they will have a hard life ahead of them – they know it and we know it – and if they do find peace, then it will only be the peace of the grave. But I am thinking not just about the characters I have seen, but about myself and some of the people I know. On stage, we saw Serebryakov: an academic who writes about art, who is respected (to some degree) by his family, but about whom there is some doubt whether he really knows very much or has contributed anything to the academy or to the world beyond. Vanya sums it up: 'all he ever does is write nonsense, grumble and feel jealous.'[1] An academic spectator who hears this description and does not wonder, at least for a moment, if it applies to her is probably not an academic whose writings I would bother to read. There are other characters whose concerns do not directly relate to my own, but who remind me of other people I care about – be they bored, depressed, hopelessly idealistic, ill or elderly. I am also filled with admiration and respect for some of the actors and, perhaps, I am mildly frustrated with others. And there is a familiar feeling after seeing a Chekhov play: I wonder in a vague and general way whether humans can make progress, whether they can achieve anything meaningful or be fulfilled by their work and by their relationships with each other. Undoubtedly, these are sad thoughts, even if I do not draw exclusively negative conclusions (and I don't normally draw any conclusions at all); and it would not, I don't think, be completely unjust to say that there's something unsatisfyingly pleasurable in having the occasion to wallow in them. I am also aware of a kind of general gloominess or moroseness, which may be linked with all my other, various feelings, but which is certainly distinct from all of them. At the same time, I wonder what I have missed in the translation and what it would have seemed like to an audience in 1897, and perhaps I am a little nervous that we may have missed the last bus home.

This description is hardly complete; perhaps some of it rings a bell, and perhaps not. But I hope it is not completely incomprehensible, at least to those who have not immersed themselves in too much philosophical discussion of art and emotion. I mention the various kinds of emotions produced by the play in order to emphasise that a single theatrical performance does not produce a single emotion, any more than, say, a funeral or an ordinary day at work produces a single emotion. Our emotions during and after the performance may well relate to characters, to actors, to themes; to ourselves, to our friends, to others in general; some seem more like moods, lenses onto the world that don't have any particular object or focus.[2] Some of them may be broadly characterised as positive emotions, others negative, others not obviously either. It is true that we are not, in general, very good at describing and expressing our emotions. Nor are we very good at defining them, understanding what they are and how they work. There are occasions when we know what we feel when we feel it; but there are plenty of occasions when we don't know until later, and plenty when we need others to help us to understand or when we never know at all. But in as much as we do feel, it seems evident that theatre can produce such feelings, often to a surprising and powerful degree.

So theatre moves us. Not always, of course; but often. Most philosophers who have written about theatre have agreed about that. But they have disagreed about pretty much everything else. Some, for example, have held that the production of certain feelings is the definitive feature of art in general. This was Tolstoy's view: 'Art is that human activity which consists in one man's consciously conveying to others, by certain external signs, the feelings he has experienced, and in others being infected by those feelings and also experiencing them.'[3] If, say, a performance does not permit the communication of feeling from the artist to the audience, then that performance simply is not art. The result of this strong definition is that 'art which does not move us' is a kind of contradiction in terms – the 'art' in question is not really art at all, but rather something else, perhaps a kind of intellectual confidence trick. This result was hardly accidental: Tolstoy's definition is offered en route to claiming that new so-called 'art' (by which he means late nineteenth-century art, which includes, for example, late Ibsen plays) should not really qualify as art at all, precisely because it leaves audiences completely unmoved.

Aristotle's definition of tragedy, as we have seen, names not the production of feeling in general, but that of two feelings in particular (and their catharsis) as the goal of tragedy:

> Tragedy is an imitation of an action that is admirable, complete and possesses magnitude; in language made pleasurable, each of its species separated in different parts; performed by actors, not through narration; effecting through pity and fear the catharsis of such emotions.[4]

For both Aristotle and Tolstoy, in rather different ways, the production of feeling must lie at the heart of theatre. However, it is possible to admit that art produces emotion, but to deny that this is central either to its definition or to its success. If one thought, for example, that the role of theatre lay in the transmission of certain truths, then the effect that theatre has on the emotions might seem relatively insignificant. Hegel wrote that feelings are 'the indefinite dull region of the mind'; hence, he thought, a study of art that places emotion at its core inevitably 'becomes tedious from its indefiniteness and vacancy, and repulsive from its attentiveness to little subjective peculiarities'.[5]

As we have already seen, a similar spectrum of views is represented in accounts of the relationship between theatre, morality and emotion. For some, the production of emotion at a theatrical performance is (at least) an extremely useful contribution to moral development; for others, the ability of the theatre to 'feed and enflame' the emotions is the subject of intense suspicion.[6] Here again, of course, the fact that theatre moves us is not in question – it's just a matter of whether the effects it has are positive or negative in moral terms. So emotions may be central to the definition and value of theatre; or they may be peripheral, even immoral. But just the fact that we feel strongly, or that we can feel strongly in response to theatre, has been the subject of much philosophical debate – regardless of what the value or significance of this emotional response is taken to be.

This chapter treats three problems in relation to the emotions that, as we've seen, all can agree are produced by theatre (at least some of the time). First, the problem of emotional responses to fictions; second, the problem of tragic pleasure; third, the problem of catharsis. These problems may well be related and we will have a chance to think about their connection; but they are distinct and therefore deserve independent attention.

Emotional responses to fiction

Put as simply as possible, the first problem is this: why do we care about the characters in the play, when we know that they don't exist? I know that Vanya and Sonya are Chekhov's creations, played by actors; the actors may or may not have similar general life concerns, but that is completely irrelevant, and in any case they are hardly stuck in a country estate, condemned to slave away in misery for the rest of their lives. And yet it came naturally to me to say that I pitied them. And not just to me: recall the centrality of pity to Aristotle's definition of tragedy.

This is an old problem: Plato was aware of it; Hamlet comments on it.[7] It continues to bother us. It has become conventional to set it out in the form of three claims, each of which looks intuitive, but that cannot all be true together:

3 claims

1 We are moved by the fate of the characters in the play.
2 We know that the characters in the play do not exist.
3 We are moved only by that which we believe to exist.

Problem

To say that these three cannot be true together is to say that they cannot be true in such a way that we are perfectly consistent or rational. One response, then, is simply to accept all three claims and accept, therefore, that we aren't rational: sometimes we do things that we know to be irrational; one of these things might be weeping over the fate of fictional characters. Hence Radford concludes, from his discussion, that the way we respond emotionally to artworks 'involves us in inconsistency and so incoherence' – but no more so than fearing death when we believe it to be a 'dreamless sleep'.[8] Radford's claim is appealing in many ways. But we can probably admit that if there's a simple explanation of my pity for Vanya, which doesn't make me fundamentally irrational, then that's the explanation I would prefer to go for. Responses that seek to avoid irrationality may be broadly divided into those that aim to deny or modify the first, second or third claim, such that all three sit nicely together (and also do justice to the phenomena). We shall look at each in turn.

Denying 1: we are not moved

Translation

Looking back to the description of my response to *Uncle Vanya*, it's clear that plenty of other things move us, which have nothing to do with the characters. One thing (amongst many others) that Chekhov is doing with his play is drawing our attention to a set of concerns that, quite simply, bother us: can we get meaning or fulfilment from our lives? If we feel emotional about these concerns, it is nothing to do with Vanya or Sonya in particular; perhaps we simply see them as media, as messengers who pass these concerns from Chekhov to his audiences. We don't care about them as such; we care about the questions they raise. And because the questions they raise are all too real, there is no problem reconciling this with the second and third claims, above. But this won't quite do. Nobody, I think, would deny that these general kinds of question can stir us as part of watching a play. Furthermore, the distinction between what I feel specifically *for Vanya* and what I feel (say) for myself is always going to be blurry. But, in order for this to be a successful resolution of the problem, it's not enough to say that the emotions stirred up by the play are often connected with real-life concerns. To resolve the problem, one must also deny that we *ever* feel for the characters. After all, I might well care about Vanya's particular concerns and also care about how not to waste my life. The one does not exclude the other.

The question would be, then, whether we can explain all of what we feel in relation to the performance, without making reference to feelings about the characters. This would involve a kind of translation between claims about the characters and claims about something else. Thus, when I say that I pity Vanya, I am really saying that I pity (say) people who reach a certain age having dedicated their lives to something they no longer believe in and who feel it is too late to make anything meaningful out of their existence. Because the latter undoubtedly exist, there is no problem in meeting the third criterion. Hence, although saying I pity Vanya (the character) sounds a lot like saying that I care about my (real) niece, Anya, my two claims are actually completely different in kind. One is about a person – the other refers to general concerns.

But could we really translate every claim about the character into a general claim? This seems doubtful. One thing I might care about, for example, is whether or not Helen (the professor's wife) and Michael Astrov (the doctor) will have their affair or whether they will part without seeing each other again. A 'translation' of this might then go as follows: that I care, in general, about affairs between professors' wives and doctors. But that is false – I don't. Or perhaps: I care about affairs between beautiful, bored, unhappy women and aging, overworked, proto-environmentalists with ridiculous moustaches. But, again, I don't. Now it is true, of course, that many people have general feelings of various kinds about the role of infidelity in their lives and the lives of others. Some theatrical performances may well offer us the opportunity to work through our own thoughts and feelings – a platform for understanding ourselves. But, watching *Uncle Vanya*, I care about the specific outcome of the conversations between Helen and Michael; I want to know whether or not they'll meet in secret in the forest reservation (which, as it happens, I also know to be non-existent). And these specific concerns don't seem connected to any general concern I have about infidelity. To put it bluntly: whether or not Helen and Michael get together won't tell me very much (say) about whether my partner is cheating on me, or whether my own infidelity is justifiable, and so on. Yet, still, I want to know what happens to them. And, because I know that they don't exist, we haven't resolved our problem.

Make-believe

A different way of denying that we are moved (denying 1, above) would be to deny that what we understand to be an emotion in response to a character is really an emotion at all. We have already said something

imitation

about Kendall Walton's theory of make-believe in the context of the discussion of *mimesis*. For Walton, once we view plays (and others works of art) as games of make-believe, it turns out that apparent emotions in response to artworks are not real emotions, but make-believe emotions. Walton holds that genuine emotions are connected to existential beliefs (as stipulated in 3, above). Thus, to fear X is to believe that X exists.[9] If I do not believe that X exists, then by definition I cannot fear X. But Walton does not deny that we have certain psychological and physiological responses to fictions. In such cases, it's not that we believe that X exists (and then have certain psychological and physiological responses to X) it's that we *make-believe* that X exists (and then have certain psychological and physiological responses to X). Whatever the response to our make-believing, it cannot be a genuine emotion; instead, it is a make-believe emotion. There are examples (notably, it must be said, examples of uncontroversial make-believe[10]) in which this seems plausible. When children play a game in which they are being chased by the 'vampire' (someone wearing fake vampire teeth), and they scream as the vampire chases after them, it might make sense to say that they are not really afraid, they are make-believing that they are afraid of a make-believe vampire.[11] Walton extends this to all (supposed) emotional responses to artworks. Fictions license us to respond to them in a certain way; thus, just as it is fictional that Willy Loman is a failed salesman or that Iago tricks Othello, so 'it is only fictional, not true, that we feel for Willy Loman or detest Iago'. Hence, there is no 'loss of touch with reality' and we should reject the first claim – namely, the claim that we are moved by theatre.[12] Indeed, Walton goes further, claiming that reports of emotional responses to fictions are themselves a kind of make-believe in accordance with the rules of the game; so when I say 'I pity Vanya', it would be somewhat equivalent to the child who says 'I see a vampire'.

In one sense, then, Walton places all my feelings about Vanya on the same level as the child's 'fear' of the vampire-teacher: a kind of playful playing-along to a game, rather than a genuine, emotional experience. Given the strength and depth of emotion that theatre can produce, it is certainly tempting for any theatre-lover to throw Walton's book out of the window at just this point. But we need to be careful here. It's not that my subjective state – the one that I intuitively call my 'pity' for Vanya (although Walton would not call it 'pity') – is weaker, or less troubling than my pity for a real person with a similar biography. It is merely a claim about the cause of the two instances of so-called 'pity' (make-belief versus belief). It has nothing to do with their strength, or depth, or about how they seem to me subjectively. Thus one and the same subjective experience (my heart beating faster, my fists clenched, a feeling of heightened agitation and so on) would be one of genuine fear or one of fictional fear, depending on whether I believe in or make-believe in the existence of the threat. In both cases, I am experiencing the subjective state associated with fear (what Walton terms 'quasi-fear'); sometimes quasi-fear is brought about by belief, but sometimes it isn't. So it is no problem (in principle) for Walton that fictional fear is very distressing, seems just like real fear, has many or all of its physiological accompaniments and is 'as intense as anything you might feel outside the theatre'.[13]

Nonetheless, Walton's solution to the problem leaves a great deal to be desired from an account of my emotional response to *Uncle Vanya*. For one thing, his account leads to some very peculiar results. I mentioned not just my pity for Vanya, but also my general feeling of gloominess. The kind of moods we find ourselves in during and after performances are integral features of theatrical experience, but they don't attach themselves to particular characters or events in the play, nor do they obviously have any specific beliefs associated with them. Here, Walton effectively claims that my gloominess may be both real and fictional.[14] This looks to be unnecessarily complicated. Isn't it more natural just to say that I feel gloomy and to forget about the hunt for clearly distinguished fictional and non-fictional emotions? More importantly, one has to wonder whether all that much has been explained. After all, isn't it still odd that I experience what Walton would call 'quasi-pity' (i.e. all the subjective responses associated with that emotion) in response to the story of Vanya? Even accepting that my pity doesn't count as real pity, you might think that full knowledge of Vanya's non-existence would suffice to rule out the kind of subjective feelings associated with pity: being sorrowful, weeping and so on. So ideally we would want to have a better account of what Walton takes to be our peculiar ability (say) to make our hearts beat faster, to clench our fists, to sweat, to feel all that we would associate with fear in relation to a non-existent object. The simple explanation (which he has to deny) is that I'm experiencing the symptoms of fear because I'm afraid; likewise for pity. Make-believing that I am a millionaire does not make me rich; why should make-believing that there is a ghost make me actually tremble? Trembling and experiencing all the symptoms of terror in response to a make-believe object is still odd. Walton has hardly offered a solution if the curious phenomenon he sought out to explain is simply pushed back to the level of make-believe, rather than belief.

To emphasise some of the problems here, it might be helpful to look beyond the Vanya example, to some slightly different cases. In the Vanya example, I have watched (what I take to be) a successful performance of a great work. But, sadly, this is not always so. Sometimes plays completely fail to move us: I know I'm supposed to feel pity for Elektra, let's say, but the performance has been so unutterably dreadful that all I feel is frustration and regret. One could imagine similar scenarios for other emotions: a supposedly terrifying scene that makes me laugh instead of making me afraid. In such cases, it is not clear how the make-believe plus quasi-emotion structure could help me to understand what is happening. Naturally, one would say that it wasn't scary, or that I just didn't feel for any of the characters. But for Walton that was never a possibility. Why is it that sometimes we experience quasi-fear and sometimes we don't, given that we are just as willing to make-believe in each case? This is no less mysterious than the problem we began with.

[handwritten margin note: 2nd error]

Second, just as there are times when I do not feel anything in response to the performance, so there are times when I do feel something, but I very strongly wish that I hadn't. At a grotesquely sentimental play for children, I might weep as the naïve but war-stricken boy is finally reunited with his long-lost horse. But I hate myself for being so susceptible to this trash. Naturally, I would say what Walton cannot: that I pitied the boy and his horse, even though I didn't want to. And there is nothing strange or irrational about feeling something and wishing I didn't. Walton, however, would have to say that I make-believed not only the boy, the horse and the reunion, but also that I make-believed my own pity – the same pity that I find myself so disappointing for being unable to control. The idea that I am make-believing both a story and an emotional response to that story that both has the force of bringing me to tears and also disgusts me is, to put it mildly, not a very intuitive account of what is going on. It's much simpler to forget about the make-believe and say that the boy–horse reunion made me feel a genuine pity that I wish I hadn't felt. The position that we are seeking to reject is the irrational one of holding all three inconsistent claims, above. But it's not clear that the picture offered by Walton of me make-believing emotions that I detest is in any way more rational that the picture of me feeling sorry for characters I know not to exist.[15]

[handwritten margin note: final conclusion]

Denying 2: we don't always know that the characters aren't real

Denials of the second claim are relatively rare, but we have come across one of them already. In our discussion of theatre and illusion, we noted Stendhal's view that, for brief moments during a performance, the spectator really does believe that what she is seeing is real (moments of 'perfect illusion'). Thus, one can explain why I 'cry so copiously' at the theatre: for brief moments, I believe I am seeing Vanya, not the actor playing him; and I believe that Vanya exists. Needless to say, my belief is false; but many people are scared of plenty of things that they falsely believe to exist (hell, for example) and there is nothing strange about that.

I am very sympathetic to the idea that, for brief moments during the performance, we really are experiencing perfect illusion. We can get absorbed in plays relatively easily and it's hard work to keep reminding ourselves that it's not really happening.[16] We cannot simply argue that, because we believe it was all a fiction when the curtain goes down, we believe this at every moment during the course of the performance. Emotions arising from perfect illusion may perhaps account for some of what we feel in relation to some performance.

But it cannot be the whole story. For Stendhal admits, as he must, that perfect illusion, if it happens at all, happens only very briefly – 'a half-second or a quarter second'.[17] Well, perhaps it might last a little longer than that. But even so, the question must be whether such brief moments, be they minutes or seconds, can suffice to account for all of the emotions that we have in relation to fictional characters and events. Thus, for example, I may pity Sonya just at the moment that she learns of her rejection, because I am absorbed in perfect illusion and I believe her to be real. But if I pity her in any way after that – say, as I leave the theatre after the show is done – then we still have a problem. Intuitively, it seems as though I do pity her once the show is over. In fact, I still pity her now, as I write. If emotions arising out of perfect illusion account for all that I feel about Sonya, then either Stendhal must claim that I continue to believe that Sonya exists once the performance is over (which I don't); or he must claim that somehow the memory of the genuine emotion (but not the emotion itself) carries over, in which case I do not pity Sonya once the show is over, I merely remember pitying her (this begins to look like a denial of 1, not 2). So a denial of 2 doesn't seem to give us the full picture, even if we accept the notion of perfect illusion.[18]

Denying 3: caring for the non-existent

Could we deny that we care about things only when we believe that they exist? In some clear cases, we can. First, there is a sense in which the events of next year do not currently exist, but still I care about some of them a great deal. But, of course, this is not a helpful model for caring about Vanya.[19] The events of next year certainly will take place: assuming I am still alive, they will have a direct effect on me and on my life. Not so for Vanya. Second, there are emotions that do not appear to require any kind of belief at all. Suppose you are alone at home, and for some reason you begin to feel afraid. There has been no evident cause for this fear – no strange noises or unexplained phenomena. You cannot say exactly what it is that you're afraid of. This general kind of fear doesn't seem to require any kind of belief about the existence of something to fear; it's just a mood. So the question of belief just seems irrelevant to our understanding of this kind of emotion. As discussed, general moods caused by performances can be powerful and significant. But this can't be all there is to it. For example, the parallel with Vanya is not helpful. My pity for Vanya is not a general mood; I know exactly what the object of pity is: it is Vanya, wasting his life away working for a thoughtless, vain academic whose wife he is desperately in love with. Third, suppose you tell me a story about a girl who suffers a series of terrible misfortunes. Suppose, too, that I don't know whether or not the story is true. In such a case, before knowing whether or not the story is true, I might be justified in pitying the girl. It doesn't seem as though I need to believe in her existence in order to pity her. But here, still, we don't quite have what we're after. In the case of the story of the girl, I don't know whether she exists or not. In the case of Vanya, I know full well he doesn't exist, and still I pity him. So even if we changed the third claim such that we feel emotions for things, the existence of which is unknown to us, we haven't come any closer to understanding my pity for Vanya.

It is perfectly true that, although they help us to modify 3, none of these kinds of emotion helps us to explain how I pity Vanya, knowing that he does not exist. But they do suggest that we ought to be more liberal about the kinds of emotions we have (and their causes) than 3 would suggest. They point to the possibility of ways of experiencing emotion which are not as simple as, say, fearing the tiger that is directly before my eyes. And if all of these various ways of experiencing emotion are possible, then why is it impossible to experience emotion in relation to a fictional character? We feel things based on certain triggers. Sometimes we understand what those triggers are; sometimes we don't. Of course, sometimes when I feel fear, it's the fear that this particular tiger is going to eat me immediately. And sometimes I feel pity for a real person facing a difficult situation. But I can experience fear without there being any particular thing that I'm afraid of; and I can also feel pity for a little girl you tell me about, before I know whether or not the story is true. So why assume that I can't feel for Vanya, whose story is so pitiable, who suffers as I watch him? What we're effectively suggesting here is that my feelings for Vanya simply prove that we can feel for things that we believe not to exist. So it's just not true that we feel for things only when we believe they exist (i.e. 3 is false), just because I can experience emotions for fictional characters. Of course, sometimes when I pity a person, I believe that they exist; but sometimes I don't. As it happens, in Vanya's case, I don't. Now, it is clear that for some philosophers the fact that I know that Vanya doesn't exist means I can't pity him; but one might respond that, for others, the fact that I pity Vanya means that I can pity things when I know they don't exist. This is something of an impasse, and it's not clear where we can go from here. But we might note that, of the three claims we have considered, this third claim looks the least firmly grounded.

A pluralistic solution?

What we have set out here are some basic strategies for responding to the problem of how I might pity Vanya. Given the enormous amount of material written about this problem, these arguments have hardly been given full exposure in this chapter. But I'll end the discussion of this problem simply by pointing out that there is absolutely no reason to think that every apparent instance of an emotion directed towards a fictional character must be explained or analysed in exactly the same way. Some of these strategies are incompatible, but many are not. Perhaps sometimes, as Stendhal suggests, we get so carried away by the performance that we really believe that a character exists and we respond accordingly. Perhaps, on other occasions, our emotional response is a kind of make-believe, a pretend fright that we act out to play along with the action. Or what we first take to be a concern for a character disguises a feeling that we have about a theme or problem that they represent, or a real person whom they resemble. And perhaps, sometimes, we find ourselves genuinely feeling sorry for someone whom we know not to be real – whether we see this as an anomalous instance of sheer irrationality, or whether it is a legitimate case of sympathy for non-existents. Outside the theatre, our emotional lives are complex, varied and difficult to describe with any great accuracy; the same is probably true when we watch a play.

Tragic pleasure or the 'paradox of tragedy'

The second problem related to theatre and emotions is, in a sense, dependent on there being some kind of solution to the first. When I wrote, above, about my feelings after the performance of *Uncle Vanya*, it is notable that much (although not all) of what I described was far from positive. I feel sorry for some, I feel sad for others. Often, when we go to plays – tragedies, but not only tragedies – we watch people whom we admire or respect going through terrible misfortune: Desdemona is strangled; Hippolytus is killed; Oedipus is blinded. Put simply, the so-called 'paradox of tragedy' is this: under normal circumstances, we don't like crying, we don't like feeling sad, we don't like watching people whom we care for suffering horribly and we don't like being made to feel sorry for them. But when we watch tragedies, we experience many if not all of these things; and, in some way, we seem to like it, enjoy it, recommend it to our friends. So, if we don't like these things in everyday life, then why should we like them at the theatre?[20]

As with the other problems with theatre and emotion, the paradox of tragedy has a long history. Gorgias, Plato, Aristotle and Augustine show some awareness of it; Hume devotes an essay to it. We shall begin with

Hume, although it's clear from his essay that by his time it was already an established topic for philosophical discussion. He begins:

> It seems an unaccountable pleasure, which the spectators of a well-wrote tragedy receive from sorrow, terror, anxiety, and other passions, which are in themselves disagreeable and uneasy. The more they are touched and affected, the more they are delighted with the spectacle, and as soon as the uneasy passions cease to operate, the piece is at an end.[21]

This quotation gives us the basics of the problem, although it's worth noting straight away that Hume seems wrong to say that we are more pleased, the more we are affected.[22] After all, some tragedies may well be too painful to watch. More generally, plenty of people don't like tragedies precisely because they are so miserable and, judging by box office sales for long-running shows, comedies of various kinds continue to be far more popular than tragedies. Indeed, Hume's essay is remarkable mostly for its lack of interest in tragedy (not to mention its lack of insight), and also for its peculiar solution, which has been given far too much philosophical attention, perhaps because its author was writing in English.[23] So rather than spending too much time on Hume's particular account, let us begin with two claims, both of which require our assent if the paradox of tragedy is even to get off the ground:

1 Tragic events, when real, are not pleasing to us.
2 Tragic events, when theatrical, are pleasing to us.

There is more to the paradox than these two claims. But it is clear that a denial of either would render the problem immaterial. The paradox rests on there being a difference in our response to tragic events, when those events are on and off the stage. A denial of 1 would suggest that tragic events, whether real or theatrical, are pleasing; a denial of 2 would suggest that tragic events, whether real or theatrical, are not pleasing. In each case, there would be nothing special about theatre. Broadly speaking, we may divide responses to the paradox of tragedy into three categories: those that deny 1; those that deny 2; those that deny neither 1 nor 2, but seek to resolve the problem in another way. We shall look at examples of each of these approaches.

Denying the first commitment: sadism

It has become almost a custom in recent writings on the paradox of tragedy to open by saying that, obviously, we simply don't take pleasure in watching suffering. However, given the kinds of entertainment humans have indulged in over the years – gladiator battles, public executions, jousting, hunting, bullfights, boxing and so on – it seems that the possibility of taking pleasure in suffering (on stage and off stage) should not be ruled out without discussion.[24] Indeed, plenty of philosophers, among them Lucretius, Hobbes, Burke and Nietzsche, have thought it relatively uncontroversial that we enjoy watching people suffer, especially (as in theatre) when we know ourselves to be safe and sound.[25]

I have placed responses of these kinds under the heading of 'sadism'. But it might be helpful to make a distinction between a strong and a weak version of sadism. Both versions maintain that we enjoy watching the suffering of others. According to the stronger version, when we watch other people suffer, we feel no negative emotions at all; on the weaker version, there is some negative, perhaps painful response to watching the sufferings of others, but there is also a pleasurable response, which is inextricably linked to the suffering and which outweighs the pain. In both cases, the point is that our experience of tragedy is not especially unique and does not require a special explanation.

Burke appeals to a strong version of sadism, by way of an explanation of tragic emotion.[26] His starting point seems to be the observation (uncontroversial in his day) that the public take great delight in executions – greater, in fact, than in the best tragedies:

> [Choose] a day on which to represent the most sublime and affecting tragedy we have; appoint the most favourite actors; spare no cost upon the scenes and decorations; unite the greatest efforts of poetry, painting and music; and when you have collected your audience, just at the moment when their minds are erect with expectation, let it be reported that a state criminal of high rank is on the point of being executed in the adjoining square; in a moment the emptiness of the theatre would demonstrate the comparative weakness of the imitative arts, and proclaim the triumph of the real sympathy.[27]

As Burke realises, most people aren't going to be thrilled at the suggestion that we all want to hurt each other. After all, it's not as if we go around happily mutilating strangers. But he has a response. The key distinction, he maintains, is between, first, wanting some horrible event to happen and, second, given that it is happening, wanting to watch. Whereas the first desire would be peculiar, perhaps pathological, the second, he suggests, is almost universal. Most people don't want a horrible accident to happen on the road; but, driving past one, most people crane their necks to see. This allows for a general desire to see other people suffer without the extra (and at least *prima facie* improbable) claim that we actively seek to make them suffer whenever we can. Because enjoying tragedy doesn't involve bringing about horrible events, we can set about doing what we always do, namely enjoying watching them unfold. Note, then, that to deny 1 we do not need to claim that we like making each other suffer, nor that we like watching our friends and relatives suffer. All Burke claims is that, given the suffering of others, we often seem to like watching: and that is all that theatre requires.

Although Burke avoids one problem (the unintuitive claim that we actively try to hurt each other), he is still left with another. For as a description of the psychology of tragedy, this looks unintuitive (at least for some tragedies, in which we take a certain pleasure). We don't crane our necks to watch the characters meet their sticky ends: often the deaths do cause us some discomfort and we do find ourselves experiencing negative emotions such as sorrow, pity and so on. It's not clear where Burke finds space in his discussion to admit that some of the emotions that we feel in response to tragedy might really be unpleasant.

According to the weaker version, though, I feel some sorrow at watching Hamlet meet his end; but I also take pleasure in his suffering, perhaps for other reasons. Hobbes, for example, writes:

> As there is novelty and remembrance of own security present, which is delight, so there is also pity, which is grief. But the delight is so far predominant, that men usually are content in such a case to be spectators of the misery of their friends.[28]

Note that Hobbes isn't denying the significance of feelings of pity and sorrow, nor that the experience of such feelings is negative. It's just that pleasure from the fact of our own security trumps whatever pity we feel, and thus enables us, on balance, to enjoy the sufferings of others, including those of our friends.[29] Thus he is not faced with the same problem as Burke, for he does not deny that we feel a genuine grief at the sufferings of others.

One problem for Hobbes is that he seems to assume a psychology, according to which we normally forget about our security and are reminded of it by being shown the misfortunes of others. But there is no obvious reason why (at least for some people) it shouldn't work exactly the other way around. Why assume that my reaction would be one of relief at being reminded that some misfortune is not happening to me right now, as opposed to terror at being reminded that it might? Perhaps Hobbes (or the defender of a solution arising from his remarks) would claim that we take more pleasure, the more certain we are that the misfortunes depicted couldn't harm us. Certainly, his examples from the same section – following Lucretius, the pleasure of watching from land as a ship is tossed in a storm – suggest that we take pleasure in threats to others that aren't presently threats to ourselves. But in that case, we would expect to enjoy tragedies that show events unlikely to threaten us more than those that show real, extant threats. Thus, a Chekhov play that depicts bored, spoilt, miserable people whittling away their lives would be less pleasurable to a modern, Western audience than *Oedipus Tyrannus*, whose particular misfortunes, whatever else one may say about them, do not pose an imminent danger to most of us. However, this just doesn't seem to be true: some people prefer Chekhov; others prefer Sophocles. And, what's more, it's not always so easy to treat misfortunes at such a particular level. Thus, I might be happily going about my day, when, upon being taken to *Oedipus Tyrannus*, I am suddenly reminded (say) that human lives are frail, and that even the best and most noble individuals have little or no chance at fending off the horror that confronts them at every turn. This is made more pressing, because it's at least a reasonable interpretation of *Oedipus Tyrannus* that misfortune tends to strike just when you feel most secure and prosperous – exactly when, for Hobbes, the pleasurable response to the misfortune of others is meant to kick in. So even though some of the specifics of Oedipus' plight are unlikely to concern each audience member, it's fair to say that the general menace of deep instability and insecurity might be enough to cause them some bother. Again, why assume that pleasure at not being Oedipus would override displeasure at being reminded that the same (sort of) thing might happen to me? Of course, we haven't ruled out some instances of just the response that Hobbes outlines. It's just that, for all we know, reminding people of the dangers facing others could at least go either way.

Denying the second commitment: tragedy without pleasure

If we can't solve our problem by appealing to pleasure that we take in real suffering, then perhaps we could deny that the portrayal of tragic events on stage is pleasurable. There are two ways to deny this: (1) tragedies are not pleasurable at all; (2) tragedies, although they may be pleasurable, do not please us in virtue of the tragic events that they portray.

Tragic displeasure?

A strict denial of the claim that tragedies please is relatively hard to find. Some philosophers have argued (with justification) that 'pleasure' doesn't seem to be a good description of what it is that we value about tragedies, or of why it is that we watch them. Certainly, it seems right that the best tragedies are not necessarily the tragedies that give us the most pleasure.[30] If you had asked me how *Uncle Vanya* was, I would probably have replied that it was one of the best performances I had seen in a long time;

I might not have said, unprompted, that 'I really enjoyed it'. There's nothing particularly surprising about this: the best philosophy, the best political systems and the best computers (however one were to measure such things) would not obviously be the most pleasurable in any straight-forward sense. So it may be that what we like about tragedy should be separated from what we value about it, why we accord it a high status among art forms, or what we think it, in particular, has to offer us.[31] Indeed, some discussions of the paradox of tragedy appear to assume that we *only* do things if we enjoy them; this assumption – sometimes called 'the hedonistic theory of motivation' – has rightly been called into question.[32] But although this is an important qualification, it does not actually amount to a denial that we find tragedy pleasurable: it's just that taking pleasure isn't the most important thing.

To see why there is a problem with the full-strength claim that tragedy does not please us, it may help to recall a distinction made in Chapter 5 between pleasure as a kind of physical sensation (the opposite of pain) and a more general notion of something being pleasing to us. Some activities – such as eating, when we are hungry – bring us a physical sensation of pleasure. But there are plenty of things we do that please us, but that do not obviously give us a physically pleasurable sensation: learning, gossip-ing, travelling and so on. Then, of course, there are things that we take part in, which do not please us at all: household chores, perhaps certain kinds of paid labour, or unpleasant medical examinations. In such cases, we are doing something unpleasant for the sake of something else that we value (hygiene, money, health). It is unlikely that anyone would claim that tragedy is pleasurable in the first of these senses. It doesn't give us a physically pleasurable sensation akin to that of eating when hungry or warming up when too cold. The claim is, rather, that tragedy pleases us in a more general sense. Of course, there may be all sorts of benefits to watching a play that do not reduce to pleasure: but, if one wants to claim that tragedy doesn't please us at all, then (as with household chores or medical appointments), one had better explain why it is that we go. Normally, when I pay some money to do something that I don't find at all pleasurable, I am able to offer some plausible account of why.

It's not hard to think of possible candidates for benefits from tragedy that are independent from pleasure: truth, beauty, moral edification. It's just that, if tragedy is not at all pleasing, then we would expect going to the tragedy to be something that we perhaps felt neutral about, disliked, dreaded, or simply were bored by. This doesn't seem like a good description of those who frequent tragedies. What's more, if tragedies were not pleasurable at all, but useful for the sake of some other benefit, then, just as we praise a doctor who performs some procedure less painfully than the rest, so we would expect spectators to praise a tragedian who conveys more truth with less distress.[33] This seems all wrong: we often praise tragedies for being moving in a 'tragic' way.

Compensation

Going to the tragedy does not fit the model of a non-pleasing activity undertaken for the sake of some other benefit. But we can still deny (2) while accepting that tragedy pleases. We engage in plenty of activities that please us overall, but that have unpleasant elements. One could make this claim for tragedy: that it produces unpleasant, negative emotions that we find displeasing, but it also offers other compensating factors that make the experience, as a whole, a positive one. This would neatly dissolve the problem, because there's nothing all that strange about the benefits or pleasures of an activity outweighing the costs: so, just as one might enjoy visiting a friend despite having to make the unpleasant journey to see her, so one might go to the theatre to enjoy certain features (the beautiful lines, the performances, the complex plots, the universal themes), despite the negative emotions one will be forced to endure. But although the independence of the pleasure from the pain is an analytic possibility, it doesn't quite do justice to our experience. So, for example, it would be difficult to imagine a successful tragedy – a tragedy that we appreciated and enjoyed as a tragedy, rather than as a farce or as a play starring someone we know – that did not make us feel in any way sad or compassionate (and so on). As James Shelley points out, if we enjoy the tragedy despite the negative emotions it produces, then one wonders why we couldn't watch plays that retained the pleasing features, but that didn't make us feel sad at all.[34] What seems more likely is that there is something about the negative emotions themselves that is pleasing; but, with that, the problem of tragic pleasure has returned.

Accepting both commitments?

Could we solve the paradox of tragedy, while accepting both that tragic events are pleasurable in the theatre and that tragic events are unpleasant when not in the theatre? A number of solutions have been proposed along these lines. A prominent solution appeals to the pleasure taken in emotional catharsis. Because we shall be treating this in a separate section, I shan't discuss it here. But note that catharsis, as a concept, is just as problematic as tragic pleasure itself, so catharsis certainly can't be wheeled out, without discussion, to settle what it is we enjoy about tragedies. Nor can it be offered, with any certainty, as Aristotle's 'solution' to the paradox of tragedy: although Aristotle thinks that tragedy involves taking pleasure in pity and fear, he neither formulates the paradox, nor makes it sufficiently clear that catharsis could function in that role. Setting catharsis aside, I shall consider three proposals which appeal to truth, morality, and the nature of the emotions, respectively.

Truth

Perhaps one reason we go to tragedies is that they present us with truths. In Chapter 3, we looked at some problems with this claim; but, setting those aside, would this perhaps provide a solution? For one thing, truth can't be all there is to it. If tragedy tells us truths, but does so via negative emotional responses, then one wonders why we couldn't do without the truth altogether, saving ourselves an unpleasant evening. Or, if we are set on truth, wouldn't we be better off getting our truth via a less distressing medium? One would have to provide an explanation as to why we discover truths via tragedy (with its attendant pains) rather than by neutral or even pleasurable means (or just not at all). James Shelley's proposed solution attempts such an explanation, using the notion of repression. The truths presented by tragedy are truths that we seek to repress in our everyday lives, because they are disturbing and they conflict with how we wish the world to be. But repressing them is (somehow) unpleasant or difficult. Hence, when they are revealed to us at the tragedy, we experience the pleasure of no longer having to repress such difficult truths: 'tragedy relieves us from the pressures of thwarted truths.'[35] Shelley doesn't deny that tragedy is pleasurable, nor that watching other people suffer is unpleasant. The claim is as follows: that we repress all sorts of unpleasant truths about the world; that repressing them is unpleasant; and that releasing them (through watching a tragedy) brings the pleasure of no longer having to repress.

We have already seen that deriving truths from theatre is not straightforward. The first problem with Shelley's argument is the lack of useful examples. At one point he suggests the following, by way of a candidate: 'a good man, acting in accordance with his best judgement, acts in way that leads, unforeseeably though with astonishing ease, to his own destruction.'[36] This seems a plausible (though not unproblematic) reading of *Oedipus Tyrannus*. But plenty of people, myself included, would happily agree that this is true, without feeling the need to repress it at all. Yet, contrary to what Shelley's account would predict, I can still enjoy a performance of the play. Second, supposing the truths in question are in fact so nasty that one has to repress them: why is the joy at no longer having to repress them not outweighed by the horror at their release? If I am sitting on a box that is full to bursting with venomous snakes, then the effort of keeping them shut away may be troubling. But the pleasure at releasing them (i.e. the pleasure of no longer having to exert myself to keep them in) would surely pale compared with the discomfort of being surrounded by angry, venomous snakes; and if letting them out of the box isn't all that bad, then why did I exert myself so much to keep them shut up there in the first place? Finally, if we repress these truths outside the theatre, why don't we repress them inside it, too? Returning to Shelley's 'good man using best judgement' truth: if the everyday world is the kind of place where that holds, and Sophocles' Thebes is also a place where that holds, then why can't I repress it at the theatre just as in real life? I might, for example, deny that Oedipus is good or that he acts in accordance with his best judgement – both of which are plausible interpretations.

Morality

The next major candidate for a solution to the problem of tragic pleasure is that tragedy gives us a kind of pleasure that is related to morality. As we saw in our discussion of theatre and ethics, the case for theatre being moral in relation to the emotions has been made frequently and in different ways. Susan Feagin has argued that tragedy provides a kind of test of our sympathetic, moral responses. If we witness real, tragic events, we are overcome by sorrow at what we have seen. At the tragedy, in contrast, we know that it isn't real; nonetheless, we can see that we do have the correct kinds of sympathetic responses to tragic events and so we can take pleasure in the confirmation that we are suitably moral beings, connected with our fellow moral beings in the right kinds of ways: 'we find ourselves to be the kind of people who respond negatively to villainy, treachery and injustice.'[37] Of course, taking pleasure in being sympathetic would be completely inappropriate when faced by real, tragic events; but when the events are taking place in the theatre, we are permitted to feel 'satisfaction' at our sympathetic, moral responses.[38]

Feagin's proposed solution has the advantage that it can explain why the negative emotions (pity, fear, and so on) are necessary in order for us to experience tragedy as pleasurable: pleasure comes from appropriate sympathetic responses to the hardships of others; such responses occur in the face of troubling situations; therefore, the pleasurable experience of tragedy requires the depiction of troubling situations. However, Feagin's account still leaves a great deal to be desired. For one thing, feeling pleasurably satisfied with our moral responses to the pains of others – even to the pains of characters in play – doesn't necessarily look that moral. If the audience at *Uncle Vanya* is composed of hundreds of individuals, who have attended with the express purpose of delighting in their ability to pity plain, hardworking, lovelorn girls and their weary, hopeless uncles, then I'm not sure it reflects very well on any of them, morally or otherwise.[39] We might also recall Rousseau's point, that it's hardly a good moral test to be made to feel a certain way in relation to a situation, but not be required in any way to act upon it. More importantly, though, Feagin's understanding of tragedy seems unnecessarily restricted. For her, tragedies would appear to have plots, the sympathetic responses to which should be relatively straightforward, thus enabling a certain satisfaction at getting them right. We would predict, on her account, that morally complex tragedies – in which it is not clear how to interpret the ethics of those involved and to sympathise accordingly – would be less pleasurable, because they would not allow us to take satisfaction in our responses (we wouldn't know what 'getting it right' looked like). Clear-cut moral plots, on the other hand, would afford good tests for whether we respond in the right way to the good characters, and so on. But this is hopelessly wrong. If we *response* praise tragedies at all in relation to their morality, it is hardly because they present us with characters and plots, the ethics of which are self-evidently available to all spectators.[40] Often, following fairly standard interpretations, tragedies offer worlds that are radically incompatible with the kind of satisfaction that Feagin describes: irreconcilable opposition between conflicting but legitimate moralities (*Antigone*); the inability of human beings to make moral sense of the world and their place within it *examples* (*Oedipus Tyrannus*); the failure both of social convention and of non-conformism to provide the basis for a good life (*Ghosts*, *Rosmersholm*, or pretty much any of the late Ibsen plays). I repeat, here, my scepticism (see Chapter 5) about summing up the moralities of plays in any convincing or exhaustive way – these are merely proposed examples, which the reader can take or leave; my point is only that *if* these tragedies set our moral gears in motion, they do not do so in such a way that obviously leads to satisfaction in the way we respond. Put another way: it seems to me that tragedies might have the function of *challenging* our responses or revealing various moral commitments to be incompatible with one another, rather than simply functioning as triggers for the production of (and satisfaction with) whatever moral outlook we took with us into the theatre.

The nature of the emotions

A last attempt at explaining the pleasure of tragedy re-examines the understanding of the emotions that is presupposed by the discussion so far. Up to now, we have spoken of negative emotions, meaning sorrow, pity, fear and so on; and we have assumed that experiencing such emotions is an intrinsically negative experience. In his discussion of the paradox of tragedy, Kendall Walton challenges just this assumption.[41] Sorrow, he *argument* claims, is not intrinsically negative. But sorrow often arises in relation to very negative events – a bereavement, for example. By calling sorrow negative, we confuse the experience of the emotion with the cause of the emotion. The death of a loved one is obviously a terrible thing; but the feeling that one has in relation to that event is not necessarily in itself good or bad. At a funeral, one would not exactly take pleasure in being made to feel sad; but one might conceivably feel better as a result. Thus, there may well be circumstances in which we could say, without obvious contradiction, that it feels good to feel sad. So, for Walton, there's nothing peculiar about enjoying the feeling of pity or sorrow or fear, whether at the theatre or not. Sometimes, such emotions are pleasurable; sometimes, they aren't.

There is something appealingly simple about this solution to the problem and it has a lot going for it – not least because it is helpful to highlight the difference between the causes of our emotions and what it feels like when they are expressed. But, even acknowledging that it might sometimes feel good to feel sad, it still seems a general rule that people, on the whole, would prefer not to feel sad and would prefer to go out of their way to avoid it. The opposite is true of feeling happy: one can imagine feeling happy and not enjoying it, but this sounds like the symptom of some kind of medical condition or the side-effect of a drug, rather than a standard, everyday occurrence. Tragedy regularly produces emotions that are typically thought to be unpleasant; and yet we seem to enjoy such emotions when at the tragedy. Walton does not offer an explanation of just what it is about tragedy that enables us to enjoy the emotions that typically (if not always) are unpleasant. A more satisfying answer might be able to fill in more of the details.

Another pluralistic solution?

I'll end my discussion of tragic pleasure in much the same way that I ended my discussion of feeling for fictional characters. We should be wary of looking for one solution that completely solves the problem; the answer may well be different for different kinds of theatrical experience, and there's no reason why different spectators or different performances shouldn't fit different patterns. Thus some tragedies might appeal to a kind of sadistic voyeurism, whereas others provoke a pleasurable or stimulating moral reflection; some tragedies may not be all that pleasurable, but worth sitting through for other reasons; the feeling that you are empathising with your fellow man may on occasions be a pleasurable one, and so might finally acknowledging that the world works in a way that you had always known but tried to deny. I have given reasons why these proposals, in some of their guises, do not give a satisfactory, single solution – and some of them seem significantly less appealing than others. But they may help explain instances of tragic pleasure and it may be that explaining certain instances is all we can do. Understanding the pleasure that you get from a particular tragedy may require self-examination, or perhaps literary criticism and analysis of the tragedy in question.[42]

Catharsis

What I termed 'the problem of catharsis' at the start of this chapter is, it must be said, a different kind of problem from the other two addressed so far. In the other two cases, we were investigating concerns that are relatively easy to grasp, independently of the writings of particular philosophers. We feel sorry for people who don't exist: how strange! We seem to enjoy feeling bad: why? However, in the case of catharsis, the main question is: what did Aristotle mean by 'catharsis'? To state the obvious: we are not talking about an independent problem, which would have arisen had Aristotle's *Poetics* never been written; we are talking about a problem of interpretation.

To make matters worse, we are talking about a problem of interpretation which, most writers agree, can never be resolved to anyone's satisfaction. The reasons for this are relatively simple. First, although the word 'catharsis' appears in Aristotle's definition of tragedy (see above), that is the only place it appears, when used in this way, in the whole of the *Poetics*.[43] Not only is it not defined or explained; it isn't even mentioned, except in that one lonely sub-clause. And although it is standard to translate the relevant clause as saying that tragedy effects 'through pity and fear the catharsis of such emotions' – thus implying that catharsis is something that affects the spectators – a number of commentators have either challenged this translation or interpretation, arguing that the catharsis is something that happens not to the spectators at all, but rather something that applies to the tragic events or action.[44] The remainder of my discussion assumes that it is the spectators who experience catharsis, but the alternative views show the range of interpretations available.

Second, although Aristotle writes about catharsis in other works, he doesn't treat it in any detail and it's an open question whether the kind of catharsis that he is writing about in other places is the same as the one that he associates with tragedy. How helpful, for example, is his brief discussion, in the *Politics*, of the catharsis brought about by *music*? Tragedy, after all, had musical elements; but, in his discussion of catharsis and music, Aristotle looks to be talking about specific kinds of ritualistic singing in response to cripplingly ecstatic emotional outbursts.[45] Indeed, in the *Politics* he writes that he won't say anything more about catharsis, because it will be given a fuller treatment 'when we speak of poetry'.[46] If 'when we speak of poetry' indicates the text we call the *Poetics*, then either the fuller discussion of catharsis didn't survive, or he never wrote it (or, given that the *Poetics* is thought to be teaching material, perhaps he never wrote it *down*); if it indicates a completely different text on poetry, then that other text is lost. An answer to this riddle is as distant as an answer to the riddle of catharsis.

Third, there are a number of related interpretative problems, which, given the sparse language of the *Poetics*, we are unlikely to solve with any satisfaction. As things stand, then, we lack a solid foundation on which to build an account of catharsis. I shall give some brief examples. First, Aristotle tells us that tragedy produces the catharsis of 'pity and fear'. Some have taken it as obvious that 'pity and fear' stand in for a range of emotions, including perhaps sorrow, shame, anger and so on.[47] Others argue that, if Aristotle had meant to include those emotions, he would have done so.[48] If catharsis is something that happens only to pity and fear (but not, say, to sorrow or anger), then it's highly specific and our account of it will follow suit. Thus, it would be worth analysing what Aristotle thought about pity and fear (including what he writes about them in the *Rhetoric*).[49] But if 'pity and fear' just head up a long list, then an investigation into Aristotle on pity and fear (only) would be of limited help to us.[50] Second, there is the question of how catharsis relates to pleasure. Aristotle speaks of the characteristic pleasure of tragedy (without saying what it is);[51] and he (elsewhere, not in the *Poetics*) associates catharsis with pleasure.[52] Does this mean that tragic catharsis is the characteristic pleasure of tragedy? Most assume that it is – hence its central place in the definition of tragedy; others have argued that it is not, because Aristotle mentions several kinds of pleasure that may be related to tragedy.[53] A further and related problem, which we shall come to, is the question of who is meant to experience catharsis. Is it (1) all spectators (2) only the most virtuous spectators (3) not all and not the most virtuous? Finally, there is a question that we touched on in relation to *mimesis*: to what extent is the *Poetics* in general, and *catharsis* in particular, intended to be Aristotle's response to Plato's complaints about the effect that theatre has on the emotions?[54] How we answer any of these interpretative questions reflects on how we answer the others, leaving us with no safe starting point. For example, if *catharsis* is just for pity and fear, then it looks less convincing as a response to Plato, who was concerned with the effects of theatre on *all* the emotions.[55]

All of which might be thought sufficient to forget about the problem of catharsis altogether. Why should we devote an enormous amount of time and energy to a problem that, even if solved, would tell us what one Macedonian thought was the function of one kind of (now virtually unknowable) theatre approximately two and a half millennia ago and that will, in any case, never actually be solved? When put this way, it's hardly surprising that plenty of people think that we shouldn't and that the extensive critical interest in catharsis has been dismissed by one critic as 'a grotesque monument of sterility'.[56] Nor is it surprising that the word 'catharsis', like 'freedom' and 'justice', has been used to support pretty much any prevailing view, no matter how ludicrous or far-fetched.[57]

Nonetheless, we shall look at catharsis in a little more detail, for two reasons. First, because I suspect that part of the reason why this one word has attracted so much attention is that we think that there's something plausible about the idea that *something like* catharsis – whatever Aristotle might have meant by it – can be a feature of theatre, and especially of tragedy. It has a certain intuitive appeal, despite the critical haze. Second, because the notion of catharsis has such a long and established place in the history of philosophy and theatre, for this reason alone, we shouldn't pass it by altogether. My aim, then, is to combine a discussion of various interpretative options with our intuitive sense that something like catharsis may be a feature of our emotional experience of theatre.

What does 'catharsis' mean?

The Greek word, 'catharsis', had a variety of meanings. While it could be used in a relatively straightforward way to refer to everyday cleaning, modern scholars have tended to focus on two different umbrella terms as the starting point for their discussions. The first, 'purging', is primarily a medical notion. The second, 'purification', is primarily religious. Before we look at each term, two qualifications are important. First, *both* purging and purification relate to Greek institutions and practices – medicine and religion – which were by no means standardised, which are completely foreign to a general, modern readership and which (in many cases) remain relatively obscure even to scholars.[58] In any case (and this is the second qualification), the suggestion is not that Aristotle thought that tragic catharsis was actually medical or religious: very likely, he was using the term metaphorically, or in a technical sense. Both the medical and religious terms lend themselves to metaphors of various kinds and had already done so by the time Aristotle wrote his *Poetics*. For both these reasons, therefore, even settling on one of purging or purification won't help us enormously. Nonetheless, because they would take us in different directions, let us say something about each.[59]

Purging

For the Greeks, catharsis as 'purging' covered all sorts of different physiological processes – among them, basic bodily functions such as menstruation or the emptying of the bowels (the latter was an accepted meaning of 'catharsis' in English well into the nineteenth century) and medical procedures such as the draining of pus. Put crudely and literally, it is 'getting something out of your system', which, just as in English, could easily develop into metaphor. If vomiting is 'getting something out of my system' in a literal sense, then an intense bout of weeping may be 'getting something out of my system' in a metaphorical sense – not the tears, but the emotion. Note that getting something out of your system could be getting rid of it *completely*; or it could be draining off the excess, where only the excess was unwanted. So, in relation to the emotions, it might suggest getting rid of my fear *altogether* or getting rid of the extra bit of fear that was in some sense too much.

The modern, English use of the term 'cathartic', which probably derives from a certain interpretation of Aristotle's *Poetics*, looks to express this kind of metaphorical notion of purging. It is used to describe an experience that was emotionally difficult, but that led to a certain kind of satisfactory or even pleasurable resolution. The difficult emotions will be 'discharged' (to keep the medical metaphor alive). A 'cathartic' conversation with a friend might then be one in which certain conflicts, brewing for a long time, were finally discussed in the open and were resolved, at least for the foreseeable future. It is a term that might be used to describe the experience (or even the function) of a funeral: an opportunity to express intense emotions, which were in some sense there all along (since the death), in such a way that brings a kind of relief or satisfaction. The medical metaphor may also lend intuitive support to the sense in which catharsis might be connected with pleasure: vomiting, one supposes, is not in itself something one particularly enjoys; but, when it happens, it is often followed by a kind of pleasurable relief.

Initially, then, the notion of purging, of getting the fear and the pity out of our system, looks to be a promising one. Hence, for a long time, the notion of purging was given as the standard and relatively uncontroversial interpretation for catharsis.[60] It has also found favour with some theatre theorists, among them Artaud, who took up the idea that theatre was designed to 'drain abscesses'.[61] Indeed, 'purging' is often presented as Aristotle's intended meaning, without much further discussion.[62] We go to the tragedy; our pity and our fear are expressed; we feel a pleasurable relief. It is, in the modern, English sense of the term, a cathartic experience.

However, for various reasons, purging turns out to be problematic. As I have said, our interest here is both in what Aristotle might have meant and, regardless of what he meant, whether the interpretation in question is intuitively helpful for our understanding of theatre. To begin with, compare purging at the theatre with the other kinds of purging under discussion: in the bodily cases, there is something unwanted that is being secreted, excreted and so on; in the metaphorical cases, there is also something unwanted or uncomfortable, which is being expunged. Thus, when I go to the funeral, my weeping is 'cathartic' because my grief was always present. The cathartic conversation with the friend was such,

because there was always trouble brewing. However, in the case of theatre, there doesn't seem to be an obvious candidate for what was there *all
along*. To be sure, my pity for Vanya and Sonya is expressed during the
course of *Uncle Vanya*. But, before I saw the play, I had absolutely no idea
who they were and I certainly didn't have feelings about them that
I needed to get out of my system.

To maintain the 'purging' metaphor in relation to tragedy, we would
need to claim that either (1) the emotion that gets purged by theatre is
just the emotion that theatre itself produces or (2) before we even step
into the theatre, there are emotions that we need to get out of our system,
which theatre helps us to purge. If we opt for (1), then the significance of
catharsis is questionable: instead of getting something out of our system,
theatre puts something *in* and then gets it out of our system. In medical
terms, this would be like taking a healthy person, making them feel terribly
nauseous and then helping them to vomit. Doubtless, the latter would
produce a certain kind of relief, so there's nothing contradictory about
tragedy performing this kind of role for certain negative emotions. It's
just that it doesn't seem a terribly noble or significant role; and, in fact, it
makes the spectators sound more like emotional junkies or Roman ban-
queters than anything else. Perhaps this accounts for why this first option
doesn't seem to have been taken seriously by Aristotle critics, who generally
seek something profound and significant for the effects of catharsis.[63]

Suppose then that we opt for (2) – that there is something, all along,
that we want to purge. But, if so, then we seem to be saying that, for audience members who experience catharsis, there's some kind of unwanted or
troublesome emotional element that they bring with them into the theatre,
and that theatre helps them to expunge. In other words, if we choose this
option, we need a much broader account of human psychology. (We have
already discussed a version of this, in relation to why we might have
feelings for fictional characters.) I don't doubt that this is sometimes what
happens when we go to the theatre: we are feeling sad about something
else, and the play helps us to express that feeling: one reason I was so
moved by *Uncle Vanya* is that Chekhov puts his finger so exactly on some
of the things that worry me. But it's unlikely that everyone has that
experience or goes to theatre with that in mind and, as we have seen, it's
not exactly clear why watching a play in which what I worry about
happens to fictional others should bring *me* any particular relief or pleasure. What's more, the proposed model seems more intelligible for some
emotions than for others. Thus, I might be feeling sad and find relief in
expressing this at the theatre; but does it really make sense to say that
I might be carrying around too much pity?[64]

These were objections to the intuitive appeal of (2) as an explanation of
what happens to our emotions at the theatre. But as an interpretation of

Aristotle, the purging claim faces all of this and more. For one thing, Aristotle has a particular view about what it is to be a virtuous person: namely, a virtuous person has the right sort of emotional responses at the right time. He will be afraid when it is appropriate to be afraid, and so on. He is not somebody who doesn't have any emotional responses.[65] Thus, a virtuous person sounds like exactly the kind of person who doesn't need a purge at all; a purge might do him harm, by getting rid of the very emotions in virtue of which he is virtuous. But (2), above, suggests that the people who experience the benefits of catharsis are those who need a purge. Thus, either we say that only non-virtuous people experience catharsis, which most (although not all) Aristotle scholars wish to avoid; or we say that purging can't be the right metaphor for catharsis.[66] A second objection relates to Aristotle's claims (elsewhere) about the emotions. Fear, he suggests, is not just a feeling; it is attached to particular (fearsome) objects at particular times.[67] I don't just 'feel fear' (he thinks); I feel fear because of (say) the tiger that is coming towards me. So it's not clear how fear, in general, could be purged. I ought to be afraid of that which is fearful; because whatever was fearful before the tragedy is fearful afterwards, Aristotle probably doesn't think that purging would (or should) take place.[68]

Purification

In a religious context, 'purification' seems to have meant something like a ritual cleansing of a person or a place. We can compare this with the thought of 'washing away' sins, or purifying a place of worship with holy water or incense. In any case, the intuitive connection is between everyday hygiene and religious or spiritual hygiene: making things clean. Whereas it's fairly obvious what a purging of the emotions would involve (even if it isn't obvious that this is what Aristotle had in mind), it's not at all obvious what a purification of pity, fear or any other emotion would be. So just what exactly does Gerald mean when he tells Anabel that 'we shall hate ourselves clean at last, I suppose'?[69] The purging metaphor is one of quantity. We have a pretty good idea of what having more or less of an emotion involves: I can be more or less afraid, angry and so on. But the purification metaphor is one of quality. So what does it mean to have purer fear or purer pity? The religious context is of little use to us, because there's no obvious analogy, in the spectator's emotion, for the ritual purification of a person, place or object. More so than accepting the purge metaphor, accepting the purification metaphor in itself gives us nothing much to work with.

One thing it might mean, of course, is that the fear or the pity is somehow *better*. Thus, a more speculative account of catharsis has been

suggested, along the lines that it offers a kind of moral training or education, which makes your emotions – and therefore you, as a whole –
'purer' in that sense. This is given some plausibility by the fact that, for
Aristotle, virtue consists (at least to some degree) in having the right
kinds of emotional responses to the world: one shouldn't be afraid of
everything; one shouldn't be afraid of nothing, and so on.[70] Perhaps,
along these lines, we could imagine the spectator 'getting clearer' about
pity and fear, about the sufferings of others and so on.[71]

However, what's missing is an account (in Aristotle) of why tragedy
should in any way make our pity and our fear more appropriate, or in
what way it would morally educate. Because we have already discussed
the common but problematic view that theatre can train our moral sentiments, I shall not rehearse the general arguments here. Suffice to say,
it's not clear just how it does so, nor why theatrical 'training' would fit
with the world of everyday experience – which they would have to, if the
'education' is to be of any use.[72] So to those general concerns with theatre
as a school for the sentiments, I shall add some problems for this as an
interpretation of Aristotle. First, as with purification, there is the question
of whether virtuous people could experience catharsis. If so, and if the
virtuous man's emotions are already in harmony, then he has no need of
catharsis in this sense. You don't need to be taught what you already
know.[73] (As before, one can jettison the notion that the virtuous man
experiences catharsis. But then theatre – as moral education – becomes
something for the morally needy, not for the morally accomplished.)
Second, one of Aristotle's other remarks on catharsis seems to tell against
this interpretation. When he discusses the effects of music, Aristotle
appears to distinguish clearly between music that is useful in ethical
training and music that causes catharsis. This is the same text in which
Aristotle tells us that catharsis is to be explained in relation to poetry.[74]
If, in the case of music, catharsis and moral education are distinct, then
they are probably distinct in the case of poetry. To repeat: the word
'catharsis' in no obvious way *means* 'moral education'. Given this, and the
clear distinction that Aristotle makes between catharsis and moral education
elsewhere, it seems to me that this interpretation is on tricky ground.[75]

Conclusion

We have had the opportunity to investigate three problems, each of
which asks questions about how theatre moves us. It should be clear that
these problems may well be related. Some choose to explain the second
problem with reference to the third (tragic pleasure is the pleasure of
catharsis). More generally, how one approaches the problem of tragic
pleasure may depend on how one has answered the problem of how, in

general, we respond emotionally to fictional characters. And, before explaining how tragedy purges or purifies our fear, we might think it reasonable to get a better sense of what 'fear', in relation to a piece of theatre, actually means. The defenders of theatre, and its detractors, have often appealed to its effects on the emotions. Perhaps this chapter has helped us to understand some of the challenges that confront both sides.

Further Reading: Emotions

For a sample of pieces on emotional responses to fiction, see Radford (1975), Walton (1990: 195–204), Neill (1993), Zemach (1996), Suits (2006). On the paradox of tragedy, Hume (1965) is often used as a starting point, although he evidently did not invent the problem; see Neill (1999) for a critical analysis of Hume. For a sample of contemporary discussions, see Feagin (1983), Budd (1995), Shelley (2003), Friend (2007). On catharsis: Aristotle's *Poetics* is, of course, the source of the dispute; interpreters make frequent reference to his *Politics* (for its reference to catharsis), *Rhetoric* (for the analysis of emotions like pity and fear) and *Nicomachean Ethics* (for its discussion of ethics and the emotions) to support their various claims. For a sense of the variety of interpretations, see Halliwell (1986: 184–201) (which also features a helpful discussion of the uses of the Greek term), Schaper (1968), Nehamas (1992), Golden (1973) and Lear (1992). On the rich history of interpretations of catharsis, see Halliwell (1986: 350–6).

Notes

1 Chekhov (1980: 144).
2 Having seen a performance, it is perfectly possible to feel one emotion in relation to the actor and another in relation to the character that the actor was playing. See, e.g., Brock (2007: 217–9) for discussion.
3 Tolstoy (1995: 40).
4 *Poetics* 49b.
5 Hegel (1993: 37–8).
6 See, e.g., *The Republic* 605b–606d.
7 *Hamlet*, II.ii 229.
8 Radford (1975: 78–9).
9 Walton (1990: 249).
10 As I have mentioned in my discussion of Walton in Chapter 2, his notion of 'make-believe' is much broader than the everyday use of the term.
11 This example is developed from Woodruff (2008).
12 Walton (1990: 241).
13 The quotation is from Woodruff (2008: 164), who appears to miss this feature of Walton in arguing against him.
14 Walton (1990: 252–3).
15 For further critical discussion of Walton's view, see Neill (1991).
16 Pirandello's *Six Characters in Search of an Author* plays on exactly this phenomenon.

17 Stendhal (1962: 24).

18 For a contemporary defence of a version of this response, see Suits (2006), who argues that, given a more flexible notion of 'belief', one can believe that what one watches is real while simultaneously believing that what one watches is fictional.

19 See Eldridge (2003: 195).

20 The 'paradox of tragedy' is one of the few problems in the philosophy of art that, by name at least, is connected with theatre. But writers on the problem often argue about whether it just applies to tragedy, or whether it can be applied to other works of art. It seems clear that it also applies, say, to films and novels. Other candidates include paintings, documentary films, roller coasters, fine oratory and so on. Because our concern is with theatre, I won't spend time discussing how far the problem stretches.

21 Hume (1965: 185).

22 See Friend (2007); Feagin (1983).

23 Roughly, Hume thinks that the artistic elements of a performance 'convert' the negative emotions to positive ones. For an excellent critical analysis, see Neill (1999).

24 Lennard and Luckhurst (2002: 134) even suggest that public slaughtering of humans and animals in Rome accounts (in part) for the relative lack of appreciation and popularity of theatre.

25 Nietzsche has his prophet, Zarathustra, say that man is the cruellest animal because he enjoys tragedies, bullfights and crucifixions (in *Thus Spoke Zarathustra*, Part 3, 'The Convalescent'); a more nuanced discussion of our pleasure in the sufferings of others (and ourselves) can be found in the second essay of *The Genealogy of Morality*.

26 Burke (1998: 43–4).

27 Burke (1998: 43). Long before Burke's time, the public execution and the theatre were often compared and contrasted as public shows. Thus, in the middle of the seventeenth century: 'the association of public executions and theatre was a commonplace. Executions were staged for the edification of the audience.' (Thomson 1995: 203)

28 Hobbes (1994: 58); as Carlson (1993: 129) notes, these remarks are not explicitly about theatre, although he does speak of the 'spectator' and the 'spectacle'.

29 The view that our security is the source of our pleasure at the suffering of others is one that, as it happens, is explicitly rejected by Burke.

30 Thus I agree with Ridley that 'successful tragic drama – think of Lear, think of Oedipus – is simply not all that pleasing' (2003a: 413); and with Woodruff that 'the best theatre is not the theatre that gives us the most pleasure' (2008: 186). See also Budd (1995).

31 See e.g., Gardner (2003: 236).

32 See e.g. Neill (2003).

33 The medical example is developed from Shelley (2003).

34 See Shelley (2003: 178).

35 Shelley (2003: 183).

36 Shelley (2003: 185).

37 Feagin (1983: 98).

38 Feagin (1983: 98).

39 Friend (2007) makes a similar point.

40 We discussed this in Chapter 5.

41 Walton (1990). As he acknowledges, Walton's solution to the paradox is independent of the claims he makes about emotions and make-believe, which we discussed earlier in the chapter; I have chosen to present it without using the rest of his theoretical apparatus.

42 A further question, unexplored here, concerns the unity not of the answer but of the problem or 'paradox' that we began with: are we in fact dealing with a single 'paradox' or are we looking at a series of overlapping concerns that deserve isolated treatment? Some have suggested, for example, that the psychological question of what motivates us in going to the tragedy should be kept apart from the moral question of whether it is permissible to enjoy depictions of the suffering of others. I have treated them in a unified manner here, partly for simplicity, partly because the answers are evidently related to one another (are our psychological motivations morally permissible?). But see e.g. Neill (2003: 207–8) for elaboration.

43 The only other mention of the word describes the 'purification' of Orestes' madness as part of a tragic plot. See *Poetics* 55b.
44 Nehamas (1992) and Else (1957) give different versions of this alternative reading.
45 Compare Golden (1973), Nehamas (1992) and Janko (1992) on this question.
46 Sometimes translated as 'in the *Poetics*', for obvious reasons; see *Politics* VIII.7, 1431b, pp. 37–9. See Halliwell (1986: 190) for discussion.
47 Compare e.g. Taplin (1995: 23) and Halliwell (1986: 200f).
48 A further option, endorsed by some of the French tragedians, was that either pity or fear would do; Lessing argues strongly against this position. See Lessing (1962: Sections 75–6, p. 182).
49 For a flavour of this, see Lessing (1962: Section 74–75, pp. 175–82) and (1962: Section 78, pp. 191–2). Halliwell (2002: ch. 7) gives a detailed reading of Aristotle's account of pity.
50 Recent scholarship, it is fair to say, favours a 'pity and fear only' solution; but see Schaper (1968: 136–7) and Janko (1992: 349–350), for an argument that 'a wider range of feelings' is invoked. Lessing (1962: Sections 74–75, pp. 175–82) tries to reconcile both positions, by suggesting that pity and fear accompany all the emotions that we feel for the characters; pity, in the sense of feeling what the character feels, makes it possible to get (say) angry and our pity is related to the fear that what happens to the character might happen to us.
51 *Poetics* 53b.
52 *Politics* VIII.7, 1431b.
53 See Heath (1996).
54 See Chapter 2 for general discussion. On *catharsis* in particular, compare Halliwell (1986) with Nehamas (1992).
55 See Nehamas (1992: 306).
56 Quoted in Halliwell (1986: 184).
57 See Halliwell (1986: 350–6).
58 See, e.g. the discussion of Aristotle on 'homeopathic' treatment in Halliwell (1986: 192–3). The claim is that curing pity and fear *using* pity and fear (following the medical 'purging' metaphor) wouldn't have made sense in the light of Aristotle's own medical theory, even although others frequently made use of it.
59 It is true, of course, that the metaphor of catharsis might somehow have been intended to combine purging and purification: getting rid of some and purifying the rest. In the absence of a compelling account of such a combination, I won't pursue this here.
60 It is associated with the pioneering work of J. Bernays, discussed in Janko (1992).
61 Quoted in Balme (2008: 76).
62 E.g. Lennard and Luckhurst (2001: 62); Balme (2008: 72) (although Balme considers other interpretations elsewhere).
63 Exceptions include Nehamas (1992) and Heath (1996).
64 Nietzsche, to be sure, thought that nineteenth-century Europe was, in general, suffering from too much pity; he takes Aristotle to be offering a 'purging' account of catharsis and prescribing tragedies precisely in order to curb the dangerous excesses of pity. See, e.g. *Antichrist*, section 7.
65 See Aristotle's *Nicomachean Ethics* II.6 1106b, pp. 40–1.
66 Compare Heath (1996) with Lear (1992: 316–7) and Halliwell (1986: 191).
67 See *Rhetoric*, 1382a–1383b.
68 Lear (1992: 317); for more general criticism of the 'purging' view, see Golden (1973).
69 D. H. Lawrence's *Touch and Go* (III. i. 72). I feel as though I know exactly what he means, but it's not easy to explain.
70 See Aristotle's *Nicomachean Ethics* II.6 1106b, pp. 40–1.
71 Nussbaum (1992: 280–3). One could present 'moral education' interpretations, not as a species of 'purification', but under a heading of their own – and indeed, some do. But because 'catharsis' doesn't mean 'moral education', interpreters who favour the latter as a kind of interpretation tend to develop it out of the notion of 'purification'.
72 See Nehamas (1992: 303–4) for more on this problem, specifically in relation to Aristotle.

73 Nussbaum (1992) rejects the idea that the virtuous person doesn't need training – a virtuous person, she supposes, would be open to correction, and she provides some evidence from Aristotle to support this intuitive idea.

74 *Politics* VIII.7, 1431b.

75 Halliwell (1986: 195) tries to answer this concern; but see Lear (1992: 319) for critical discussion.

7   Collective Action: Theatre and Politics

Caryl Churchill's *Seven Jewish Children: A Play for Gaza* premiered at the Royal Court Theatre in early 2009. The play was about ten minutes long; it was free to all spectators, but a collection was taken at the end for 'the people of Gaza', via an organisation called 'Medical Aid for Palestinians'. Free entry, followed by a collection for Medical Aid for Palestinians is, in fact, a condition on any performance of Churchill's play. The play text itself consists of seven speeches by unspecified adult relations, parents perhaps, of seven Jewish girls. The speeches correspond to different times in the prehistory or history of Israel; in each speech, the adult relative debates or agonises over what the girl should or shouldn't be told.

The play was billed as a response to the Gaza War of 2008–9, which ended shortly before the first performance. The publicity material suggested (although this is not explicit in the play text itself) that the final, seventh speech was that of a contemporary Israeli relative during the Gaza War. In any case, in the most controversial and concluding part of this speech, the seventh relative says:

> Tell her we're the iron fist now, tell her it's the fog
> of war, tell her we won't stop killing them till we're safe, tell her I
> laughed when I saw the dead policemen, tell her they're animals
> living in rubble now, tell her I wouldn't care if we wiped them out,
> the world would hate us is the only thing, tell her I don't care if
> the world hates us, tell her we're better haters, tell her we're
> chosen people, tell her I look at one of their children covered in
> blood and what do I feel? tell her all I feel is happy it's not her.
> Don't tell her that.
> Tell her we love her.
> Don't frighten her.[1]

The controversy surrounding Churchill's play – and the wide range of responses it provoked – could hardly come as a surprise: the play was accused of anti-Semitism in some quarters, just as it was praised for its accuracy and insight in others. Reviewers also took the opportunity to discuss, albeit in passing, the role of political theatre. Readers familiar with the British press may not be astonished at the outcome. The *Guardian*'s critic found Churchill's play 'a heartfelt lamentation for [...] future generations', which confirms 'theatre's ability to react more rapidly than any other art form to global politics'. The *Sunday Times* described it as typical of the 'enclosed, fetid, smug, self-congratulating and entirely irrelevant little world of contemporary political theatre'.[2]

The term 'political theatre', together with the idea that political theatre could be an independent theatrical genre, is frequently associated with the pioneering work of Erwin Piscator, who published a book called *The Political Theatre* in 1929.[3] Clearly, though, the political significance of theatre stretches back before the twentieth century. Broadly speaking, the topic of this chapter is the relationship between theatre and politics. To understand Churchill's play and the controversy that surrounded it, one would have to research the play itself, its alleged invocation of antisemitic tropes, the history and context of the Gaza War, along with that of the playwright and the Royal Court Theatre, not to mention the singular and incendiary role that Middle Eastern conflicts play in the British public sphere. The point of this chapter is not to attack or to defend Churchill's play – or any other specific attempt to combine theatre and politics. Nor do I offer an account of whether plays ought or ought not to encourage political actions of various kinds. Given the volume and variety of material on this subject, my aim is rather more modest: to give a sense of some of the different issues that arise when thinking about theatre and politics and to explore one of the better known accounts of this relationship. Churchill's play, together with the reactions it produced, reminds us that political theatre is still with us, that it still provokes, that it touches on the most controversial, most inflammatory issues of the day. It also reminds us that the relationship between theatre and politics is often not a matter of eternal rules, but frequently of specific encounters between playwrights, companies and spectators at a specific place and time, which deserve consideration in their own terms. The analysis of political causes and effects for some particular performance, or set of performances, might want to take into account facts about how that performance is funded, who creates and performs it, who sees it and how it is received. Nonetheless, there is a place for some analysis at a theoretical level. We'll begin by making some distinctions that will help to give a shape to the discussion.

Three distinctions

Politics in the narrow and the broad sense

A first distinction to make is that between what I'll call 'politics in the narrow sense' and 'politics in the broad sense'. The narrow sense of politics covers what one might expect to find, for example, in the 'Politics' section of a newspaper: parliamentary debates, elections, domestic and foreign policy, taxes, budgets, the internal affairs of specific political parties and organisations, and so on. If one hears, as is often claimed (at least in England), that it is 'rude to talk about politics', then presumably it is this narrower sense that the speaker has in mind. But there is a broader sense of 'politics' – much broader than the affairs of government: this broader notion covers the power relations between people and the organisations and institutions that shape their lives and that, to some degree, give them meaning. Thus, to take an obvious example, a church *might* be political in the narrow sense – it might express views about fiscal policy or immigration rates – but it certainly will be political in the second sense, because it organises groups of people and structures the relations between them. Obviously, the kinds of activities that fall under these two categories are not distinct from one another, and each can and does have a great impact on the other. Thus, say, government legislation can affect religious organisations or power structures in the workplace, just as churches can and frequently do have an effect upon how the members of their congregations are likely to vote. Finally, the question of what counts or ought to count under 'politics in the narrow sense' is itself a highly charged political question and is liable to depend on the context. Thus, for the Greeks, certain religious and artistic duties (theatrical festivals, of course, counted as both) were self-evidently affairs of the *polis*, whereas, in modern Western democracies, religious and artistic institutions are often held to be beyond the purview of politics in the narrow sense.

When it comes to politics in the broader sense, a theatrical event obviously is already a political event, so the question is not whether theatre is political but in what ways. The fact that theatre at least typically (if not necessarily) requires more than one person may be seen to give theatre a specially political dimension as an art. Compare the potentially solitary activities of playing the piano, looking at a painting or watching a film. There is no standard, theatrical event involving just one person. Indeed, when Hannah Arendt writes that theatre is 'the political art par excellence', it seems that this is partly what she has in mind. Theatre offers action and interaction among characters and, of course, the audience.[4] It both represents and is already an instance of politics in the broader sense. Primarily, our interest in this chapter is in politics in the narrow sense. But discussions of political theatre must not ignore the attempt of theatre not only to convey certain political messages to spectators, but also, in order to do so, to gather them together in an ordered group of some kind. In sixteenth-century England, Robin Hood plays – traditional plays in which Robin Hood's followers are imprisoned by the sheriff, but then turn the tables and imprison the sheriff himself –

were eventually suppressed by Henry VIII. The idea was partly to discourage the notion of robbing the rich to feed the poor and the ritual overturning of authority (i.e. the content of the plays); but it was also to stop certain kinds of people gathering together, playing, marching, revelling and so on.[5]

Politics and political philosophy

Second, it may be helpful to draw a distinction between politics (in either the narrow or the broad sense) and political philosophy. Political theatre might be theatre that 'does politics' or theatre that 'does political philosophy'; those two things are different. Political philosophy is the attempt by philosophers to think systematically about politics. Where that is politics in the narrower sense, philosophers typically address questions that directly affect some element of government. Well-known examples include questions of authority (who gets to tell whom what to do?) or questions of resource distribution (who gets what?). There are also, as one might imagine, plenty of further questions about what those questions, in turn, might mean, assume or imply.

The relationship between politics and political philosophy is not altogether straightforward. It is clear that, in principle, if a political philosopher argues that the redistribution of resources is justifiable only under certain conditions and in a certain way, then that would (if it were taken seriously by those in power) have an impact on politics in the narrower sense. However, instances of such direct influence are extremely rare; where there is influence from political philosophy to politicians, it tends to be indirect and to require the transformation beyond recognition of the philosophy in question.[6] In any case, politics in the narrower sense has always involved ad hoc decision-making in response to specific circumstances – decisions in relation to which no political philosophy could offer anything but the slightest hint of guidance. What, for instance, would a utilitarian view suggest should be *done* about the Cuban Missile Crisis?

Although this is the usual, contemporary sense of 'political philosophy', plenty of philosophers also want to think about the relations between people indicated by politics in the broader sense: philosophers of this kind might ask, say, what kinds of power there are operating in a particular social context or what kinds of concepts and ideals guide or inhibit the activity of the people concerned. A philosopher might therefore be political in the latter sense, without necessarily drawing any conclusions about political philosophy of the narrow kind. Indeed, it would be possible to draw from a political philosophy of the broader kind the view that politics of the narrower kind (and the philosophy devoted to it) is somehow an inappropriate or fundamentally unworthy activity. Nietzsche, it has been suggested, might represent a view of this kind. Alternatively, one might form a view that government policy should not have any impact upon labour contracts or religious organisations, in which case one's political philosophies in the broad and narrow sense would be forced into some kind of alignment.

Although it is helpful to keep 'politics' and 'political philosophy' apart from one another, the distinction shouldn't be overemphasised. Evidently, one's political philosophy can and should be influenced by politics, and vice versa. What's more, a claim about what ought to be done in the narrow sphere of politics may well appeal to or imply a broader philosophical or theoretical outlook. A politician may claim to have no particular guiding philosophy, but such a philosophy may be implied by her actions, or derived retrospectively by looking at the way in which she has voted. One does not need, in other words, an explicitly articulated 'political philosophy' in order to display, in one's actions, theoretical views about politics that can be reconstructed externally.

These brief distinctions and discussions may enable us to look more clearly at what might be implied in a discussion of theatre and politics. If an act (including a theatrical act) is 'political' it may be affecting politics in its narrow or broad sense and it may be an attempt at discursive or reason-based activity which takes politics as its subject. So strikes and sit-ins are not obviously contributions to political *theory*; but, first of all, they are obviously political acts in the narrow sense; and, second, if they are sufficiently widespread and powerful, it may be that political theories should adapt in response to them. Conversely, a highly theoretical tract on the foundations of government may be an esteemed contribution to political philosophy, yet have little or no political impact in the narrow sense. If we speak of 'political' theatre, or of the relationship between theatre and politics, then keeping these distinctions in mind may be useful. A play that has an impact on politics in the narrow sense is not the same as a play that offers spectators new conceptual tools with which to theorise about politics (in the narrow or the broad sense).

Politics in text and performance

So far we have discussed politics in the narrow and broad sense, together with the distinction between politics and political philosophy. However, the distinction we shall use to structure the remainder of our discussion is that between politics in the play text and politics in performance. As frequently in discussions of theatre, it is useful to keep these apart when thinking about theatre and politics, even if a crystal-clear distinction isn't always possible. Theatrical performances, as we have said, are inherently political in the broad sense, because they bring together groups of people, structure them and direct their attention towards certain kinds of action. But a play text itself doesn't do that. Similarly, there may be features of play texts that are not inherently or intentionally political, but that can be brought out as such in a particular performance or that can be interpreted in such a way by an audience. Thus, for example, the text of Churchill's *Seven Jewish Children* relates to recent political events directly in virtue of its words – an Israeli adult speaking of her happiness when confronted by pictures of dead Palestinian children. But each performance asks audience members whether they would like to contribute money to Medical Aid for Palestinians – something that the play text itself doesn't directly ask of the reader. A performance of *Seven Jewish Children* is therefore also a fundraising event for a particular organisation as well as an attempt to bring people together to think about a particular issue from a particular point of view. We'll begin with politics and play texts, before moving on to politics and performances.

Political features, themes or interventions in play texts are widespread and well documented. Some take the form of specific protests or interventions in the narrow world of politics; others explore certain theoretical themes and conflicts; others, needless to say, merge both. In much modern discussion of 'political theatre', the phrase is regularly used almost as a term of abuse. Often, the notion of 'political theatre' is taken to be an unwanted or unwelcome intrusion on the part of playwrights and directors into politics in the narrow sphere – unwelcome either because playwrights are considered ill qualified or because political plays are considered somehow inferior. One cause of hostility to political theatre is the fact that, at least in the English-speaking world, 'political theatre' is code for 'left-wing political theatre'; thus, an objection to theatre that mixes in politics can often amount to an objection to left-wing views, appearing in a theatrical guise. Of course, there is no reason why a play that is overtly political should be left wing; but in as much as this is the complaint that lies behind objections to political theatre, it is more a matter of politics than of theatre.

A different but equally common argument against theatre mixing with politics (in the narrow sense) is an aesthetic claim about art and its purpose. The idea is that art should have something eternal about it; it shouldn't be put to use for a particular narrow purpose. By meddling in current affairs – in issues that will fade from the public consciousness in a matter of years – the playwright ensures that a play won't have any longevity, thus won't be any good by the standards of posterity. This is a common enough criticism that we should take some time to consider some objections to it. First, as a descriptive claim about theatre and what it is and isn't for, this is misleading. There is nothing odd or peculiar per se about theatre being used instrumentally. Theatre theorists use the general term 'applied theatre' as a broad term to indicate the use of theatre for particular practical purposes.[7] Applied theatre is widespread, although it often escapes the heading of 'theatre' altogether. Frequent examples include theatre as training or as therapy. As for the former, role-play training techniques may be used to help people learn to deal with certain typical situations: I have had training as a teacher, which uses techniques of this kind; I have also made use of it to train graduate students. Therapeutic theatre is also widespread; it is given a brutally frank treatment in David Foster Wallace's story, *The Depressed Person*. The 'depressed person' takes part in therapeutic applied theatre, during which

> ... other members of her small group had role-played the depressed person's parents and the parents' significant others and attorneys and myriad other emotionally painful figures from her childhood, and had slowly encircled the depressed person, moving in steadily together so that she could not escape, and had (i.e., the small group had) dramatically recited specially prepared lines designed to evoke and reawaken trauma, which had almost immediately evoked in the depressed person a surge of agonizing emotional memories and had resulted in the emergence of the depressed person's Inner Child and a cathartic tantrum in which she had struck repeatedly at a stack of velour cushions with a bat of polystyrene foam and had shrieked obscenities and had reexperienced long-pent-up wounds and repressed feelings.[8]

In addition to therapy and training, theatre may be applied to awareness-raising, such as the use of so-called 'AIDS-plays' to raise awareness and promote debate about AIDS and HIV.[9] Some of these take place in front of a 'street' audience, who do not realise that what they are watching is a play and are therefore not engaged in assessing the performance as a work of art.

Those who object to political theatre on the grounds that, being instrumental, it is bad art are assuming, of course, that it is the production of 'good art' that's at stake. In some of the cases just discussed, the success criteria are obviously completely different and the artistic achievement hardly comes into consideration. Needless to say, where theatre has been primarily used as a quick and economical mass tool for education or propaganda – as, for example, were the 'Blue Blouse' troupes who spread the word to workers and peasants after the Russian Revolution – it would be open to the creators and performers simply to accept that aesthetic value has at most a secondary or instrumental role in their plays. But this still leaves political theatre open to the charge that it is bad art. This, as we have seen, depends on the notion that good artworks last the longest or stay relevant, and I shall now turn to some objections to this claim.

First, the idea that a play that focuses on achieving a certain practical political outcome – fundraising, changing how people vote, demanding industrial action – must therefore not have any duration as an artwork assumes a dichotomy between political relevance and endurance, such that the playwright must choose between the two. One response, then, would be to deny that this dichotomy exists. A play might have a great deal to say about its own time, using contemporary issues as a focus, but also have resonance with later spectators – just as, by analogy, a historian might hope that her work would both educate readers about some particular issue and, perhaps, tell them something general about human affairs. Still, one might think that a play that looks to bring about a highly particular, focused set of actions with respect to a particular deadline – an election or a protest – might lose much of its significance once that deadline is passed.

Thus, a second thought accepts the dichotomy – i.e. that a play must be either eternal or politically relevant – and argues that aesthetic value should lie with the latter. George Bernard Shaw claims that Ibsen's play, *A Doll's House*, which highlights (amongst other things) the plight of wives and daughters who are not afforded the same legal rights as their husbands and fathers, will probably not endure in the way that *A Midsummer Night's Dream* has endured; that doesn't matter, Shaw suggests, because the former will have 'done more work' and is a better play.[10] In his own work, Shaw did not shy away from claiming to be encouraging specific, political actions from the spectators of his plays: his first play, *Widowers' Houses*, is (he wrote) 'deliberately intended to induce people to vote on the Progressive side at the next County Council election in London'.[11] If we accept the dichotomy, then it is a necessary concomitant of the view that artworks should be eternal that they shouldn't deal exclusively or primarily with current affairs. As Shaw's claims illustrate, the reverse is also true: if you think dramatists should have something to say about contingent features of their world, then obviously you won't think that the best artworks are those that audiences at all places and all times can easily relate to. Following Shaw's line, if plays can have an effect on politics in the narrow sense, then the view that plays should be judged solely by their longevity is as much a conservative's view of politics as it is an aesthete's view of art.

A final word about longevity and aesthetic value: there may be many reasons why a play endures (or not), which don't have much to do with the subject matter of the play or the intended political effect on the audience or, in general, the aesthetic qualities of the work. If Aristophanes' comedies rely on untranslatable Greek puns, then they will find it harder to appeal to audiences once Greek has become a dead language. That does not, it seems to me, make his plays any the worse. It is a contingent fact about the language he uses, which has now become obsolete. Furthermore, plenty of the Greek works that do speak to us are liable to contain references to contemporary events that are missed by the modern audience. To take one minor example: *Oedipus Tyrannus* opens with a plague devastating the city of Thebes, which acts as the catalyst for Oedipus' terrible discoveries; when it was performed, in Athens, a plague was devastating the Athenians, killing many of their finest citizens.[12] That people can appreciate the play without knowing about some of the contemporary events to which it may have referred strikes me as an accident of history as much as an aesthetic triumph on the part of the playwright.

Textual politics

Setting aside the idea that, because of concerns about longevity, engaging with politics necessarily damages the value of the play, we can ask in what ways a play text could engage with politics. To do so, we'll consider four ways that a play text might want to contribute to politics: statements; morals; questions; commands.

Statements and morals

A 'political play' may be one that makes a statement – a factual claim – about a contemporary political issue. The play amounts to a communication of a certain kind of knowledge – or, at least, the attempt to convey a certain kind of belief. Such beliefs may be about concrete political current events or they may be about general political views or theories. There are, broadly speaking, two ways of construing how such a claim could be made. First, it could be a claim that the author is making, through the play, to the audience. Second, we might prefer to leave out the author and speak of a play making claims in its own right. (There are many different ways to understand this, but the basic thought is that plays can end up 'saying things' or 'meaning things' that the author didn't necessarily put in there.) Thus one might take Churchill – and some reviewers certainly did – as making a claim about what Israelis think about the death of Palestinian children during the Gaza War; or one might prefer to leave Churchill out of the picture and speak of the claims made in the play. In what follows, I'll speak primarily in the first way – that is, in terms the playwright making political statements through the play; but it seems to me that these remarks apply more or less to the second construal as well.

In as much as political drama is a matter of an author making statements through the play text, it is open to some familiar objections and concerns. We have, in previous discussions, already found reasons to be suspicious of the ability of theatre to transmit an author's beliefs. We saw, in Chapter 2, that deriving an author's claims about the world from a play text or theatrical performance is hardly a simple matter. To state the obvious: writing a play in which a character makes a statement is not the same as making that statement yourself, nor is it (*contra* Aristotle) the same as stating that characters of that kind always or typically make statements of this kind. Take the controversial speech at the end of *Seven Jewish Children*, quoted above: does this represent Churchill's view of how Jews think about Palestinian children, how Israelis think, how at least some Israelis think, how some Israeli settlers *sometimes* think? Is it her idealised portrayal of a way of thinking that informs Israeli foreign policy and represents a stage in the history of Israel, even if no individual would ever think or utter these words? Or is she equating what Jews suffered during the Holocaust with what Palestinians suffer in Israel? ('I wouldn't care if we wiped them out ... ') The answers to these questions are not forthcoming from the text or from theatrical performances of the text, and it's not clear that they *need* to be for aesthetic purposes. But, obviously, if we want to take Churchill (or, more generally, her play) as making a political *claim* – the kind that could be true or false – then we'd want to be pretty sure which of these options to begin with. All of them may be wrong; but some are more plausible, and some are more incendiary, than others.

Even supposing we could derive a statement, we would still be faced with another familiar concern, stemming from Plato's arguments against *mimesis*. The Platonic objection would be that playwrights don't really have any special expertise when it comes to politics, so there is no reason why they should pretend to or why, if they do, we should listen. As discussed in relation to *mimesis*, Plato's fear is that audiences will fail to appreciate the ignorance of the playwright and will be taken in by various elements of the performance. Where the play makes claims about politics, the thought that an ignorant and opinionated artist, especially a gifted one, could influence the views of an audience becomes a cause of some concern. The use of theatre – and of art more generally – as propaganda in the service of certain authoritarian regimes has helped to give a modern twist to this ancient concern.

Contrary to this Platonic thought, though, it's not clear that all contributions to politics must be in the form of making statements, or of the amassing and communicating of *knowledge*. If what politics needs is another discursive article or another set of statistics, then perhaps theatre is not the best forum for such a contribution. But there are many instances of 'contributions' to politics in the narrower sense, which don't take this form and which probably wouldn't have been nearly as effective if they had. A black woman who refuses to give up her seat on the bus is not obviously communicating knowledge to those around her.

A further thought, which might now count against the Platonic objection, relates to our conception of democracy. Plato expresses his views about theatre in *The Republic*, which, as we have seen, is primarily a discussion of politics. Ideal political activity, for Plato, is philosophically informed and based on knowledge – but poets don't know. Then again, it's not just the poets who don't know what they're talking about; it's the people, too. Thus, citizens without any special training shouldn't have any say in the running of the ideal city. Plato, then, is consistent in his view that neither the people (in general) nor the poets should be able to influence political affairs. However, if we now hold that democracy is legitimate – that the general public, no matter how much or little they know, must have a say – then the case for being suspicious of political theatre in this sense looks a bit shaky. Why object to a playwright expressing political views in a play text, and not object to that same playwright casting a valid vote in a general election, or to her standing for public office, to be elected by the very public whom, as a playwright, you feel she is liable to mislead?

Furthermore, this platonic criticism of political theatre does not necessarily sit well with the initial objection, namely that plays should be treating universal subjects and therefore should last through the ages. If you hold the latter view, then that may well be because you think that playwrights have something valuable to contribute to our thinking about such matters. But the first, Platonic criticism was that playwrights don't know what they are talking about. If artists are supposed to deal with 'eternal' themes, then presumably their knowledge and treatment of such themes are open to the same criticisms as their treatment of political affairs: what expertise do they have about either? Plato is consistent, it seems, that they have none whatsoever. But the critic who claims that plays should keep out of politics because they should be dealing with eternal or universal themes presumably thinks that artists have something to bring to the table with regard to such themes. And if an artist is permitted to speak of eternal concerns, then why not of specific ones?

Finally, even if a relatively clear statement is conveyed, we should be clear that predicting an audience's response to it – how politically effective it turns out to be – is a completely different matter. Whatever the intent of Beaumarchais' *The Marriage of Figaro* – and he clearly intended to ruffle a few feathers – the speech in which Figaro denounces the aristocracy as lazy, conceited good-for-nothings was greeted with tumultuous applause by the aristocrats who had waited overnight to see it. Given the date of the performance (1784), they might have listened more carefully.[13]

One might take a political play to be encoding or expressing a moral principle or 'moral of the story', which relates in some way to a contemporary political issue. Obviously, if this moral principle is one that the author believes to be true and is trying to transmit through her play, then it is just a specific instance of the general statement, and what we have already said about political statements applies here too. But, as we have seen in our discussion of the school of morals, playwrights have taken themselves not merely to be communicating facts to their audiences, but in some sense training them or educating them to be better or more moral people. Aristotle's notion of 'catharsis' has sometimes been interpreted in this way; versions of the 'school of morals' view have been repeated by various defenders of theatre, and were attacked by Rousseau in his letter to D'Alembert. Because we have discussed these arguments in detail in another chapter, I do not propose to repeat them here; but note that much of what was said in relation to theatre and general moral principles may also apply to specific political claims about what ought and ought not to be done.

Questions and imperatives

Hegel calls the work of art a question. Indeed, it may be that where political plays are asking political questions, they are easier to defend than where they appear to be making statements or claiming to offer moral training. If I make a statement to you, then the implication is that I know more than you; but in a typical case, if I ask you a question then I think you can help me with the answer. A question, as we noted in Chapter 2, is not the kind of thing that is true or false. Thus, if the political playwright thinks of herself as a questioner, then she does not have to answer Plato's charge of where she gets her special information from. She's just asking.

Asking questions can be an important philosophical and political activity. Plato's Socrates – who in *The Republic* demands knowledge from the rulers – is perhaps the best model here. Socrates claims to know nothing and assumes that those around him know more than he does. But he is disappointed with the answers, and concludes that none of the Athenian experts really knows about the things that most concern him. Socrates' insistence on asking why the Athenians are doing what they are doing and questioning their responses has obvious political implications. In one of the most important instances of this kind of conversation (in Plato's *Meno*), Plato has Socrates question someone called 'Anytus'; as a result of this questioning, Socrates concludes that politicians don't really know what they're doing – when they get a decision right, it's really a matter of luck, not skill or knowledge.[14] Written after but set shortly before Socrates' trial and execution, the significance of this conversation – and the series of questions that brings about Socrates' conclusion – is that Anytus will go on to be one of Socrates' chief accusers and will try, successfully, to have Socrates put to death. Anytus, in other words, concludes that Socrates' questions are a danger to the city.

To take an example from the history of theatre: one historian has argued that the court plays performed in front of the absolutist king, Charles I, frequently found ways of asking questions like 'what is it that makes a king?' or 'must one deserve to be a king?'[15] Even asking such questions, let alone asking them in front of the king himself, has obvious political importance, no matter whether the plays offer answers or what those answers were. If questioning can be an important political and philosophical activity, then how does the political play as a question fare against some of the objections we've been considering? Regarding Plato's concern about knowledge, we've said that asking a question doesn't obviously rely on the questioner knowing more than the questioned. In the case of Churchill's *Seven Jewish Children*, one question we might derive from the text could be: what would Israelis who support the Gaza War think when confronted with footage of children who have died as a result of this war? This is not an illegitimate question and there's no reason why someone would have to be qualified in any particular way to ask it. It may be, of course, that this is not the best question, or that it is merely one question among many, but clearly the playwright's supposed ignorance is no longer the problem. If Churchill is telling us what she thinks an Israeli parent would say, then we should ask her how on earth she knows that. But if she's asking us to think about what such a parent would say, or asking us what we think such a parent would say (if not that), then shutting down this question looks more difficult.

As well as avoiding Plato's concern – that playwrights don't know what they're talking about – the model of the political playwright as asking a particular question may also do something to answer the other concern that we had about political statements: namely, how do we know which statements are being made? Often, it's much easier to agree on what a playwright is asking us than it is to agree on what she is claiming to be true. And there's also more acceptable room for error. Churchill might, one suppose, consider it a failure on her part if she was attempting to convey a particular statement in her play and most spectators took her to be claiming the contrary. But 'getting it wrong', in the case of the question, wouldn't be such a disaster.

Another way of thinking about a political play would be as a kind of imperative, or order. Like a question, a sign that says 'Beware!' or 'Keep quiet!' is not exactly claiming any particular kind of knowledge. Like a question, an imperative is neither true nor false. Aeschylus' *Oresteia* trilogy gives a founding myth for an Athenian jury-court that works together with the goddess, Athena, and will serve the city of Athens for all time. The terrifying, wild 'Furies' (roughly, demons of vengeance) who have been pursuing Orestes are tamed and put into just service of the city. Aeschylus offers, according to one interpreter, an 'urgent plea for the avoidance of *stasis* [civil strife or civil war]' at a time when tensions were high, following the assassination of a prominent democratic reformer: Gods and citizens must work together for the preservation of civil harmony, although the details, of course, are left unspecified.[16] Needless to say, there's a great deal more to the *Oresteia* than the plea: don't let Athens be dragged into civil war! But when one recalls who would have been watching Aeschylus' trilogy – thousands of Athenian citizens, many of whom would be directly involved, in one way or another, in the troubles – this interpretation has a certain plausibility. To make this plea, and imperatives like it (Stop! Help!), one does not have to be an expert of any kind. The main qualification for whether such a plea is successful is, first of all, whether you have an audience at all and, second, whether that audience is well disposed in the right ways to do your bidding. (This relates to the performance just as much as to the text – see, for example, the discussion of 'Access', below.) Of course, discerning the particular imperative being made in a particular play text is hardly a simple matter, and many critics might want to disagree, say, with this interpretation of Aeschylus: perhaps the reliance on the divine intervention in the *Oresteia* suggests that the plea is not addressed to the human spectators but to the immortals? But a broader imperative is often implied in a political play text, which is easier to spot. The theatre, as we have seen, is originally the 'place for viewing'; hence, the imperative from the playwright is: 'Look at this!'

Just like questioning, demanding that attention be paid to something doesn't necessarily require prior knowledge or expertise (although doubtless that can help). If politics is partly about responding to the issues of the day, then making something an issue – demanding that people pay attention to it – is rightly considered political. Anybody who has been involved in administration of any kind, including political administration, knows that completely ignoring things is an important tool for ruling, directing or governing. Making things hard to ignore is thus a perfectly reasonable response from those who are ruled, directed and governed. So a play that purports to represent how peasants actually live – miserably, in filth – can raise awareness or draw attention to a social concern that would have been far from the mind of the average spectator; but even if the playwright in question didn't really know about the condition of the peasants, a play that presents a starkly different vision of how peasants actually live from what spectators are used to might motivate them to find out more. Thus, it might bring about more knowledge or more concern, even if it was written in ignorance.[17]

This is not to say, of course, that there's no such thing as a 'wrong' or faulty question or command. Questions can encode certain assumptions: the standard example is the prosecutor's question, 'When did you start beating your wife?', which rules out the possibility that the wife was never beaten. Blundered orders, in particular, can cause severe harm to those who obey them ('Charge for the guns!'). In both cases, we could well expect the questioner or commander to be able to justify what they have said in terms of some kind of knowledge. But in both of these cases, the harm done by the mistaken question or command is clear: a false conviction, perhaps, or the death of the soldiers. The theatre is neither a court of law nor a battlefield. We might, for all sorts of reasons, prefer the questions or demands of one play to those of another; my point is that, by moving away from thinking about the political play as *informing* us towards thinking about it as demanding certain kinds of attention or thought, we place different and perhaps less stringent demands on its creators. Playwrights may not deserve the authority to tell us about the world, but anyone can ask us to look or to think.

Politics in performances

We have been talking, so far, about political features of play texts. But, as I said at the start, discussions of political theatre must also look beyond the words, to the performances. There, *at* the theatre, we find a number of features that make theatrical performance a tool for political engagement. Given, as we have said, that political issues are highly context dependent, there may be little to be said that is completely general about relations between theatrical performances and politics. A Greek tragedy, organised by and performed in front of the citizens of Athens at a Dionysian festival, is obviously already not the same kind of event – political or otherwise – as a West End production of Shakespeare. The following categories and examples are intended to give a sense of some of the variety in question.

Location

A first thought looks to the theatre itself – the location of the performance – as a venue. Theatres typically gather large numbers of people together and unify their attention on a particular action or event. Such gatherings of people, as we have said, are de facto political in the broad sense. They also have the potential to be political in a narrower sense. The Greek example illustrates this neatly. There were two Athenian venues that had the capacity to hold thousands of citizens and enable them to focus on the speeches of just a few: the Theatre of Dionysus and the *ekklesia* (Assembly), in which democratic debate took place. Scholars have noted their comparable structure, capacity and, perhaps, spectators' seating arrangement.[18] One early Greek text on Athenian politics, the treatise of the so-called 'Old Oligarch', strongly connects the institution of comedy in particular with the process of democratic decision-making (to which he objects).[19]

Theatres in the later Greek world did, in fact, serve as venues for political debate and decision-making.[20] We find echoes of this in later eras: when English playhouses were closed in 1642, one cause was the Puritanism of parliament; but another was the fear of the 'lawless assembly'.[21]

Access and public expression

Theatre has traditionally been a place where powerful people – famous spectators or notables – can be seen and accessed by those who wouldn't normally have the chance. Obviously, this can be a vehicle for the display and reinforcement of political power, but it can also be an opportunity for the direct expression of dissatisfaction from the company or from the audience. As for the former: it has been suggested that the set-designs of the architect Inigo Jones were constructed so that only from the seat of the King could they be fully appreciated; other spectators would therefore be constantly reminded of their inferiority.[22] The tradition of having spectators sitting on the stage at French classical drama meant that arriving late at a theatrical performance could itself become an ostentatious performance. As for the latter: that the presence of powerful political figures can be an opportunity for the expression of dissatisfaction is shown, at the extreme, by a long tradition of high-profile political assassinations at theatres. Two of the most significant, in terms of their historical impact, are, first, the assassination of Philip II of Macedon at the theatre of Aegae in 336BC – which allowed his son, Alexander, to take control first of Macedon and then of the known world; and, second, the assassination of Abraham Lincoln in Ford's Theatre, Washington, D.C. at a performance of Taylor's *Our American Cousin*. Although the theatrical venues of these assassinations may seem insignificant, they point to a broader trend: theatres and theatrical performances have frequently offered access of various kinds to the rich and powerful. Criticism may therefore be expressed through the content of a particular play – as when a play performed in front of Charles I criticises absolutist monarchy.[23] A crowd can also express its approval or disapproval for a political figure in the audience, without the threat of being singled out and punished. Thus, according to Cicero, a particular line uttered by an actor and taken out of context – 'our misery has made you *great*' – could be taken by the crowd to be a criticism of the unpopular Pompey the Great and thus cheered and applauded.[24]

   Where a governing regime places severe restrictions on what can and can't be expressed in a public setting, the presence of a Pompey or of a Philip II is not required: simply the public expression of approval or disapproval amounts to something powerful and political. At performances of Chekhov's *Three Sisters* in Soviet-ruled Czechoslovakia, it was known for Masha's line, 'the army is leaving', to make the entire audience rise to its feet. In the context of the play, the departure of the soldiers from their small town is, to say the very least, not a cause for celebration in the eyes of Olga, Masha and Irina; it isn't meant to express the hope that an occupying military force will soon be on the way out. This very fact, however – that a line may be accidentally relevant and used to promote the group expression of a political sentiment – strikes me as an important part of the political power of theatre. It isn't just the intentions of the author in the carefully chosen words of the play text; nor is it the well-rehearsed scenes of the company. It's a gathering of people, often of strangers, drawn together and given the opportunity to think and to express themselves.[25]

The Chekhov anecdote also indicates two further features of theatrical performances that, in this context, we ought not to forget. The first is that political theatre needn't come from a new play – newly written, directly addressed to present political concerns. Churchill's play, of course, was all of those things; but the performance of *Three Sisters* was permitted precisely because Chekhov plays were considered part of a literary canon, thought to be in some way safe or approved by the Soviets. Safe, classic plays can turn into something political in virtue of the live performance. Indeed, a number of authoritarian governments have shown themselves reluctant to be seen to ban (say) Shakespeare or Chekhov, because that would make them seem barbaric; it's much easier to exclude or censor the work of living artists. The second point is that, compared with written, published literature (including, of course, play texts), theatrical performances are much harder to censor. One reason for this is that reading a text – if indeed there is one – gives only a partial sense of what a particular performance would be like. Puns, for example, are particularly easy to miss. According to one anecdote, a clown called Durov, performing in 1907, trained a pig to fetch a helmet (German: *Helm*). As the pig fetched the helmet, Durov would use ventriloquism to make the pig say 'I want helmet' (*'Ich will Helm'*); because, in German, 'I want helmet' sounds exactly like 'I [am] Wilhelm', audiences who began by laughing at a pig chasing a helmet suddenly found themselves laughing at calling the Kaiser a pig. Would a censor, looking at a text, have been able to pick this up?[26] Generally, of course, the same text can produce an infinite variety of performances. It's also extremely difficult to tell, just from reading it, how an audience might respond to a particular line ('the army is leaving'). When you add in effects of lighting, sound, vocal emphasis and so on, the text becomes a pretty poor guide to a performance. Elsom puts this nicely in his discussion of Cold War censorship: 'a line which looked innocent when read by the censors in Moscow took on a different meaning when played against a lighting change which turned the set blood red.'[27] Even sending a censor to a dress rehearsal of every performance – a time-consuming and expensive procedure – isn't guaranteed to pick up on what a large audience would respond to. Nor is there any guarantee, of course, that what the censor sees at the dress rehearsal will in fact be repeated at each performance, or that what he chooses to censor will in fact be left out. Compared with a print run, in which each copy is identical, the performances that make up a theatrical production show much more internal variation.[28]

Event

A final, but by no means less important consideration is that theatrical performances are themselves events and, as such, they can and frequently are locations for activity that would otherwise be illegal or impossible. This can be a feature of the *mimesis*: it has often been noted that the Theatre of Dionysus, in notable contrast to the Greek Assembly, gave a public 'voice' both to female characters and to slave characters, whose real-life counterparts would not in fact have had a chance to speak to an assembled audience of Greek citizens. Because the words uttered by these characters were written by male citizens and the actors who played these characters were male citizens, there is a question about how much of an anomaly or a liberation this really was.[29] Certainly, the traditional cries of mourning found in tragedies would not have been heard in any public setting other than the theatre.[30] Leaving the mimetic elements aside, though, theatre has often been the venue for public actions that, if not legitimised by the institution of theatre, would be illegal or at least highly provocative. We have already mentioned cases of spectators publically expressing political opinions in response to particular lines, taken out of context (as in the *Three Sisters* anecdote). In Shakespeare's time, dressing up like a king or a nobleman would have been a highly questionable, perhaps illegal act; actors, though, were exempt from such restrictions.[31] On contemporary public stages, it's often permissible for actors to smoke cigarettes, even though this would be banned in almost any equivalent public indoor gathering.[32] A more significant instance of this kind was the staging of *Othello* in apartheid South Africa, with a black actor playing Othello and a white actor playing Desdemona. A kiss between Othello and Desdemona – fully warranted in the text of the play – was also a kiss, in public, shared between a black man and a white woman. Certainly, outside the theatrical context, a public kiss between a black man and a white woman would have been provocative. It was recognised as such by spectators at the time, some of whom walked out at that moment.[33] Perhaps the most extreme example comes from the realm of performance art: in his performance piece, *Shoot*, Chris Burden was shot in the arm.

Brecht's political theatre

Up to this point, we've looked at some general ways in which theatre can interact with politics. This has been a piecemeal approach, taking examples from across the history of theatre in Ancient Greece, Rome, Tudor England, Soviet-ruled Czechoslovakia, Apartheid South Africa and twenty-first-century Britain. I've said that politics is specific to a time and a place, so a final account of politics and theatre won't be possible. Nonetheless, one playwright and theatre theorist has had an incomparable influence on the way we think about politics and theatre: Bertolt Brecht.[34] In developing his theories, Brecht combined his own political philosophy with an account of the contribution that the right kind of theatre can make to this project. To understand Brecht's political and artistic goals, it will help to begin with how he characterised his opponents.

Aristotelian drama

When Brecht tried to carve out a theoretical space for his theatrical practice, he found it helpful to contrast what he was aiming at with something he termed 'Aristotelian drama'.[35] Aristotle, of course, made a number of different claims about drama, and there is a question about whether it's really Aristotle who is the target of Brecht's criticisms, or the naturalistic techniques that were so popular in his time. In any case, three features of 'Aristotelian' drama seem salient to Brecht (although he doesn't always keep them apart). First, it presents the kind of stories in which the emotional responses of individual human beings provide the key moments of the drama, and other features of human life tend to be omitted or ignored. Thus, a typically 'Aristotelian' piece might have, in its climactic moment, an agonising and emotional decision for the main character. Thus, to use an example from a playwright active in Brecht's lifetime: should John Proctor (in Arthur Miller's *The Crucible*) lie to save his life or tell the truth and die? To get more of a sense of what Brecht might mean here, consider what a Hollywood biopic would do with the story of a famous political leader. One could easily imagine the complexities of political and social history sacrificed to more 'dramatic' elements: an inner, personal struggle against adversity; a battle against a childhood nemesis; a secret love story; a monumental decision. Brecht's view seems to be that this is true of much of the theatre of his time: it tends to ignore or simplify just those things it should be representing (complicated social and political states of affairs), whereas it emphasises just those things it should play down (personal, emotional struggle). In fact, he argues, to understand the contemporary world one must look far beyond such crude relations.[36]

A second element of the Aristotelian drama is that it takes itself to present universal truths – truths that hold for all people at all times. (One can find traces of this view in the *Poetics*, of course, in Aristotle's claims about poetry and universals.) Thus, once presented with purported universal, unchanging truths, the Aristotelian audience concludes that this is just the way things are for human beings, and there's nothing to be done about it: 'a few circumstances may vary, the environments are altered, but man remains unchanged.'[37] The result is resignation and inaction. Brecht's objections to this are philosophical: according to his Marxist view (about which more later), the central or most important truths about human beings change as their stage of technological development changes. Of course, human beings still eat and breathe and so on, but they hardly need theatre to tell them that; it's what's changed – the economy, industry, political structures – that matters. These changes have been brought about by human beings and could potentially be changed by human beings. To resign oneself to the universal, negative fate of 'human nature' is therefore to make a mistake. Genuine progress is possible: positive and negative.

One can see how these first two thoughts might relate in Brecht's view: the theatre he objects to turns everything into a matter of oversimplified emotional interactions and, therefore, makes it seem as though all people at all times face the same kinds of emotional dilemmas. We watch the play or film set in Ancient Rome and think to ourselves: they were just like us! If the Hollywood biopic were forced to spend more time on the specific, historical details then perhaps it wouldn't be able to reduce everything to the love story or the personal struggle.

The third feature of Aristotelian drama is empathy. 'Empathy', as many have noted, is hardly a clearly defined term and Brecht is not always unambiguous in the way he uses it. Broadly speaking, the kind of empathy that characterises the Aristotelian drama occurs when the spectator feels what the principal character feels. In doing so, she identifies with the situation of the principal character. Thus, each spectator at an Aristotelian performance of *Oedipus Tyrannus* is transformed into a little Oedipus and feels equally trapped in Oedipus' fate. This kind of empathy, Brecht sometimes suggests, is the single most important feature of the Aristotelian drama.[38]

For Brecht, all of these elements are related. They come together in the Aristotelian drama: the play simplifies human conflict, presenting it as an individual's emotional suffering at the hands of fate; absorbed in the action, I suffer the pains of the main character and imagine myself as that character; I conclude that this is just how life is and has always been and I feel pleasurably resigned to this fate. We have already suggested how the first two features might be connected (emotional simplification and universal truths). What about empathy? The connection between empathy and the first feature (reduction to emotional conflicts) is reasonably clear: however empathy works, it's going to be much easier to feel what the main character feels if his situation is familiar than if it is different from my own. I don't have a clear or intuitive sense of what social, economic or theological forces were at work among farm-workers, their wives and their daughters in seventeenth-century Salem, but I might know what it feels like to be torn between telling an upsetting truth and shamefully concealing it. So by minimising the former and highlighting the latter, Arthur Miller can write an emotionally powerful play.[39]

One might think, therefore, that the route between empathy (the third feature) and the presentation of universal truths (the second) would be via emotional simplification (the first). By simplifying dramatic situations such that emotional conflicts are at the fore, the playwright can make us empathise with the characters and also convince us that the situation of the characters and our own situation just is the human condition and there's nothing to be done about it. But Brecht's writing often suggests a more intimate connection between empathy and the conclusion that there are fixed, unalterable human conditions. This more direct connection between empathy and resignation or inaction in the face of universal truths is not so clear-cut. After all, empathy is often posited as a force for good, a spur to helping others. If I see someone hurt and, to some degree, feel the hurt that she feels, then I may be motivated to try to relieve her suffering (and my own). One might think that, without empathy, I would walk on by in blissful ignorance. Feeling someone's pain needn't mean completely and inescapably identifying with her and it might well be a spur to thinking critically about the situation she is in. In any case, there's no obvious reason to think that empathy, in this simple case, would lead to resignation or to the conclusion that humans suffer and there's nothing I can do about it.

One thought in Brecht's favour might be that, as in the case of Oedipus, the fate of the main character may be extremely well known; thus, to empathetically 'become' Oedipus (to identify with him and feel what he feels) just is to become trapped in a well-known and inescapable fate. Perhaps I'm more likely to believe that there are unchangeable, universal facts about man if I have imagined myself into and felt with someone who is trapped in an unchangeable, fated scenario. It's certainly true of Oedipus that there's nothing he can do to change his fate; perhaps, by feeling what he feels, I am more likely to imagine that the same is true about me. More generally: if theatre (particularly tragic theatre) tends to present people inevitably destroyed, no matter what they do, how good they are, and no matter what kind of social framework they inhabit, then perhaps repeated empathetic engagement with such characters would drill that message home. Nonetheless, the connection suggested here is pretty weak. Even Oedipus, one might suppose, could have done things differently – reacted with less suspicion, accepted his fate with more dignity. And, if this is what Brecht had in mind, then it's not exactly *empathy* that's the problem, but rather empathising with particular kinds of characters in particular kinds of plots, or drawing certain kinds of conclusions as a result of feeling what the characters feel. This, I think, is closer to Brecht's view: that empathy is a concern only when enmeshed with the other Aristotelian elements explored above, empathy as part of the ritual of conventional theatre. What, for him, are interconnected elements may in fact be separable. This does pose a challenge to the unity of his view.

A final, and possibly related, feature of Aristotelian drama is the behaviour and attitude of the audience. This seems to have had two features. First: the quiet, reverential audience. It is a curious historical fact that, probably around the start of the twentieth century, audiences began to become quieter and more reverential at theatrical performances. One suggested cause is the dimming of the house lights so that more attention could be focused on the stage (a trend Brecht was keen to reverse). Whatever the cause, Brecht clearly objected to the effect. A quiet, reverential audience might well be the kind of audience that would happily and submissively wait to have universal, unchanging truths thrust down its throat. Second: going under the spell. In the earlier discussion of theatrical illusion, I used the term 'going under the spell' to describe the state of an audience as it gets absorbed or lost in the action. One might think that going under the spell would be easier if in a darkened room, surrounded by other quiet, meek spectators – thus, there might be a connection between these two features of audience behaviour. In Brecht's view, going under the spell leads to a reduced capacity for critical thinking: 'they look at the stage as if in a trance: an expression which comes from the middle ages, the days of witches and priests'. What's more, Brecht clearly thinks that going under the spell enables empathy, thus connecting to some of the previous concerns.[40] Once again, though, to isolate Brecht's theoretical objection to 'illusion' would be to lose its connection to other elements of his view.

Epic theatre

To get a clearer picture of what Brecht objects to (and what he aims at correcting in his own work), it will be helpful to turn away from how he characterised his opponents (i.e. as Aristotelian) and towards how he characterised his own work. The various terms that Brecht used for his work – most notably the 'epic drama' (or 'epic theatre') and the 'theatre of the scientific age' – require some explanation before we can see why he thought they might be useful.[41] I'll begin with the 'epic drama'. To begin with, recall that the terms 'epic' and 'dramatic' describe, for the Greeks, two different styles of poetry: hence Plato's discussion of what makes dramatic (especially tragic) poetry distinctive, compared with epic. Epic poetry combines *mimesis* (roughly: imitation) with narration; dramatic poetry has no narration; it is pure *mimesis*. The epic is thus a story that is reported to its audience by a storyteller (or perhaps to its reader). The storyteller (or rhapsode) – the performer or reciter of the epic – isn't meant to be confused with the characters whose adventures he reports on, although he may do impressions of them at various points. But in dramatic poetry – and, by extension, in what Brecht terms the 'Aristotelian drama' – the actors are not 'telling' the story: they *are* the story. Thus, the actor playing Hamlet isn't best described as 'telling you the story of Hamlet'; that would imply a kind of separation between actor and character that, according to Plato's discussion, isn't possible.[42] For the purposes of the performance, the actor playing Hamlet just is Hamlet. The notion of an 'epic drama', then, is meant to sound contradictory at first glance, because one is supposed to think that the defining characteristic of a drama is such that it can't be an epic. This desired jarring effect has, of course, been lost – especially to modern, English-speaking students; but, once restored, we can see that it is a helpful term.[43] Brecht's productions are meant to put together these opposed modes of storytelling: he's doing drama as if it were an epic. Thus, actors both 'are' the characters and also 'report' on the characters as if in the third person (as would the rhapsode, telling the story of Odysseus). As Brecht puts it: 'the actor must not only sing but show a man singing'.[44]

Brecht doesn't want to abandon the dramatic mode altogether, so it's not that he just prefers the epic mode. Otherwise he would have written epics – which he didn't. On the contrary, he obviously thought that the dramatic elements were valuable, as long as they were combined with the epic elements in the appropriate ways. Seen this way, conventional theatre and epic theatre are not mutually exclusive modes of presentation: there is a spectrum running from the purely dramatic mode of presentation (character and actor are inseparable; no sense of third-person storytelling) to the purely epic mode, in which there is no dramatic action whatsoever. Brecht was keen to point out that his plays could use different techniques within this spectrum in different scenes, depending on what he felt was required.

In one of his most helpful essays on this subject, Brecht likens the techniques he is using to the techniques used by the eyewitnesses of a street accident, who are trying to explain what happened to some newcomers to the scene.[45] He suggests that his own theatre is much closer to the street scene than to conventional, Aristotelian theatre. The eyewitnesses are ultimately trying to get a certain point across – to explain what happened, how and why. Sometimes it may help them to act out elements of the accident; but, as they do so, they might explain what they are doing, what each thing represents and why. There is, therefore, a three-part relation: spectators (the newcomers); actors (the eyewitnesses); 'characters' (i.e. the real victims, who are no longer present). On the street, the distinction between all three will be evident to all concerned at all times.

When we look back to what Brecht objects to in so-called 'Aristotelian' drama, we can see that the differences between that and the street scene are significant for him. In the Aristotelian case, the gap between the actors and the characters is closed: the actor is the character. What's more, the role of empathy is, in a sense, to close the gap between the spectator and the character: via empathy, the spectator becomes Oedipus. What in the street scene is a relation between three viewpoints – victim, eyewitness/actor and newcomer/spectator – has been reduced to one. Brecht's most celebrated theatrical concept – the so-called 'alienation effect' – is a general label for a series of devices aimed at breaking up this unity between character, actor and spectator: devices including songs, actors directly addressing the audience, documentary projections.[46] In this light, it is better understood as an effect that makes the spectator, actor and character 'other' or foreign in relation to each other – thus preserving the distance between them. The actor will 'do all he can to make himself observed standing between the spectator and the event'.[47] It's not meant to make the spectator feel awkward or shocked – or, better, that's not the final goal; rather, it's meant to create an 'otherness' in two different directions: between the actor and the character; between the character and the spectator.

Think, for example, of how the newcomers (i.e. the audience) at the street scene would respond to the eyewitnesses (i.e. the actors). This differs from what one might expect of a typical (twentieth-century) audience member in both the respects identified above: first, the reverential silence of a typical, twentieth-century spectator would be unlikely and perhaps inappropriate; one would expect the newcomers to be asking questions, seeking to understand what was going on. If something didn't make sense in the explanation, one would expect them to say so. Second, the newcomers wouldn't sit back and get lost in the performance (what I termed going 'under the spell' in the discussion of theatrical illusion). They would be attentive, but they wouldn't lose sight of the point of the exercise, in a state of dream-like absorption. For Brecht, the 'epic' elements are clearly meant to undermine (which is not to say eliminate altogether) the spell, or absorbed illusion.

Epic elements of a performance might also be thought to counteract empathy. Recall the simplest case of empathy: I see someone hurting and I feel her pain. If empathy tends to be provoked by the *sight* of someone in pain, then reminding me that the person I am seeing is not in fact in pain – that she is an actress, or a storyteller – might be a way of blocking that empathetic response. With the empathetic response blocked, I may be able to take a more critical stance towards the performance: instead of becoming Oedipus and experiencing his sufferings, I am being told the story of Oedipus by a group of gifted storytellers and I am able to reflect upon it.

The theatre of the scientific age

A second term Brecht used for his new theatre was the 'theatre of the scientific age'. Again, some discussion may be helpful. Brecht considered his age 'scientific' in two senses, which are now so distinct that one would hardly imagine them together. Indeed, one of them would hardly be considered 'scientific' at all. The first sense is the one that is still typically used today: the scientific age was an age of great technological advancement. Brecht, after all, lived through both World Wars and saw the advent of the aeroplane, the cinema, and eventually the atom bomb. He was certainly conscious of the significance of such technological changes.[48] Brecht's view is clearly that theatre should keep up with science, in other words that it both make use of new pieces of technology (projection screens, new kinds of lighting, use of film as part of theatrical performance) and scientific research (statistics given to audience members). This accounts for his interest in science in the first sense.

Note, though, the German term for science, *Wissenschaft*, is much broader, and may be used for any organised body of scholarly knowledge or activity. And one of the intellectual approaches that counted as 'scientific' for Brecht – no less scientific than the physics behind the bomb – was Marxist economic and political theory. For as well as living through the invention of the aeroplane, he also lived through the Soviet revolution of 1917 and, like many, he came to see this as a kind of proof. Thus the theatre of a scientific age is also an appropriately Marxist theatre. Within this notion, there are two separate elements that it is helpful to disentangle. First of all, theatre may be 'scientific' in the sense that it should communicate the truths discovered by Marxist theory. Thus, a play might in various ways be able to set the record straight. Telling the truth – making true claims about how the world is – was explicitly part of the Brechtian project; and the most important truths he thought he could tell were those relating to 'the materialistic dialectic of economy and history'.[49] As we have seen, this is hardly uncomplicated in the context of a theatrical performance – as Brecht clearly recognised. It's hard enough to know what's true; one also has to communicate it in the appropriate way, to the appropriate people and so on. Plus, putting oneself in a position of the truth-teller suggests that one is in a position of superiority in relation to the audience – something that Brecht accepts, albeit in a qualified way. For that can't be all there is to it: one of the truths contained in Marxism – at least this is clearly Brecht's take on it – is that the governing ideas must be generated by the workers themselves. In other words, the plays can't just be a matter of telling the workers what they ought to think. Thus, a second feature of Marxist 'science' was the necessity of worker-guided action. Brecht sees his plays as helping to bring that about.[50] 'Science', then, was a matter of communicating certain truths and aiding certain kinds of actions. Aiding such actions meant not merely dictating facts to an audience (although there is no doubt that Brecht was willing to do so when he thought it necessary), but also asking the right kinds of questions to the right kinds of people – namely, the workers. Looking back to the distinctions made earlier in the chapter, Brecht clearly conceives of his plays as mixtures of statements, questions and commands. What is more, his focus on who the spectators are reflects a version of the concern with theatre as 'access', which we discussed above. After all, on Brecht's account, it's the workers who will come to take control; thus, getting access to a theatre full of worker-spectators gives the playwright an important kind of access. (One might wonder, as many did, why one had to exhort workers to achieve what was scientifically inevitable. This was a common problem – if not a theoretically unsolvable one – for many socialist thinkers of this era.)

Although I have tried to pull apart some of the notions that are wrapped up in the concept of a theatre for the 'scientific age', it is important to see that, for Brecht, they very much fit together. It's not, that is, that he was confusing natural science and speculative political philosophy, or trying to pass one off as the other; it's that, as far as he was concerned, they were intimately connected.[51] The workers find themselves in a new position relative to their capitalist employers, precisely because of the technological advances of the new era. Thus, in making plays more technologically advanced, Brecht brings before the workers the same technology that makes possible their liberation. (In doing so, he also takes himself to be counteracting a capitalist necessity – namely, to keep all matters of importance hidden from the workers.) Marxism, on his account, just was turning an appropriately scientific eye to the effects of modern technological development. His view, like those of many Marxist (and Hegelian) art theorists, is that art in some sense reflects the developmental stage of a society. What was true about Shakespearean England (in terms of its sociopolitical structure) is not true about Weimar Germany; thus, one would expect the art, including the theatre, to be different. If art has the function of communicating the truth about relations between people (as Brecht suggests it does) and those relations are characterised by new technology, then it isn't unreasonable for theatre to make use of that technology. And if theatre doesn't explore and represent those relations, then it risks becoming obsolete or irrelevant.[52]

The notions of the 'scientific' theatre and the 'epic' theatre thus point us in the direction of different features of Brechtian practice. His theatre is 'epic' in the sense that actors, to some degree, are 'telling' the story, not being the story; thus spectators (Brecht suggests) are less likely to get caught up in the action and go under the spell of the theatre. His theatre is scientific in relation to his political philosophy (the Marxist science of human relations) and his aesthetic practice (making use of technology).

The use of technology in the scientific theatre is meant to count against another of the objectionable features of the Aristotelian drama: namely, the reduction of complex social situations to simple, individual, emotional conflicts. By reminding the audience of new scientific facts, and also reminding them that so much scientific progress has been made, Brecht tries to prevent them from coming to universal (and false) conclusions about what it is to be human. Finally, of course, by communicating certain Marxist ideas to the spectators – notably about labour relations in capitalist societies – Brecht opens the way for the spectators to criticise what they see and suffer from outside the theatre, instead of passively accepting it as part of the human condition into which they have (via empathy) been drawn.[53]

In examining the implications of Brecht's terms – the epic theatre and the theatre for the scientific age – we have seen how he tries to challenge what he takes to be the objectionable features of the Aristotelian drama. Brecht's theatre (in theory, at least) does not reduce complex social scenarios to simplistic emotional conflict; it does not claim to communicate universal truths for all people at all time; it does not rely on empathy; it does not require a passive, respectful audience, half-dreaming under the spell of illusion.

Challenges to Brecht

Many of the claims that Brecht makes about the effects of Aristotelian versus epic theatre are open to debate. I have already highlighted one area of concern for Brecht's view: namely, the way he wants to connect empathy with the resigned acceptance of universal truths. There doesn't seem to be a strong enough link established between feeling what a certain character feels and concluding, in resignation, that what is happening to her is inevitable and a necessary feature of human existence. The flip-side of this criticism relates to Brecht's own work: if it's not the empathy that leads to uncritical acceptance of supposed universal truths, then why think that, by blocking empathy, the epic theatre will make its audiences more critical? Indeed, a common and not unreasonable criticism of Brecht is precisely that his plays don't offer much to stimulate critical thought and action in response to the problems presented. There are other elements of his theory that might lie open to challenge: even supposing empathy were the problem, do we agree that empathy is blocked by the epic mode? Epics (and their modern counterparts, novels) often give rise to empathetic responses, so there's no special reason to think that epic theatre should prevent empathy. It's clear, for example, that the rhapsodes (the reciters of epics) could get their audiences caught up in the action, doing much of what Brecht seems to want to avoid.[54]

Many of the concerns that were discussed in relation to theatre and politics in general also relate, of course, to Brecht's views. Unsurprisingly, he was frequently criticised for didacticism, for using art to communicate political messages rather than for other, supposedly more lofty ends. His response came partly from his philosophical views and partly from his views about art. First of all, he argued, as many politically active artists have argued, that supposedly 'apolitical' art is, in fact, conservative art. Brecht never lost sight of the fact that, as we have said, a theatrical performance is already a political event of some kind. When a group of people are gathered together, focusing their attention, listening and thinking, those in charge of what they see and hear (the playwright and company) are already making a political decision. If they choose not to make an overt political statement, then this opting-out is a form of conservatism.[55] Second, Brecht sought to defend himself against the claim that didactic theatre is inferior because it is less entertaining. This is a claim one still hears today, not always without reason. Again, Brecht's defence appealed to his Marxism. The choice between either learning something or enjoying yourself – the idea that it was strictly one or the other – was, he thought, a product of a capitalist attitude to education. According to this attitude, one learns enough to compete on the market; but, once on the market, learning has a negative association, because needing to learn is equivalent to not being a competitive product. Compare the company that boasts that its forthcoming product will have new and exciting safety features with the company that recalls its current product for safety updates.

This leads us, of course, to a more pressing and central charge: namely, that many of the Marxist assumptions behind Brecht's writings have been shown to be false. There is no doubt that this is the case – at least, by any reasonable standard. For not only was Brecht a Marxist; his Marxism was of a particularly utopian kind; his faith in a glorious time soon to come for the emancipated workers (especially one beginning with the Bolshevik Revolution) is often enough a cause for embarrassment to the modern reader, as well as nostalgia for a time when such views were not confined to a dwindling, fanatic minority. Indeed, Brecht's views were attacked by contemporary Marxists at least as vehemently as by non-Marxists.

Theodor Adorno, for example, offers a cluster of criticisms of Brecht: that he is too simplistically utopian; that he is arrogant and wrong to think that he could explain or represent the complexities of contemporary life with any kind of accuracy or significance; that instructing audiences to act upon such representations is therefore irresponsible and liable, in a corrupted world, to lead to disaster if indeed it leads to anything at all.[56]

For modern readers and theatregoers, the question remains what to make of Brecht after the fall of communism. There is no doubt that many of Brecht's theatrical techniques stand alone as aesthetic developments, which can be used with or without any commitments to Brecht's political programme. A company can do an 'epic' production of *Hedda Gabler* without giving any reasons why; and that production can be a significant aesthetic achievement.[57] What's more, there's plenty of evidence that Brecht's theories didn't actually inform his practice as much as he might have suggested.[58] Many of Brecht's innovations were already favoured by him before his full commitment to the Marxist cause. Finally, one can question whether his performances ever really had the effect that he desired and sometimes claimed on their behalf. A contemporary review of one performance of *The Mother* described it as 'a field-day for the like-minded [...] but idiotic for the outsider'.[59] Elsom describes the opening of a Brecht production of *The Caucasian Chalk Circle* as follows:

> The proscenium arch was apparently made of solid marble but, as the lights rose, that frame seemed to dissolve and [the spectator] saw through the pillars, which were made of gauze, to the wings [...]. At a stroke, Brecht sent out three signals – that there would be no attempt to sustain a naturalistic illusion, that bourgeois pretensions were gossamer-thin and that fantasies of empire were sustained by the working classes, who could say no.[60]

One may sincerely doubt whether any but the 'like-minded' would have been able to interpret Brecht's signals, based on this performance alone.

With all of this in mind, one can perhaps construct a counterfactual Brecht who never got distracted by Marx, and stuck to writing plays and poems. Brecht commentator Eric Bentley, who worked with Brecht for a while, prefers to see him in this light: as a one-off artistic genius, who should be remembered not for his theories, but for his poems, plays and theatrical techniques, as well as for his insights into human nature. The latter is particularly ironic, as Bentley no doubt realises, because, as we have seen, Brecht *particularly* wanted to avoid giving the impression that he was offering insights into human nature. Bentley describes teaching a class on Brecht:

> Before we even began, the students were throwing technical terms at me that they had picked up from old Brechtians or from the Meister's own

essays [...] I told them a story I thought was well known, though they hadn't heard it. Back in the early twenties, Brecht's plays were not getting much attention. "What you need," a friend told him, "is a theory. To make your stuff important." So Brecht went home and got himself a theory, which now is known to more people than are the plays.[61]

Bentley is just one among several critics who take Brecht's better-known and more successful plays to be bad examples (even refutations) of his theory – indeed, this view may represent the considered opinion of many theatre theorists and historians. The analysis of Brecht's individual plays cannot be undertaken here.[62] However, I would like to warn against one common criticism: it is often claimed – mistakenly – that Brecht is anti-emotion, that he doesn't want his audiences, or indeed his actors, to feel anything, but rather to think and criticise. Thus, emotionally charged scenes in Brecht's plays – of which there are plenty – are taken to be failures or relapses. But this criticism represents a misunderstanding of Brecht's position, as he himself remarks.[63] What he wants is informed action on the part of spectators, aided by actors. Sometimes, this requires critical thought; sometimes, it might require making them feel a certain way. Brecht is happy to use either or both.[64] What really concerns him, as we have seen, is a kind of unthinking empathy, which, on his view, leads to resignation and inaction. There are plenty of grounds for criticism on that score – some of which we have discussed – but his suspicions of empathy should not be mistaken for a desire to cut feeling out of the spectator's experience.

Conclusion

Because of the shifting nature of politics, any far-reaching analysis of political theatre will have to consider the relationship between politics and theatre at particular times and places. Nonetheless, we began this chapter by trying to draw some general distinctions that might help to map out the territory, looking first of all at the various meanings of 'politics' and then some of the ways that play texts and theatrical performances may have political import. Brecht's theories – like those of many of the philosophers we examined – cannot ultimately offer what they claim to, especially in the light of historical developments during and after Brecht's lifetime. But what we can see, even from our brief discussion, is something of why Brecht has remained so influential. What he offered was not merely a new critique of contemporary theatrical practice – a critique that has been likened in influence and to some extent in content to that of Plato; he also offered a vision for a new kind of theatre that would combat these effects, which combined developments in technology and in philosophical thinking; *and* he worked hard and experimented, trying to bring such a theatre about. This is an intoxicating mixture, the possibility of which had not been known before, and Brecht's attempt to realise it, despite his failings, has not been rivalled since.

Further Reading: Collective Action

For reasons we have discussed, studies of theatre and politics often focus on particular times and places. On the relationship between Greek theatre and politics, see various essays in Easterling (1997) and Winkler and Zeitlin (1990), while Halpern (2011) offers an excellent critical account of some recent attempts to think about the Greeks, theatre and democracy; Butler (1987) examines theatre under Charles I on the eve of the Civil War; McConachie (2006) gives a historical overview of political theatre from 1920 to 1970, including a case study of Brecht directing *Mother Courage*; Kershaw (1992) looks at post-war British political theatre. On theatre and political theory in general, Kottman (2008) is an ambitious and, in places, quite difficult attempt to establish the notion of the 'dramatic scene' as a fundamental political category. A selection of Brecht's writings on theatre are collected in Brecht (1964), although this certainly does not contain everything of interest. Jameson (1980) collects and presents theoretical writings on art and politics by Brecht and his peers, including Adorno and Lukács. Benedetti (2005: 183–220) features accounts of Brechtian practice from those who worked with him – a useful counterweight to the more theoretical approaches. Sacks and Thomson (1994) offers a good selection of scholarly essays.

Notes

1   Churchill (2009).
2   'Seven Jewish Children', the *Guardian*, 11 February, 2009; 'The Stone and Seven Jewish Children: A Play for Gaza', *Sunday Times*, 15 February, 2009.
3   Piscator was, amongst other things, Brecht's teacher and collaborator; his influence on the development of Brecht's ideas is unparalleled.
4   Arendt (1958: 188); see also Kottman (2008: 23–5 and 116–7); Halpern (2011). Unrelated to Arendt's remark, Bentley expresses a similar thought about the significance of dialogue: 'Talking involves the whole man, and talk between persons involves the whole society.' (1964: 73)
5   Wiles (1995: 90–1).
6   Curiously, this has done equally little to subdue political philosophers or to damage this conception of their purpose.
7   See Prentki and Preston (2009).
8   From 'The Depressed Person', *Harpers Magazine*, January 1998, p. 60.
9   Lennard and Luckhurst (2002: 104); Balme (2008: 180–1).
10   Quoted in Carlson (1993: 239).
11   Quoted in Bentley (2008: 253).

12 This example was taken from Cartledge (1997), which contains many others related to tragedy. It's clear that Greek comedy offered as much if not more direct social commentary. For a helpful analysis, see Henderson (1990).

13 Holland and Patterson (1995: 276).

14 See Plato's *Apology* for Socrates' description of his philosophical method; see Plato's *Meno* for his conversation with Anytus. Socrates' argument is that politicians, if they know how to act well, would be able to teach others to do so; and they would undoubtedly make a priority of teaching this valuable knowledge to their children; but the children of the best politicians are often foolish; so obviously politicians don't know how to teach what it is that they're so good at; so they don't really know what they're doing.

15 For Butler (1987), they were frequently highly critical of the king. See e.g. Butler (1987: 24, 44).

16 Cartledge (1997: 24).

17 This example is taken from Ziolkowski's account of the 1889 premiere of Hauptmann's *Vor Sonnenaufgang*, which depicted peasants living in squalor at a time when Socialist meetings were banned by law. See Ziolkowski (2009: 38–48). In Ziolkowski's view, Hauptmann did present something of the reality of peasant life and ultimately had an effect on government policy.

18 Winkler (1990: 22); Halpern (2011: 545).

19 See Henderson (1990).

20 Wiles (1995: 56); Halpern (2011: 555).

21 Thomson (1995: 203).

22 Lennard and Luckhurst (2002: 86).

23 See e.g. Butler (1987: 35–42).

24 Wiles (1995: 56).

25 The *Three Sisters* incident is described in Brown (1995: 522). See Elsom (1992: 78) for similar accounts of unusual and prolonged applause for the death of Hastings at a performance of Richard III in Soviet-era Poland. The anonymity provided by the darkness of the auditorium – something, as we shall see, that bothered Brecht – may also be a factor here.

26 Kershaw (1992) pp. 1–2. It's unlikely, of course, that Durov would have provided a 'text' in the first place.

27 Elsom (1992: 81).

28 See Chapter 1. This goes some way to explaining the particular attention given to theatre by censors in various different regimes. For a helpful overview of theatre censorship, see Stephens (1995).

29 Also, note that male Athenian citizens were almost never represented as characters on stage, even although they held all the power; so perhaps this isn't a good measure. See Hall (1997) for discussion.

30 Halpern (2011: 561).

31 Thomson (1995: 180).

32 My thanks to Gabriel Doctor for this example.

33 'Othello' causes stir in Johannesburg Theater', *Chicago Tribune*, October 29, 1987. Lennard and Luckhurst (2002: 211) go further, suggesting that the kiss may also have been illegal.

34 This influence is very much still with us. To take one anecdotal example: in a review of recently published books on philosophy and theatre, I noted that, although they generally had very little in common, all of the reviewed books included discussions of Brecht.

35 See e.g. Brecht (1964: 57, 60, 87). Brecht uses the term 'drama' broadly, and it's clear that his plays must count as 'dramas' under any usual understanding of that term; he certainly referred to his work, on occasions, as 'epic drama' (1964: 45). But he also uses the adjective 'dramatic' as a synonym for 'Aristotelian' in his particular sense – i.e. he wants to contrast his own 'epic' theatre with traditional 'dramatic' theatre (1964: 37).

36 See Brecht (1964: 70, 77); see also Brecht (1980: 76–9). Brecht (1964) is collection of many of Brecht's most important theoretical writings. For convenience, I'll refer to this edition where possible.

37 Brecht (1964: 97).

38 Brecht (1964: 87, 91).This is broadly what Woodruff terms 'fantasy identification' (2008: 176), which he takes to be the key concern lying behind Brecht's objections to empathy. The idea that the spectator becomes Oedipus is still a popular view – see e.g. Nehamas (1992).

39 I am using Miller's play by way of example. But Miller obviously had some contemporary political targets in mind when he wrote *The Crucible*.

40 Brecht (1964: 187); see also (1964: 27, 44).

41 The meaning of some of Brecht's preferred terms for his theatrical practice changed over time, as did the terms themselves, as did the practice itself. What I offer is an overview of what I take to be the most central and long-standing elements. No doubt that this account is simplified. Bradley (2006), for example, carefully traces how his theory and practice changed in relation to one play (*The Mother*).

42 Note that Brecht doesn't think that people *really* get confused between the actor and the character; he just thinks that character–actor identity is a kind of ideal in 'Aristotelian' drama.

43 The first time I taught Brecht, I began by asking what made something 'epic'. The two answers I got were: it has to be 'really long' and 'awesome'.

44 Brecht (1964: 44–5).

45 The essay is called 'The Street Scene: A Basic Model for an Epic Theatre'; see Brecht (1964: 121–9).

46 Brecht (1964: 125–6).

47 Brecht (1964: 58).

48 See, e.g., Brecht (1964: 67, 184).

49 See Brecht (1966: 136).

50 Brecht (1966: 137).

51 See in particular his 'Short Organum for the Theatre', sections 16–23, reprinted in Brecht (1964).

52 See Brecht (1964: 67, 121). Hegel's view, roughly, was that art could no longer perform the function of representing, explaining and embodying this kind of information and thus it has become, in an important sense, obsolete.

53 Brecht (1964: 70–71).

54 See Plato's *Ion*, in which Socrates converses with a rhapsode.

55 Brecht (1964: 196).

56 See, e.g., Adorno (1980). Partly, of course, such criticisms come from Adorno's own Marxist views, which were even more idiosyncratic than Brecht's.

57 For how they might: Hamilton (2007: 44–5). Mumford (2009: 130–65) offers practical 'Brechtian' exercises.

58 See e.g. Brecht (1964: 243). For accounts and discussions of Brechtian practice, based on the experience of actors, see Benedetti (2005: 183–220) and Eddershaw (1994).

59 Quoted in Brecht (1964: 61).

60 Elsom (1992: 38).

61 Bentley (2008: 10).

62 For a selection of essays on particular plays, see Sacks and Thomson (1994).

63 E.g. Brecht (1964: 145, 227).

64 What Brecht demanded from his actors seems to have changed over time, as one would expect from an experimental theatre practitioner. But it's clear that actors, like spectators, were permitted or even encouraged to engage emotionally with the characters and plot as part of their preparation for the role. See Rouse (1995) for discussion.

Bibliography

Adorno, T (1980) 'Commitment' in Jameson, F. (ed.) *Aesthetics and Politics*. London: Verso, 1980, pp. 177–195.

Aeschylus (1961) *Prometheus and Other Plays*, trans. P. Vellacott, London: Penguin.

D'Alembert (2004) 'Geneva' and 'Letter of M. D'Alembert to M. J. J. Rousseau' trans. Bloom, Butterworth and Kelly in *Jean-Jacques Rousseau: Letter to D'Alembert and Writings for the Theatre.*, Hanover and London: University Press of New England.

Arendt, H. (1958) *The Human Condition*, Chicago, IL: University of Chicago Press.

Aristotle (2004) *The Nicomachean Ethics*, trans. J. A. K. Thomson, London: Penguin.

——(1996) *Poetics*, trans. M Heath, London: Penguin.

——(1991) *The Art of Rhetoric*, trans. H. C. Lawson-Tancread, London: Penguin.

Artaud, A. (2010) *The Theatre and its Double*, trans. V. Corti, Richmond: Oneworld Classics.

Augustine (2008) *Confessions*, trans. Henry Chadwick, Oxford: Oxford University Press.

Auslander, P. (1999) *Liveness: Performance in a Mediatized Culture*, London: Routledge.

Balme, C. (2008) *The Cambridge Introduction to Theatre Studies*, Cambridge: Cambridge University Press.

Barish, J. (1981) *The Anti-Theatrical Prejudice*, Berkeley, CA: University of California Press.

Barthes, R. (1981) 'The discourse of history', trans. S Bann, *Comparative Criticism* 3, pp. 7–20.

Beardsley, M. (1981) *Aesthetics: Problems in the Philosophy of Criticism*, Indianapolis, IN: Hackett.

Beardsmore, R. (1971) *Art and Morality*, London: Macmillan.

Belfiore, E. (1984) 'A Theory of Imitation in Plato's Republic', *Transactions of the American Philological Association*, 114, pp. 121–146.

Benedetti, J. (2005) *The Art of the Actor*, London: Methuen.

Benjamin, W. (2007) 'The Work of Art in the Age of Mechanical Reproduction', trans. H. Zohn in *Illuminations*, New York: Schocken Books, pp. 217–251.

Bentley, E. (2008) *Bentley on Brecht*, Evanston, IL: Northwestern University Press.

——(1964) *The Life of the Drama*, New York: Atheneum.

Bial, H. (ed.) (2004) *The Performance Studies Reader*, London: Routledge.

Blanning, T. (2007) *The Pursuit of Glory: Europe 1648–1815*, London: Penguin.

Boal, A. (1995) 'Forum Theatre' in P. Zarrilli (ed.) *Acting (Re)Considered*, London: Routledge, pp. 251–261.

Booth, M. (1995) 'Nineteenth-Century Theatre' in J. Brown (ed.) *The Oxford Illustrated History of Theatre*, Oxford: Oxford University Press.

Bradley, L. (2006) *Brecht and Political Theatre*, Oxford: Clarendon Press.

Brecht, B. (1980) 'Against Georg Lukács' in F. Jameson (ed.) *Aesthetics and Politics*. London: Verso, pp. 68–85.

——(1966) 'Writing the truth: five difficulties' trans. Richard Winston, reprinted as 'Appendix A' in B. Brecht, *Galileo*, E. Bentley (ed.), New York: Grove Press, 1966.

——(1964) *Brecht on Theatre*, London: Methuen.

Brinker, M. (1977) 'Aesthetic Illusion', *The Journal of Aesthetics and Art Criticism*, 36:2, pp. 191–196.

Brock, S. (2007) 'Fictions, Feelings, and Emotions', *Philosophical Studies*, Vol. 132: 2, pp. 211–242.

Brockett, O. and Hildy, F. (2010) *History of the Theatre*, Tenth Edition (International), Boston, MA: Pearson.

Brook, P. (2008) *The Empty Space*, London: Penguin.

Brown, J. (1995) 'Theatre after 1970' in J. Brown (ed.) *The Oxford Illustrated History of Theatre*, Oxford: Oxford University Press, pp. 499–535.

Bruisov, V. (2001) 'Against Naturalism in the Theater' in B. Cardullo and R. Knopf (eds) *Theater of the Avant-Garde, 1890–1950: An Anthology*, New Haven, CT: Yale University Press.

Büchner, G. (1993) *Danton's Death* in *Complete Plays, Lenz and Other Writings*, trans. J. Reddick, London: Penguin.

——(2006) *Werke und Briefe*, Munich: Deutscher Taschenbuch Verlag.

Budd, M. (1995) *Values of Art: Pictures, Poetry and Music*, London: Penguin.

Burke, E. (1998) *A Philosophical Enquiry*, Oxford: Oxford University Press.

Burnyeat, M. (1999) 'Culture and Society in Plato's *Republic*' in G. Peterson (ed.) *The Tanner Lectures on Human Values*, vol. 20, Salt Lake City, UT: University of Utah Press.

Butler, M. (1987) *Theatre and Crisis 1632–42*, Cambridge: Cambridge University Press.

Cain, R. (2012) 'Plato on Mimesis and Mirrors', *Philosophy and Literature* 36, pp. 187–195.

Carlson, M. (1993) *Theories of Theatre: A historical and critical survey, from the Greeks to the Present*, Ithaca, NY: Cornell University Press.

Carroll, N. (1990) 'Interpretation, History and Narrative', *The Monist*, 73.

——(2001) 'Art, Narrative and Moral Understanding' in J. Levinson (ed.) *Aesthetics and Ethics: Essays at the Intersection*. Cambridge: Cambridge University Press, pp. 126–160.

Cartledge, P. (1997) '"Deep Plays": Theatre as process in Greek civic life' in P. Easterling (ed.) *The Cambridge Companion to Greek Tragedy*. Cambridge: Cambridge University Press. pp. 3–35.

De Certeau, M. (1988) *The Writing of History*, New York: Columbia University Press.

Chekhov, A. (1980) *Uncle Vanya* in *Five Plays*, trans. Ronald Hingley, Oxford: Oxford University Press.

Churchill, C (2009) *Seven Jewish Children*, London: Nick Hern Books.

Collingwood, R. (1994) *The Idea of History (Revised Edition)*, J van der Dussen (ed.), Oxford: Oxford University Press.

Craig, E. G. (1911) 'The Actor and the Über-Marionette' in his *On the Art of the Theatre*, London: William Heinemann.

Currie, G. (1995) *Image and mind: film, philosophy and cognitive science*, Cambridge: Cambridge University Press.

Dancy, J. (1995) 'Arguments From Illusion', *The Philosophical Quarterly* Vol. 45, No. 181 (1995), pp. 421–438.

Danto, A. (1965) *Analytic Philosophy of History*, Cambridge: Cambridge University Press.

Day, M. (2008) *The Philosophy of History*, London: Continuum.

Diamond (1982) 'Anything but argument?' *Philosophical Investigations* 5:1, pp. 23–41.

Diderot, D. (1936) *Diderot's Writings on the Theatre*, Cambridge: Cambridge University Press.

Dorsen, A. (2010) *Hello Hi There*, available online at: http://www.anniedorsen. com/showproject.php?id=6. Accessed July 2013.

Easterling, P. (ed.) (1997) *The Cambridge Companion to Greek Tragedy*, Cambridge: Cambridge University Press.

Eddershaw, M. (1994) 'Actors on Brecht' in G. Sacks and P. Thomson (eds) *The Cambridge Companion to Brecht*, Cambridge: Cambridge University Press, pp. 278–96.

Eldridge, R. (2003) *An Introduction to the Philosophy of Art*, Cambridge: Cambridge University Press.

Else, G. (1957) *Aristotle's Poetics*, Cambridge, MA: Harvard University Press.

Elsom, J. (1992) *Cold War Theatre*, London: Routledge.

Ferrari, G. (ed.) (2007) *The Cambridge Companion to Plato's Republic*, Cambridge: Cambridge University Press.

Feagin, S. (1983) 'The Pleasures of Tragedy', *American Philosophical Quarterly*, 20, pp. 95–104.

Fine, G. (1993) *On Ideas: Aristotle's Criticism of Plato's Theory of Forms*, Oxford: Oxford University Press.

Fogle, R. (1960) 'Coleridge on Dramatic Illusion', *The Tulane Drama Review*, Vol. 4, No. 4 (May, 1960), pp. 33–44.

Frayn, M. (2010) *Plays: 4*, London: Methuen Drama.

Frede, D. (1992) 'Necessity, Chance and "What happens for the most part"' in A. Rorty (ed.) *Essays on Aristotle's Poetics*, Princeton, NJ: Princeton University Press.

Freud, S. (1961) *The Interpretation of Dreams*, trans. James Strachey, London: George Allen & Unwin.

Friend, S. (2007) 'The Pleasures of Documentary Tragedy', *British Journal of Aesthetics*, 47:2.

Gale, R. (1971?)'The Fictive Use of Language', *Philosophy* vol. 46, pp. 324–340.

Gardner, S. (2003) 'Tragedy, Morality and Metaphysics' in S. Gardner and J. L. Bermúdez (eds) *Art and Morality* (2003), London: Routledge, pp. 218–259.

Gendler, T. (2003) 'Pretense and Belief' in M. Kieran and D. Lopes (eds) *Imagination, Philosophy and the Arts*, London: Routledge.

Geuss, R. (1999) 'Introduction' to F. Nietzsche, *The Birth of Tragedy*, trans. R. Speirs, Cambridge: Cambridge University Press.

——(2005) *Outside Ethics*, Princeton, NJ: Princeton University Press.

Goffman, E. (1956) *The Presentation of the Self in Everyday Life*, Edinburgh: University of Edinburgh, Social Sciences Research Centre.

Golden, L. (1973) 'The Purgation Theory of Catharsis', *Journal of Aesthetics and Art Criticism*, 31, pp. 473–9.

Gombrich, E. (1978) *Meditations on a Hobby Horse*, London: Phaidon.

——(2002) *Art and Illusion*, London: Phaidon.

Grotowski, J (1969) *Towards a Poor Theatre*, London: Methuen.

Hall, E. (1997) 'The Sociology of Athenian Tragedy' in P. Easterling (ed.) *The Cambridge Companion to Greek Tragedy*, Cambridge: Cambridge University Press, pp. 36–53.

Halliwell, S. (1986) *Aristotle's Poetics*, Chicago, IL: University of Chicago Press.

——(2002) *The Aesthetics of Mimesis: Ancient Texts and Modern Problems*, Princeton, NJ: Princeton University Press.

——(2007) 'The Life-and-Death Journey of the Soul: Interpreting the Myth of Er' in G. R. F. Ferrari (ed.) *The Cambridge Companion to Plato's Republic*, Cambridge: Cambridge University Press.

Halpern, R. (2011) 'Theater and Democratic Thought: Arendt to Rancière', *Critical Inquiry* Vol. 37, No. 3, Spring 2011, pp. 545–572.

Hamilton, C. (2003) 'Art and Moral Education' in S. Gardner and J. L. Bermúdez (eds) *Art and Morality* (2003), London: Routledge, pp. 37–55.

Hamilton, J. (1982) '"Illusion" and the Distrust of Theater', *The Journal of Aesthetics and Art Criticism*, Vol. 41, No. 1, pp. 39–50.

——(2007) *The Art of Theater*, Oxford: Blackwell Publishing.

Haslanger, A. (2011) 'What happens when pornography ends in marriage: the uniformity of pleasure in *Fanny Hill*', *English Literary History* Vol. 78:1, pp. 163–188.

Heath, M. (1996) 'Introduction' in Aristotle's *Poetics* trans. M. Heath, London: Penguin, pp. vii–lxvii.

Hegel, G. (1977) *The Phenomenology of Spirit*, trans. A. V. Miller, Oxford: Oxford University Press.

——(1993) *Introductory Lectures on Aesthetics* trans. B. Bosanquet, London: Penguin.

Heller, A. (2002) *The Time is Out of Joint: Shakespeare as Philosopher of History*, Lanham, MD: Rowman & Littlefield Publishers.

Henderson, J. (1990) 'The *Dēmos* and Comic Competition' in J. Winkler and I. Zeitlin (eds) *Nothing to do with Dionysus?*, Princeton: Princeton University Press, pp. 20–62.

Herodotus (2007) *The Histories* trans. A. Purvis, New York: Pantheon Books.

Hobbes, T. (1822) *The History of the Grecian War, Written by Thucydides*, London: Whittaker, Parker and Bliss.

——(1994) *Human Nature and De Corpore Politico*, Oxford: Oxford University Press.

Holland, P. and Patterson, M. (1995) 'Eighteenth-Century Theatre' in J. Brown (ed.) *The Oxford Illustrated History of Theatre*, Oxford: Oxford University Press, pp. 255–98.

Horace (1995) *Ars Poetica* trans. L. Golden in L. Golden and O. B. Hardison (eds) *Horace for Students of Literature: The Ars Poetica and its Tradition*. Gainesville, FL: University Press of Florida, pp. 7–23.

Hoy, J. (2009) 'Hegel, *Antigone* and Feminist Critique: The Spirit of Ancient Greece' in K. R. Westphal (ed.) *The Blackwell Guide to Hegel's Phenomenology of Spirit*, Oxford: Wiley-Blackwell, pp. 172–189.

Huhn, T. (2004) *Imitation and Society: The Persistence of Mimesis in the Aesthetics of Burke, Hogarth and Kant*, University Park, PA: Pennsylvania State University Press.

Hume, D. (1965) 'Of Tragedy' in *Of The Standard of Taste and Other Essays*, London: Bobbs-Merrill.

Jacobson, D. (1997) 'In Praise of Immoral Art', *Philosophical Topics*, Vol. 25: 1, pp. 155–199.

Jameson, F. (ed.) (1980) *Aesthetics and Politics*, London: Verso.

Janaway, C. (ed.) (1998) *Willing and Nothingness: Schopenhauer as Nietzsche's Educator*, Oxford: Clarendon Press.

Janko, R. (1992) 'From Catharsis to the Aristotelian Mean' in A. Rorty (ed.) *Essays on Aristotle's Poetics*, Princeton, NJ: Princeton University Press.

Jones, E. (1949) *Hamlet and Oedipus*, London: Victor Gollanz.

Kershaw, B. (1992) *The Politics of Performance: Radical Theatre as Cultural Intervention*, London: Routledge.

Kierkegaard, S. (1992) *Either/Or: A Fragment of Life* trans. A. Hannay, London: Penguin.

Kirby, M. (1995) 'On acting and not-acting' in P. Zarrilli (ed.) *Acting (Re)Considered,* London: Routledge, pp. 43–58.

Kleist, H. (1978) 'Über das Marionettentheater' in (1978) *Werke und Briefe*, Berlin und Weimar: Aufbau-Verlag.

Kottman, P. (2008) *A Politics of the Scene*, Stanford, CA: Stanford University Press.

Lamarque, P. and Olsen, S. (1994) *Truth, Fiction and Literature*, Oxford: Clarendon Press.

Lear, J. (1992) 'Katharsis' in A. Rorty (ed.) *Essays on Aristotle's Poetics*, Princeton, NJ: Princeton University Press.

——(2006) 'Allegory and Myth in Plato's *Republic*' in G. Santas (ed.) *The Blackwell Guide to Plato's Republic*, Oxford: Blackwell, pp. 25–43.

Lennard, J. and Luckhurst, M. (2002) *The Drama Handbook: A Guide to Reading Plays*, Oxford: Oxford University Press.

Lessing, G. (1962) *Hamburg Dramaturgy* trans. H. Zimmerman, London: Dover Publications.

Levinson, J. (ed.) (2001) *Aesthetics and Ethics: Essays at the Intersection*, Cambridge: Cambridge University Press.

Lopes, D. (2003) 'Out of Sight, Out of Mind' in M. Kieran and D. Lopes (eds) *Imagination, Philosophy and the Arts*, London: Routledge.

Lukács, G. (1983) *The Historical Novel*, trans. H. and S. Mitchell, Lincoln, NE: University of Nebraska Press.

——(1971) *History and Class Consciousness*, trans. R. Livingstone, London: The Merlin Press.

Mason, J. (1982) *The Irresistible Diderot*, London: Quartet Books.

McCollom, W. (1947) 'Illusion in Poetic Drama', *The Journal of Aesthetics and Art Criticism*, Vol. 5, No. 3 (Mar., 1947), pp. 183–188.

McConachie, B. (2006) 'Theatres for reform and revolution, 1920–1970' in G. Williams (ed.) *Theatre Histories*, London: Routledge, pp. 425–56.

Mink, L. (1970) 'History and Fiction as Modes of Comprehension', *New Literary History*, Vol. 1, No. 3, pp. 541–558.

Moss, J. (2007) 'What is Imitative Poetry and Why is it Bad?' in G. R. F. Ferrari (ed.) *The Cambridge Companion to Plato's Republic*, Cambridge: Cambridge University Press.

Mumford, M. (2009) *Bertolt Brecht*, London: Routledge.

Nails, D. (2002) *The Plato of the People: A Prosopography of Plato and Other Socratics*, Indianapolis, IN: Hackett.

Nehamas, A. (1992) 'Pity and Fear in the *Rhetoric* and the *Poetics*' in A. Rorty (ed.) *Essays on Aristotle's Poetics*, Princeton, NJ: Princeton University Press.

——(1988) 'Plato and the Mass Media', *Monist 71*, pp. 214–234.

——(1982) 'Plato on Imitation and Poetry in Republic 10' in J. Moravcsik and P. Temko (eds) *Plato on Beauty, Wisdom, and the Arts*, Totowa, NJ: Rowman and Littlefield.

Neill, A. (1991) 'Fear, Fiction and Make-Believe', *Journal of Aesthetics and Art Criticism*, 49, pp. 47–56.

——(1993) 'Fiction and the Emotions', *American Philosophical Quarterly*, 30, pp. 1–13.

——(1999) 'Hume's "Singular Phaenomenon"', *British Journal of Aesthetics*, vol. 39, pp. 112–125.

——(2003) 'Schopenhauer on Tragedy and Value' in S. Gardner and J. L. Bermúdez (eds) *Art and Morality* (2003), London: Routledge, pp. 204–217.

Nietzsche, F. (1999) *The Birth of Tragedy* trans. R. Speirs, Cambridge: Cambridge University Press.

Norton-Taylor, R. (ed.) (1997) *Nuremberg*, London: Nick Hearn Books.

Nussbaum, M. (1992) 'Tragedy and Self-sufficiency: Plato and Aristotle on Fear and Pity' in A. Rorty (ed.) *Essays on Aristotle's Poetics*, Princeton, NJ: Princeton University Press.

——(1990) *Love's Knowledge*, Oxford: Oxford University Press.

O'Connor, D. K. (2007) 'Rewriting the Poets in Plato's Characters' in G. R. F. Ferrari (ed.) *The Cambridge Companion to Plato's Republic*, Cambridge: Cambridge University Press.

Palmer, F. (1992) *Literature and Moral Understanding*, Oxford: Oxford University Press.

Pinkard, T. (1996) *Hegel's Phenomenology: The Sociality of Reason*, Cambridge: Cambridge University Press.

Plato (2000) *Republic*, trans. T Griffith, Cambridge: Cambridge University Press.

Plutarch (2001) *Plutarch's Lives*, trans. J. Dryden, New York: Random House.

Prentki, T. and Preston, S. (eds) (2009) *The Applied Theatre Reader*, London: Routledge.

Puchner, M. (2010) *The Drama of Ideas*, Oxford: Oxford University Press.

Pushkin, A. (2007) *Boris Godunov and Other Dramatic Works*, trans. J. Falen, Oxford: Oxford University Press.

Racine, J. (1991) 'Preface to *Phèdre*' in *Phèdre* trans. M. Rawlings, London: Penguin, pp. 18–23.

Radford, C. (1975) 'How can we be moved by the fate of Anna Karenina?', *Proceedings of the Aristotelian Society*, Supplementary Volumes, Vol. 49, pp. 67–80.

Reynolds, S. (2000) 'The Argument from Illusion', *Noûs*, Vol. 34:4, pp. 604–621.

Ridley, A (2003) 'Against Musical Ontology', *The Journal of Philosophy*, Vol. 100, No. 4, pp. 203–220.

Ridout, N. (2006) *Stage Fright, Animals and Other Theatrical Problems*, Cambridge: Cambridge University Press.

Ridley, A. (2003a) 'Tragedy' in J. Levinson (ed.), *The Oxford Handbook of Aesthetics,* Oxford: Oxford University Press.

Rokem, F. (2000) *Performing History*, Iowa City, IA: University of Iowa Press.

——(2010) *Philosophers and Thespians: Thinking Performance*, Stanford, CA: Stanford University Press.

Rorty, A. (1992) (ed.) *Essays on Aristotle's Poetics*, Princeton, NJ: Princeton University Press.

Rouse, J. (1995) 'Brecht and the Contradictory Actor' in P. Zarrilli (ed.) *Acting (Re)Considered,* London: Routledge, pp. 228–241.

Rousseau, J.-J. (2004) 'Letter to D'Alembert on the Theater' trans. A. Bloom in A. Bloom, C. Butterworth, and C Kelly (eds) *Letter to D'Alembert, and Writings*

For the Theater, vol. 10 of *The Collected Writings of Rousseau*, Hanover, NH: University Press of New England.

Ryle, G. (1933) 'Imaginary Objects', *Proceedings of the Aristotelian Society, Supplementary Volumes* Vol. 12, 1933, pp. 18–70.

Sacks, G. and Thomson, P. (eds) (1994) *The Cambridge Companion to Brecht*, Cambridge: Cambridge University Press.

Saltz, D. (1995) 'When is the Play the Thing? – Analytic Aesthetics and Dramatic Theory', *Theatre Research International* Vol. 20:3, pp. 266–276.

——(2001a) 'What Theatrical Performance Is (Not): The Interpretation Fallacy', *The Journal of Aesthetics and Art Criticism*, Vol. 59, No. 3, pp. 299–306.

——(2001b) 'Why Performance Theory Needs Philosophy', *Journal of Dramatic Theory and Criticism*, Fall 2001, pp. 149–154.

Sandford, M. (ed.) (1995) *Happenings and Other Acts*, London: Routledge.

Santas, G. (ed.) (2006) *The Blackwell Guide to Plato's* Republic, Oxford: Blackwell.

Sartre, J.-P. (2004) *The Imaginary* trans. J. Webber, London: Routledge.

Schaper, E. (1968) 'Aristotle's Catharsis and Aesthetic Pleasure', *The Philosophical Quarterly*, vol. 18, No. 71, pp. 131–143.

Schiller, F. (1979) *The Robbers and Wallenstein* trans. F. Lamport, London: Penguin.

——(1962) *Schillers Werke: Nationalausgabe*, Weimar: Hermann Böhlaus Nachfolger.

Schopenhauer, A. (2000) *Parerga and Paralipomena* trans. E. F. J. Payne, Oxford: Oxford University Press.

Shakespeare, W. (1995) *King Henry V*, T. W. Craik (ed.), London: Arden Shakespeare.

——(2006) *Hamlet*, A. Thompson and N. Taylor (eds), London: Arden Shakespeare.

——(2005) *The Tragedy of King Lear*, J. Halio (ed.), Cambridge: Cambridge University Press.

Sharpe, L (2007) 'The Young Dramatist' in P. Kerry (ed.) *Friedrich Schiller: Playwright, Poet, Historian, Philosopher*, Bern: Peter Lang.

Shelley, J. (2003) 'Imagining the truth: an account of tragic pleasure' in M. Kieran and D. Lopes (eds) *Imagination, Philosophy and the Arts*, London: Routledge.

Snowdon, P. (2004) 'Knowing How and Knowing That: A Distinction Reconsidered', *Proceedings of the Aristotelian Society*, New Series, Vol. 104, pp. 1–29.

Sophocles (2006) *The Theban Plays*, trans. G Young, Mineola, NY: Dover.

——(2003) *Oedipus Tyrannus*, trans. I. McAuslan and J. Affleck, Cambridge: Cambridge University Press.

Sparshott, F. (1952) 'Mr. Ziff and the "Artistic Illusion"', *Mind*, Vol. 61, No. 243, pp. 376–380.

Stendhal (1962) *Shakespeare and Racine*, trans. G Daniels, The Crowell-Collier Press.

Stephens, J. (1995) 'Censorship' in M. Banham (ed.) *The Cambridge Guide to Theatre: New Edition*. Cambridge: Cambridge University Press, pp. 178–186.

Stern, T. (2012) 'History Plays as History', *Philosophy and Literature,* vol. 36: 2, pp. 285–300.

Stern, T (2013) 'Review Article: Theatre and Philosophy', *European Journal of Philosophy*, vol. 21:1 (March, 2013), pp. 158–167.

Suits, D. (2006) 'Really Believing in Fiction', *Pacific Philosophical Quarterly*, vol. 87, pp. 369–386.

Taplin, O. (1995) 'Greek Theatre' in J. Brown (ed.) *The Oxford Illustrated History of Theatre*, Oxford: Oxford University Press, pp.13–48.

Thakkar, J. (2013) *Can There Be Philosopher-Kings in a Liberal Polity? A Reinterpretation and Reappropriation of the Ideal Theory in Plato's Republic*, Ph.D. Dissertation, University of Chicago, 2013.

Thomson, P. (1995) 'English Renaissance and Restoration Theatre' in J. Brown (ed.) *The Oxford Illustrated History of Theatre,* Oxford: Oxford University Press, pp. 173–219.

Tolstoy, L. (1995) *What is Art?* trans. R. Pevear and L. Volokhonsky, London: Penguin.

Urmson, J. (1976) 'Fiction', *American Philosophical Quarterly*, vol. 13: 2, pp. 153–7.

Vogler, C. (2007) 'The Moral of the Story', *Critical Inquiry*, Vol. 34, No. 1, pp. 5–35.

Walton, K. (1990) *Mimesis as Make-Believe: On the Foundations of the Representational Arts*, Cambridge, MA.: Harvard University Press.

White, H. (1980) 'The Value of Narrativity in the Representation of Reality', *Critical Inquiry* vol. 7, no. 1, pp. 5–27.

Wiles, D. (1995) 'Theatre in Roman and Christian Europe' in J. Brown (ed.) *The Oxford Illustrated History of Theatre*, Oxford: Oxford University Press.

Williams, B. (1973) *Problems of the Self*, Cambridge: Cambridge University Press.

Williams, G. J. (ed.) (2006) *Theatre Histories: An Introduction*, London: Routledge.

Williams, T. (2000) *Plays, 1937–1955*, New York: The Library of America.

Winkler, J (1990) 'The Ephebes' Song: *Tragōidia* and *Polis*' in J. Winkler and I. Zeitlin (eds) *Nothing to do with Dionysus?* Princeton, NJ: Princeton University Press, pp. 20–62.

Winkler, J. and Zeitlin, I. (eds) (1990) *Nothing to do with Dionysus?*, Princeton, NJ: Princeton University Press.

Woodruff, P. (1992) 'Aristotle on *Mimesis*' in A. Rorty (ed.) *Essays on Aristotle's Poetics*, Princeton, NJ: Princeton University Press.

——(2008) *The Necessity of Theater*, Oxford: Oxford University Press.

Zamir, T. (2007) *Double Vision: Moral Philosophy and Shakespearean Drama*, Princeton, NJ: Princeton University Press.

Zarrilli. P. (ed.) (1995) *Acting (Re)Considered*, London: Routledge.

Zemach, E. (1996) 'Emotion and Fictional Beings', *Journal of Aesthetics and Art Criticism*, 54, pp. 41–8.

Ziolkowski, T. (2009) *Scandal on Stage: European Theatre as Moral Trial*, Cambridge: Cambridge University Press.

Index